Beyond Windrush

CARIBBEAN
STUDIES
SERIES

Anton L. Allahar and Natasha Barnes
Series Editors

Beyond Windrush

Rethinking Postwar Anglophone Caribbean Literature

Edited by

J. Dillon Brown and Leah Reade Rosenberg

University Press of Mississippi / Jackson

www.upress.state.ms.us

The University Press of Mississippi is a member
of the Association of American University Presses.

Copyright © 2015 by University Press of Mississippi
All rights reserved
Manufactured in the United States of America

First printing 2015

∞

Library of Congress Cataloging-in-Publication Data

Beyond windrush : rethinking postwar anglophone caribbean
literature / edited by J. Dillon Brown and Leah Reade Rosenberg.
pages cm. — (Caribbean studies series)
Includes bibliographical references and index.
ISBN 978-1-62846-475-7 (hardback) — ISBN 978-1-62846-476-4
(ebook) 1. West Indian literature (English)—History and criticism. 2. Caribbean literature (English)—History and criticism.
3. National characteristics, Caribbean, in literature. I. Brown, J.
Dillon, 1971– editor. II. Rosenberg, Leah, editor.
PR9210.B49 2015
810.9'9729—dc 3   2014045132

British Library Cataloging-in-Publication Data available

Contents

Part Three: The Politics of Literary Production and Reception

Part Four: Alternate Geographies

Acknowledgments

The editors wish to thank, first and foremost, the contributors to this volume for their erudition, enthusiasm, and patience over the long process of bringing this project to fruition. Without their hard work and good spirits, this book simply would not exist. We would also like to thank the two editors at the University Press of Mississippi who have, with warmth and efficiency, serially shepherded us through the publishing process: Walter Biggins and Vijay Shah. Gratitude is due, as well, to the anonymous readers of the proposal and the manuscript, who offered excellent insight and direction to the individual essays and the book as a whole. We would also like to express our appreciation to Frances Salmon and the staff of the West Indies and Special Collections at the University West Indies Libraries Mona, Jamaica, who identified Roger Mais's watercolor of France and granted us permission for its use as the cover illustration. Conference meetings of two scholarly organizations—the Modern Language Association and the Caribbean Studies Association—have allowed many of the contributors to the volume to meet and try out their ideas collectively, for which we are also grateful.

Individually, Leah would like to acknowledge Kenneth Kidd, Marsha Bryant, the National Humanities Center, the College of Liberal Arts and Sciences and the English Department at the University of Florida, and the Digital Library of the Caribbean (www.dloc.com) for helping facilitate her work on this book. Dillon would like to give thanks to the Department of English and the Center for the Humanities at Washington University in St. Louis for providing research support that has been crucial to the volume's completion.

Chapter 11 incorporates material previously published in Raphael Dalleo, *Caribbean Literature and the Public Sphere: From the Plantation to the Postcolonial* (copyright 2011 by the Rector and Visitors of the University of Virginia). We thank the University of Virginia Press for permission to reprint brief portions from that book.

Beyond Windrush

Introduction: Looking Beyond Windrush

J. DILLON BROWN AND LEAH READE ROSENBERG

The term "Windrush" has become a potent signifier in scholars' understanding of both British and Anglophone Caribbean cultural history. It finds its etymology in the SS *Empire Windrush*—a ship that carried almost 500 West Indians to England in 1948 (including, famously, the calypsonian Lord Kitchener) and thus inaugurated the large-scale postwar migration from the region to Britain—but its import resonates well beyond this now legendary historical watershed.[1] In contemporary Britain, "Windrush" stands metonymically as a marker for the emergence of an increasingly multicultural national polity, in which the old self-understanding of Englishness as racially white gradually cedes prominence to a newer conception of Britishness—one that strives to include the burgeoning population of citizens who trace their heritage back to the once-colonized spaces of the British Empire.[2] Reflecting on the moment of the ship's arrival, Stuart Hall concludes that "the history of the black diaspora in Britain begins here."[3] In the Caribbean, "Windrush" signals the heady midcentury period in which tens of thousands of Caribbean migrants made their way to Great Britain, challenging the long-standing verities of empire in what Louise Bennett has canonically celebrated as "colonization in reverse."[4] The extensive migration of these postwar years took place in tandem with the formation of the West Indies Federation, which served as the official channel of the region's aspirations for political independence until its untimely collapse four years after its 1958 inception. Thus the Windrush years—effectively 1948 to 1962—mark an especially poignant period for the English-speaking Caribbean, rich with dreams and controversies about migration, identity, national culture, regional unity, and decolonization. Although the ramifications of this era are still discernible today, 1962 offers a crucial point of closure to the period, as that year saw not only the acrimonious end of federation but also the independence of both Trinidad and Tobago and Jamaica, as well as passage of a deeply restrictive immigration act in Britain that decisively slowed the in-flow of migrants from the Caribbean.[5]

In literary terms, the period has become important because among the metropolitan migrants of these early, exciting postwar years were a remarkable number of authors: for literary critics, "Windrush" now also denotes a generation of particularly productive and visible West Indian writers who migrated to Great Britain to ply their trade at this time. As Anne Walmsley has detailed, this cadre of migrant writers was diverse in social background, nationality, and chosen genre, and included poets such as Ian McDonald and John Figueroa and the playwrights Errol John and Evan Jones.[6] Most prominent, however, were the novelists of the time, including Michael Anthony, Jan Carew, Wilson Harris, John Hearne, George Lamming, Roger Mais, Edgar Mittelholzer, V. S. Naipaul, V. S. Reid, Andrew Salkey, and Samuel Selvon, all of whom enjoyed a relatively high profile in the 1950s and early 1960s. Often encouraged or employed by the BBC radio program *Caribbean Voices*, this generation of male, exilic authors brought international acclaim and regional recognition to Anglophone Caribbean literature as a tradition, and the concepts and themes articulated in their work have decisively shaped Caribbean literary criticism for over half a century. Certainly, these writers believed that they were the vanguard producers of an "intellectual revolution" in Caribbean literature, in much the same way as the Windrush generation of West Indian immigrants could be seen as catalysts for a fundamental transformation of Great Britain as a nation.[7]

In his influential *The Pleasures of Exile* (1960), Lamming observes that "we have seen in our lifetime an activity called writing, in the form of the novel, come to fruition without any previous native tradition to draw upon." He goes on to assert that he and his fellow West Indian novelists "are to the new colonial reader what Fielding and Smollett and the early English novelists would be to the readers of their own generation . . . the first builders of what will become a tradition in West Indian imaginative writing: a tradition which will be taken for granted for the purpose of critical analysis by West Indians of a later generation."[8] Lamming's bold (and generically specific) prediction has proven prescient: the narrative of Windrush writers as the founding generation of Anglophone Caribbean literature has often been taken for granted by critics. As this collection hopes to show, however, various institutional and critical biases have decisively shaped the characterization of this period, pruning out much of its diversity and interest in favor of a simplified account of regional-national literary triumph. Indeed, over time the wide range of the Windrush era's authors has been narrowed into a core group of canonical figures—Lamming, Naipaul, Selvon, and Harris—who, along with their generational counterparts in poetry, Edward (Kamau) Brathwaite and Derek Walcott, have dominated curricula and scholarship since the establishment of Anglophone Caribbean literary studies in the early 1970s.[9] In this way, the critical predilections of this influential set of postwar writers have largely set the terms of debate for understanding both the force and nature of West Indian literature in scholarly terms.

In recent years, however, the critical winds have begun to shift: scholars (including, not coincidentally, many of this collection's contributors) have turned increasingly to the corpus of Caribbean literature written before Windrush. Attention has also been focused on a much broader spectrum of more contemporary authors in regard to gender, ethnicity, and sexuality, as well as genre. Selwyn Cudjoe, Alison Donnell, Evelyn O'Callaghan, Leah Reade Rosenberg, and Faith Smith, for example, have all persuasively argued for the recognition of a West Indian literary culture well before the postwar "boom," one that is often at odds with that era's demands for nationalist political orthodoxy.[10] A growing body of scholarly work has begun to rethink the Windrush legacy from other directions as well. Belinda Edmondson has traced the strong continuity between the era's male writers and the Victorian authors they purportedly refuted, as well as, more recently, arguing for the importance of a long-standing Caribbean-based middlebrow culture often overlooked by the Windrush-inspired focus on a diaspora-enabled high culture.[11] Patricia Saunders and Kezia Page have pointed out the gender and geographical biases instigated by an account of West Indian literature that privileges exiled male authorship, and, even more recently, both Raphael Dalleo and Michael Niblett have offered pan-Caribbean approaches to literature of the 1950s and 1960s that seek to dislodge the Anglocentric constrictions inherent to a critical lens intent on the binary colonial relation.[12]

Clearly, then, for many critics working today, Lamming's vision of himself and his contemporaries as heroic literary pioneers has become a rather too-orthodox critical straitjacket. As Donnell observes in discussing this traditional, triumphalist Windrush narrative, "it was a powerful and sustaining myth of origin but, like other myths of origin, it held other stories and other claims in suspicion and abeyance."[13] It is within this productive critical turn that *Beyond Windrush* positions itself, likewise insisting that it is necessary to uncover and go beyond the ideological blind spots and biases that arise from the core Windrush writers' sense of their own aesthetic mission (and its subsequent acceptance by later commentators). The collection is anchored in a belief that it is only by unsettling and overturning the potent originary myths surrounding this generation's writing that a properly comprehensive view of the Caribbean literary landscape can emerge. However, even as *Beyond Windrush* is premised on the need to critique the dominant vision of the most canonized postwar writers, it should be observed here that these figures *were* instrumental in catapulting West Indian literature onto the international literary stage—a fact testified to not least by the Nobel Prizes in Literature awarded to two authors who emerged in the 1950s, Walcott and Naipaul. Further, the group's large-scale publishing success was essential to the establishment of Caribbean literary studies and to the inclusion of West

Indian literature in curricula in the Caribbean, the United Kingdom, and the United States, as well as in Africa, where it was particularly influential in the emergence of national literatures.[14] Even the critical attention increasingly devoted to questioning the legacy the core Windrush writers bequeathed to Anglophone Caribbean literature testifies to the continuing influence of their self-defined aesthetic and political purpose.

The most noticeable component of this purpose is its tendency toward an all but exclusive focus on the articulation of a forceful anticolonial nationalism based in the folk. For example, Lamming provocatively positions his generation's novelistic achievement as one of only three truly transformative events in the entirety of Caribbean history, grouping it with Columbus's "discovery" of the New World and "the abolition of slavery and the arrival of the East—India and China—in the Caribbean Sea."[15] For Lamming, the era's novels were so signally important because they represented West Indian peasants in their full humanity, for the very first time: they constituted a literature grounded in the individual lives and culture of the region, elements that had remained imperceptible within the self-serving dictates of British colonial discourse.[16] Lamming thus holds his contemporaries' novels up as unprecedented counterpoints to the pernicious myth of English superiority that permeated West Indian society to its very core—so powerful that he compared it to "the nutritive function of milk which all sorts of men receive at birth"—naming postwar novels as perhaps *the* essential catalysts of the effort to decolonize the collective West Indian mind and set it on the road to a salutary independence.[17]

This characterization of the post–World War II generation of Caribbean writers, however vulnerable to charges of self-aggrandizement, captures much of the events and spirit of the historical moment, in which the seeds of the region's 1930s labor rebellions were flowering into an increasingly irresistible demand for political autonomy (first envisioned as a multiterritory federation). The initial focus on the anticolonial nationalist drive of West Indian literature has been echoed by critics ever since. In his introduction to *Caribbean Literature: An Anthology* (1966), for example, G. R. Coulthard notes that "there was definitely a connection in the British Caribbean between the awakening of a national consciousness and a desire for independence and the burgeoning of a new national literature."[18] Bruce King's *West Indian Literature* (1979), an early and important critical text in the field, similarly observes that "during the immediate post-war years, West Indian literature was a reflection of growing nationalism, hopes of a regional federation, feelings of anticolonialism, and interest in local culture."[19] Sandra Pouchet Paquet echoes this scholarly consensus in describing the emergence of West Indian literature, arts, and historiography in this period all as "major steps in challenging the attitudes of an inherited colonial relationship."[20]

Indeed, Norval Edwards has recently argued that Caribbean literary studies continues to be based on a cultural nationalist paradigm, asserting that since the 1930s, Anglophone Caribbean literature and criticism have

> been largely dominated by a concern with imagining and authorizing an aesthetic founded on a politics of identity and difference, conceptualized as a response to the problem of colonialism, contextualized within the anti-colonial and early postcolonial conjuncture, and articulated in cultural nationalist terms that posit race and language as consanguineous figures of nation and history.[21]

As Edwards goes on to illustrate, this cultural nationalist framework was adopted by critics of all political beliefs, geographical locations, and ethnic identities, serving as the grounding limit of textual debate. Sylvia Wynter, for example, lambasted Louis James's 1968 *The Islands In Between: Essays on West Indian Literature* for producing West Indian literary criticism that was part of the colonial and capitalist enterprise rather than a challenge to it; however, both Wynter and James saw West Indian writers who imitated British literary aesthetics as, in James's terms, "constricting" the achievement of an independent West Indian culture, and indeed both shared a basic understanding of who was important to the canon.[22] Kenneth Ramchand, in turn, criticized Brathwaite's call for an Afro-Creole folk-centered culture for the West Indies, famously quipping that he did not want to "folk up the literature" and decrying such politicized criticism as "a turn away from literariness, thus making itself almost indistinguishable from the sociology of literature."[23] Nevertheless, Ramchand himself specifically developed the 1966 *West Indian Narrative* as a reader for West Indian schools to provide their students with an accessible literature through which they might "become aware of the social and political problems of [their] own country." In fact, Ramchand concludes his introduction, addressed to this "national" body of students, with a testament to the tangible social and political power of literature, which, properly realized, "becomes a powerful magic which helps us to discover and give shape to our lives and to our world."[24] Thus even the most literarily inclined critics of West Indian literature can be seen to ply their trade from within the confines of a paradigm characterized by the pragmatic goal of cultural-national uplift.

Undoubtedly, a further, explicitly marked inheritance of the Windrush era has been the privileging of the status of the writer as exile. There was, of course, as the title of Lamming's essay collection intimates, a paradox at the heart of this generation's writing: if they were building a West Indian literary tradition, they were doing so in a location quite remote from the land and people they were hoping to represent. Summarizing the publishing geography of the postwar years, Ramchand baldly asserts that, during this time, "London is indisputably the West Indian literary capital."[25] Painfully aware of this irony, Lamming advanced rueful arguments for its necessity. In his view, the idea that only Europeans could produce literature was so entrenched in colonial Caribbean culture that writers were obliged to seek exile in England, the hub of English-language publishing, and thus a place where financial survival and critical acclaim were at least conceivable. As Lamming puts it: "If we accept that the act of writing a book is linked with an expectation, however modest, of having it read; then the situation of a West Indian writer, living and work-ing in his own community, assumes intolerable difficulties."[26] Writing in 1963, Brathwaite expressed confidence in what now seems like an unlikely antidote to what he saw as the dominant, stultifying influence of exile on West Indian literature—the writing of Naipaul—opining that in the latter's *A House for Mr. Biswas*, "we have the first novel whose basic theme is not rootlessness and the search for social identity."[27] Despite Brathwaite's apparent optimism on this front, however, Ramchand's 1970 paradigm-setting *The West Indian Novel and Its Background* endorses Lamming's assessment of exile, suggest-ing that a properly local West Indian literature could only emerge after "the creation of a literate and responsive West Indian public."[28] Although authors and critics often conveyed an anguished sense that Caribbean writers' great physical distance from the people about and for whom they wrote threatened to dilute the power and relevance of their work, the tension emerging out of exile was nevertheless seen as inescapable: simultaneously making Win-drush literature possible and threatening its raison d'etre, exile became fun-damental to an understanding of the region's writing.[29] As Dalleo has recently observed, among the set of stories most influential in literary histories of the region, "few [are] as enduring as the idea of 'exile' as an organizing logic for Caribbean literature," a phenomenon that can be traced directly back to the emplacement and self-presentation of the Windrush writers.[30]

The critical privileging of a specific group of postwar male authors has also inflected Caribbean literary studies with the gender and sexual impera-tives characteristic of most modern nationalisms. Not the least of these is the assumption that authors would necessarily be men. The gendered nature of this generation's literary output has by now been assiduously addressed and dissected.[31] The need to assert or construct Caribbean manhood was very strong in the wake of slavery, indenture, and colonialism, all of which had denied Caribbean people the attributes commonly associated with mas-culinity—the ownership of self and of one's work, and the ability to be the patriarch of one's family. As Rhonda Cobham has argued, reestablishing these attributes was such an imperative that the recognition of women, women writers, and feminist concerns became unimportant, and was even seen as an outright threat to the era's nationalist projects.[32] Even Wynter, the most revered female cultural critic of the 1960s and 1970s, did not present women and feminism as issues of primary importance, privileging instead the struggle against colonialism, and "western humanism and the consequences of its racially based definition of 'man.'"[33] Although it is belied by the presence of early postwar female writers such as Louise Bennett, Lucille Iremonger, Una Marson, Ada Quayle, and Phyllis Shand Allfrey, among others, the conventional story of West Indian literature portrays "the female voice" emerging in the 1980s, well after its 1950s male precursor. In assessing West Indian literary production of the 1980s, Laurence Breiner observes that many new voices emerged, but he remains "most impressed with how many of these new voices are female."[34] Hena Maes-Jelinek and Bénédicte Ledent observe a similar progression, asserting that "if the emergence of a new generation of novelists may be viewed as one of the main developments of Caribbean literature since the seventies, the long-awaited recognition of writing by women was an even more striking phenomenon."[35] Although they note Merle Hodge's 1970 *Crick Crack, Monkey* as an early forerunner, Maes-Jelinek and Ledent otherwise concentrate, like Breiner, on female-authored novels from the 1980s, suggesting a narrative of progression in which women writers only emerge in the region's literature three decades after the postwar boom.[36]

Another consequence of the concentration on a specific set of (masculine, heteronormative) postwar works has been the overlooking of literature that presents homosexuality as a legitimate element of Caribbean culture. If they represented it at all, canonical Windrush authors such as Lamming and Selvon tended to present homosexuality and lesbianism as a sign of perversion or comedy. Accordingly, like women's writing, queer writing and the serious representation of homosexuality have been viewed by critics as recent phenomena, emerging in the 1980s and 1990s with writers such as Makeda Silvera and Michelle Cliff. However, queer desire and identity were of significance to Caribbean writers much earlier, including, most notably, Claude McKay in the early twentieth century and, as Nadia Ellis's contribution to this collection makes clear, Andrew Salkey in the Windrush era itself.[37]

A further salient interpretive inheritance of the period's dominance has been the elevation of the novel as the principal literary vehicle of Caribbean experience. The triumph of the West Indian novel in the postwar literary marketplace led to its being considered the pinnacle of formal achievement, such that other genres—the short story in particular—became viewed as an early, simpler phase in the tradition's development. Even in the cases in which an earlier novelistic tradition was recognized, critics tended to view the situation as a teleological process, moving from ostensibly imitative works such as Thomas MacDermot's 1903 *Becka's Buckra Baby* to the "mature stage" of anticolonial aesthetics found in the postwar writers. Such narratives almost always also assumed, simultaneously, a progression from short fiction to the novel. Lucy Evans's introduction to *The Caribbean Short Story: Critical Perspectives* presents the book's essays as an attempt to address such a tendency, in which "a privileging of the novel over the short story as the subject of Caribbean literary criticism" has obscured a vibrant and enduring practice that "rendered the short story form central to the development of a regionally based Caribbean literary tradition."[38] A look at the titles of some of the most formative books for Anglophone Caribbean literary criticism—Ramchand's *The West Indian Novel and Its Background* and Michael Gilkes's *The West Indian Novel* (1981), for example—or the contents of James's *The Islands In Between* (with its sole focus on novels, excepting an essay on Walcott) and King's *West Indian Literature* (whose "significant authors" are all novelists except for the usual poetic talents Walcott and Brathwaite, and the Jamaican playwright Trevor Rhone) suggests how long the critical emphasis on novels has endured.

The framework set by the core Windrush writers—characterized by its investments in cultural nationalism, the folk, exile, masculinity, and the novel form—was both powerful and exclusionary. For one thing, of course, it assumes that all West Indian literature must be dedicated to challenging British colonialism, leaving aside innumerable thematic orientations in preference to one political orthodoxy. The emphasis on the folk likewise functioned to marginalize authors who focused on the middle class and elite, such as John Hearne, or who were themselves white creoles, like Geoffrey Drayton and Jean Rhys, and thus appeared to belong to the colonizing classes.[39] Ramchand's *The West Indian Novel and Its Background* is an important case in point. Although it sought to establish a canon that extended to literature of the early twentieth century, its roster of such works is united by a shared focus on the peasantry and urban poor. Ramchand includes white creole authors—particularly focusing on Allfrey and Rhys—only under Frantz Fanon's rubric of terrified consciousness, defining their work primarily with regard to their unbelonging and vulnerability in the period of anticolonial nationalism.[40] Similarly, in its Herderian desire for a singular national ethnicity or race—despite all the talk of creolization—West Indian literature and criticism often overlooked the prominent Indo- and Chinese-Caribbean as well as indigenous aspects of its production.[41] Perhaps the most influential critic in this regard is Brathwaite, who, in *Contradictory Omens: Cultural Diversity and Integration in the Caribbean*, employed his vast archival research on the development of creole society to argue that Afro-Creole folk culture was and should continue to be the foundation and center of the region as it developed its own culture after independence.[42]

In a contemporary context, the other exclusions inhering in the Windrush paradigm seem equally unsustainable. An insistence on exile, perversely, enhances the centrality of the imperial metropole, relegating local and regional production to second-class status. The elision of women from an account of midcentury literature likewise does an injustice to the rich variety of literary production by women at this time, even as it tacitly accepts the norms of gender and sexuality advanced by the male Windrush coterie. Undoubtedly, the formal hierarchy in which the novel reigns paramount can be seen to express an ideological hierarchy as well, in that the public, ostensibly national concerns of the novel take precedence over anything more private, lyrical, personal, or domestic that different forms of literature might be found to express.

The essays that follow, then, are interested in addressing the elisions and eschewals upon which the traditional Windrush storyline implicitly relies. However, and importantly, these essays do not engage in this task by looking to earlier moments that prefigure the Windrush writers and thus undermine that generation's claims to uniqueness. Nor do they look to a later moment, in which a more ecumenically minded field of literary production can be seen, perhaps, to redeem the blind spots of the Windrush writers, allowing for a broader diversity of voices from the region to be heard. Instead, the essays gathered here are intent on applying a much broader interpretive lens to the texts and contexts *within* the immediate postwar period itself. In her *Twentieth-Century Caribbean Literature: Critical Moments in Anglophone Literary History*—one of the most overt and persuasive critical efforts to reformulate the Caribbean canon in recent years—Donnell is forthright in abjuring any discussion of the "core body of writers and texts so favoured by general survey works."[43] As she explains, in her monograph, the major canonical figures of Anglophone Caribbean literature, especially the writers of the 1950s, "are not given sustained attention ... precisely because I am arguing that the profile, prestige, and platforms accorded to these literary voices at various stages of literary history have served to drown out the more subtle, strained, and sometimes discordant tone of many others."[44] Clearly, this collection is in sympathy with Donnell's reformative impulses; however, it is also keen to illustrate that the postwar years themselves contain subtle, strained, and sometimes discordant tones of authors normally drowned out by the usual canonical giants. That is, instead of taking the influential figures of Harris, Lamming, Naipaul, and Selvon as wholly definitive of the era's literary production, this collection argues that the postwar moment contained but cannot be reduced to the rise of anticolonial nationalism and the West Indian novel. In bringing these essays together, *Beyond Windrush* aims to make visible a new landscape of the era's writing in which far more than a metropolitan-based, novelistic focus on national independence can be discerned. Excavating forgotten facets of genre, gender, sexuality, ethnicity, transnationalism, and the local in the era's writing, the essays that follow all attest to the plain fact that much has, until now, been overlooked in critical accounts of the Windrush era, and thus that much more remains to be said about this postwar period so crucial to Caribbean literature in English.

The first section of the book, "Negotiating National Belonging," speaks to the ways in which representations of ethnicity, gender, and sexuality disrupt the buoyant views of national belonging characteristic of the traditional Windrush story. The first two essays examine the complex dynamics of belonging represented in Indo-Caribbean writing of the period.[45] In "Indianness and Nationalism in the Windrush Era," Lisa Outar identifies a palpable strain of doubt about the nationalist credentials of Indo-Caribbean people in the prominent Windrush novels of the period. The essay first illustrates how, overtly or otherwise, the period's literary emphasis on a unified national body offered little room for the region's diasporic Asian population. Outar then points to substantial archival evidence from the two major Indo-Caribbean periodicals of the postwar years—the *Observer* and the *Spectator* (famously and libelously lampooned by Naipaul in *The Mystic Masseur*)—to indicate how, far from their portrayal in the period's novels, Indo-Caribbeans were intricately and earnestly engaged in imagining themselves part of a Caribbean national polity while still acknowledging their Indian inheritances.

Atreyee Phukan's "Contradictory Omens: Repatriation and Resistance in Ismith Khan's *The Jumbie Bird*" likewise delineates the multilayered Indo-Caribbean experience of the region's nationalism as it sought to balance pride in the realization of independence from Britain on the subcontinent in 1947 with a recognition of the need to forge permanent affective links within the Caribbean basin. Examining Khan's little-studied novel in the context of the influential creolization theories of Brathwaite and Édouard Glissant, Phukan argues that Khan's book advocates a version of creolized Caribbean nationalism inflected by its characters' South Asian lineage. By highlighting the novel's explicit repudiation of the "back-to-India" movement and its valorization of a syncretic Indo-Caribbean aesthetic practice, the essay reveals that Khan's political aesthetic is quite in keeping, on a structural level, with the more celebrated, more Afrocentric theories of creolization in concert with which it arose. Nadia Ellis's contribution, "Between Windrush and Wolfenden: Class Crossings and Queer Desire in Andrew Salkey's Postwar London," engages a much different angle—sexuality and social class in the Windrush migrant male experience. As her essay suggests, Salkey was—but is rarely now—recognized as a crucial figure of the generation, and her account of his only recently recuperated novel *Escape to an Autumn Pavement*, first published in 1960, provides a case for why this might be so. For Ellis, the intersection of class, race, and, above all, sexuality in Salkey's novel raises issues that interfere with the heroic male heterosexual nationalism purveyed by the more consecrated Windrush novels. In uncovering the ambivalent but powerful queer energies evoked by Salkey's text, Ellis shows how literary accounts of the period have failed to engage with the more complicated, less overtly oppositional emotions expressed in literature portraying the midcentury West Indian migrant experience.

The second section, "Genre and Gender," addresses short stories and memoirs, uncovering an important sample of nonnovelistic production composed during the postwar years. Interestingly, all three essays find a strongly gendered component in the generic privilege given to the novel in this period. In "Rescripting Anglophone Caribbean Women's Literary History: Gender, Genre, and Lost Caribbean Voices," Alison Donnell reveals that women were active writers in the 1950s and 1960s, particularly visible in *Caribbean Voices* and *Bim*. These women, however, rarely made the transition from short story to novel, and Donnell argues that a series of factors explain this: women were less likely to migrate, less likely to conceive of writing as a profession, more likely to have their work classified as folkloric (and thus not real art), and less likely to be assisted with connections to publishers' networks (themselves largely dominated by men). The essay thus maintains that a broad spectrum of work by women writers contemporaneous with Windrush has remained hidden in the archives. In its own small act of critical recovery, Donnell's article points to the need for a more sustained and systematic effort to unearth this heretofore overlooked lineage and continuity in women's writing.

Donette Francis's "'Neither Pathological nor Perfect': Joyce Gladwell's Late Autobiographical Challenge to the Windrush Generation" takes up an analysis of Gladwell's memoir, *Brown Face, Big Master*. Although its author migrated to London in the 1950s, this account of her experience of the period was not published until 1969, a point Francis uses to illustrate the marginalizing powers of the postwar publishing field. In unpacking the complicated negotiations Gladwell's memoir portrays between race, gender, class, and—crucially—Christianity, the essay shows that this text concentrates on issues far removed from the usual remit of Windrush writing, including respectability, psychology, domesticity, and femininity. As such, Francis argues, Gladwell's memoir can be seen not only as an articulation of an alternative, long-repressed experience of migration but also as an important founding text for modern feminist autobiographical writing. Similarly, Evelyn O'Callaghan's "Elma Napier's Literary Sense of Place" finds in the writing of the Scottish-born, Dominican-resident Napier a critically shunned example of Caribbean writing deeply engaged, politically and ecologically, with the individual landscape of a particular island. The essay vividly recaptures the contours of Napier's varied writing career (including journalism, the novel *A Flying Fish Whispered*, and her memoir *Black and White Sands*) and the ways it interacted with her concrete political activities in Dominica. In doing so, O'Callaghan positions Napier as a crucially important cultural producer whose authorial modes—invested in local, ecological politics rather than those of national autonomy—combined with her identity as a white, foreign-born landowner, led to the exclusion of her work from most Caribbean literary-critical discussions. Returning to this overlooked writer's work, O'Callaghan argues, reveals a midcentury protoecological discourse that assumes increasing relevance as the depredations of global capitalism continue to impact the postindependence Caribbean environment.

The volume's third section, "The Politics of Literary Production and Reception," illuminates how the variegated politics of anticolonial nationalism influenced the form, content, and canon of postwar literature. Glyne A. Griffith's "The BBC's *Caribbean Voices* and Its 'Critics' Circle': Radio Criticism and the Development of Anglophone Caribbean Literature" sheds new light on the role of *Caribbean Voices*, the BBC radio program long credited for launching the careers of the era's leading authors, in governing the texture and political alignment of postwar Caribbean literature. Griffith first argues that *Caribbean Voices* played a direct role in establishing the dominant aesthetics of the Anglophone Caribbean literary tradition—realism and the folk—by promoting literature that featured "local color" and could be easily understood through radio broadcast. Griffith goes on to show, however, that this insistence on a geographically distinct folk culture also promoted the development of individual national literary traditions in the region, directly contradicting the BBC policy of supporting a federated conception of independence. Making clear that the BBC was not merely imposing its influence on the periphery, Griffith's essay thus brings to light the subtler political tensions *Caribbean Voices* encouraged within the region, rather than reading it as the progenitor, however compromised, of regional-national self-realization that it is often made out to be.

The following two essays return to a prominent but now rarely discussed controversy of early West Indian literary criticism: would white and near-white authors who belonged to or wrote about the plantocracy or the middle class be counted among the region's leading authors?[46] As both Kate Houlden and Kim Robinson-Walcott discuss, the novels of John Hearne became the object of this heated debate in the 1960s: Lamming suggested that Hearne's aesthetics were weakened by his focus on the near-white elite, in his words "a mythological, colonial squirearchy," while Wynter impugned Hearne's political vision, claiming that he disregarded the history and legacy of slavery as well as the privileged position that he and his protagonists occupied.[47] Houlden and Robinson-Walcott revisit this debate and, taking opposing positions, demonstrate that it remains far from resolved. Indeed, both essays suggest that a political framework for literary criticism remains a vibrant element of scholarly contention. In "John Hearne's Plantation Fantasy," Houlden departs from Lamming and Wynter by claiming that Hearne offers a much more nuanced depiction of the middle class as well as an important vision of the Caribbean as part of an American culture stretching from North to South America. Ultimately, however, Houlden maintains that after his first novel, Hearne's focus on an Afro-Creole planter class—which, she argues, he depicts with an apparently unconscious nostalgia—constitutes a failure to engage with the region's political present and future. In contrast, Robinson-Walcott's "John Hearne: Beyond the Plantation" argues that Hearne's novels have great political relevance because they critique Jamaica's near-white political elite, the class that guided Jamaica through the transition to independence. In fact, for this essay, the novels' depiction of that class's shifting support for radicalism has a prophetic quality, anticipating the ambivalence of Jamaica's middle class toward radicalism and its ultimate rejection of politics. In different ways, then, both essays suggest the critical pertinence of a return to an author largely dismissed for falling outside of the acceptable political parameters of his generation's writing.

In the fourth and final section, "Alternate Geographies," the essays explore the ramifications of geographical itineraries outside the usual route from the Caribbean to Britain. Faith Smith's "Kingston Calling: Mais's Paris, 1954" investigates the semicanonical Windrush author Roger Mais with an eye toward the fraught tension between Jamaica and France that characterized his early 1950s work (in both literature and the visual arts). Mining his letters home for insight into his artistic development, the essay constructs a vision of Mais as an artist struggling to address the expectations of his middle-class Jamaican family in a milieu far outside of its immediate knowledge or formation. Illustrating the important influence that the exhilarating mix of race,

psychology, and existentialism Mais encountered in France had on his thinking, Smith opens up a new transnational view of the author as anxious son
and excited expatriate, rather than the vociferous figure of anti-British social
protest with which he is normally associated. The essay connects especially to
Francis's analysis of Gladwell. Francis and Smith both see their middle-class,
brown-skinned authors as complicating Fanon's theorization of the objectify-
ing colonial gaze by asserting the significance of the middle-class Caribbean
gaze and its colorism for writers in the postwar period. As these two essays
illustrate, postwar Caribbean writers were not merely looking to the metropole for approval or for sources of racism; they were also looking homeward
and inward.

Raphael Dalleo's "Marie Chauvet and the Writer's Exile from the Postcolonial Public Sphere," in turn, provides a much different Francophone lens
through which to view the Windrush period. Examining the Haitian writer
Marie Chauvet, Dalleo finds striking parallels between her work and that of
the core Windrush authors, despite the fact that Chauvet was producing her
literature not in exile but at home. From this observation, the essay goes on to
make a case for a much wider, regional view of the era's literary production,
one that allows critics to index an important shift in the social role of authors
across the region (and also, perhaps, globally) from anticolonial activism to
a more nebulous, compromised sense of postcoloniality. For Dalleo, placing
postwar Caribbean literature into this translinguistic comparative frame dislodges romantic accounts of nationalism, obliging a harder look at the role
that literature did and can play in the social and political circumstances out
of which it emerges.

Michael A. Bucknor's "Beyond Windrush and the Original Black Atlantic
Routes: Austin Clarke, Race, and Canada's Influence on Anglophone Caribbean Literature" also argues for an alternative geographical vision of the
period. His essay turns to Canada—long an important migration destination
from the Caribbean—as an overlooked site of postwar literary production.
Employing the example of the Barbadian-born Austin Clarke, firmly canonized in Canada, Bucknor explores the generative links Clarke's own career
exemplifies between the Caribbean, Canada, the United States, and Britain—a
multifaceted transnationalism in conversation with his Windrush peers but
equally influenced by the civil rights movement in the United States and racial
politics in Canada. In this way, Bucknor is able to show Clarke as an exemplar of literary and political processes that resist containment within an anticolonial national frame by gesturing outward, toward a differentially rooted
(and routed), insistently global politics of blackness. The final essay of the
section, Michelle A. Stephens's "Federated Ocean States: Archipelagic Visions

of the Third World at Midcentury," encourages an even broader epistemological shift in our understanding of place and history. In it, Stephens recovers some salient examples of postwar political imaginaries that can be associated with the revolutionary Bandung conference of 1955 but that diverge from the nation-based visions of decolonization that it largely authorized. Placing C. L. R. James's utopian plan for Caribbean federation alongside Indonesia's pointed self-presentation as an archipelagic state, the essay offers an enticing alternative framework for understanding the relations between land, nation, and globe, a possibility present but not taken as the twentieth century wore on (and with particular aptness for the Caribbean archipelago). Paying particular attention to James's 1953 reading of Herman Melville in *Mariners, Renegades, and Castaways: The Story of Herman Melville and the World We Live In*, Stephens maps out how differently James saw the world, from his American outpost, than did his Windrush counterparts in London. Stephens suggests that contemporary critics of Caribbean culture would do well to engage with the different vistas offered by James's perspective.

Finally, as the collection's epilogue, Edward Baugh's "Coming of Age in the Fifties" gives an invaluable firsthand account of the Windrush era as experienced by a young Caribbean intellectual and writer. It offers eloquent testimony not only to the sense of innovation and excitement generated by the literary accomplishment of the period but also to the open-ended, wide-ranging, vibrantly mobile modes in which it was experienced. For Baugh, the achievement of postwar Caribbean writing was not remotely limited to the now canonical version of Windrush writing, let alone its accepted geographical and ideological parameters. Instead, as Baugh makes clear, it was experienced as an inclusive, effervescent, and ongoing process in which new horizons appeared with steady consistency.

It is to this ecumenical and enlivening sense of the post–World War II period that *Beyond Windrush* hopes to gesture. The incompleteness of this gesture is perhaps inevitable, and though it does not excuse our inability to include any sustained treatment of poetry or drama in this collection, we hope such incompleteness will serve as an invitation to scholars to engage in a more expansive, more fluid approach to the era's Anglophone Caribbean literature long into the future. Such work is already under way, of course, whether it be found in Laurence Breiner's 2008 recuperation of the underappreciated poetry of Eric Roach in *Black Yeats: Eric Roach and the Politics of Caribbean Poetry* or in the 2013 collection *Interlocking Basins of a Globe: Essays on Derek Walcott*, edited by Jean Antoine-Dunne, which assertively recontextualizes the Anglophone Caribbean's most canonical poet within local, regional, and global settings. Promisingly, this kind of scholarly exploration has increasingly been facilitated by a burgeoning of reprints of postwar Caribbean literature, most notably in Peepal Tree Press's Caribbean Modern Classics series (begun in 2008), which has been reissuing important writing from the 1940s, 1950s, and 1960s, including works by Carew, Neville Dawes, Figueroa, Mittelholzer, Napier, Orlando Patterson, Roach, Salkey, and Garth St. Omer. Works by Allfrey, Martin Carter, Errol John, Gladwell, Mais, and Eric Walrond, among others, have also recently been published by other presses.[48] Moreover, digitization is making yet more postwar literature easier for scholars to access, such as the Roger Mais Collection in the University of the West Indies, Mona Library Digital Collection, or the midcentury Guyanese literary journal *Kyk-over-al* in the Digital Library of the Caribbean. These newly available textual resources, alongside initiatives like David Scott's *Small Axe* interviews with figures such as Lamming, Patterson, and Wynter, allow for a much more fine-tuned picture of the texts and contexts of the period to emerge, a situation that bodes well for innovative future scholarship on the era's literature.[49]

As this collection hopes to show, this innovation is a welcome, even necessary task, for the Windrush era, in becoming the predominant origin myth of Anglophone Caribbean literature, has become somewhat ossified in the critical imagination, standing too powerfully in place as the signal moment of the region's literary development. As Breiner has noted, West Indian literary history has followed a script with "a colonial period yielding to a period of embattled and then successful nationalism . . . that typically ends with the achievement of political and aesthetic independence for the literature, a golden age of self-determination conceived as persisting indefinitely."[50] Since the age of political self-determination has surely not been entirely golden, Breiner suggests here, obeying this teleology leaves the contemporary critic somewhat adrift, unwilling to ignore the cultural and political achievement of independence, but equally unwilling to endorse the postindependence dispensation as utopian fulfillment. Similarly, this collection, while agreeing that the Windrush era is—despite its weighty historical baggage—a formative one in the history of Anglophone Caribbean literature, also suggests that by attending to the lesser known registers of that period, one might begin to form different, less teleological accounts of literary history and, hence, to ask different questions about how that history might usefully speak to us today.

Notes

1. For an incisive analysis of the mythology surrounding this historical event, see Matthew Mead, "Empire Windrush: The Cultural Memory of an Imaginary Arrival," *Journal of Postcolonial Writing* 45, no. 2 (2009): 137–149. A wide-ranging account of some of the key thinkers formed by this migration experience can be found in Bill Schwarz, ed., *West Indian Intellectuals in Britain* (Manchester: Manchester University Press, 2003).

2. The official unveiling of Windrush Square in the London borough of Brixton in 2010 stands as a testament to the state-sanctioned acceptance of this narrative.

3. Stuart Hall, introduction to *The Windrush Legacy: Memories of Britain's Post-War Caribbean Immigrants*, ed. Sam Walker and Alvin Elcock (London: Black Cultural Archives, 1998), 3.

4. Louise Bennett, "Colonisation in Reverse," in *Jamaica Labrish*, ed. Rex Nettleford (Jamaica: Sangster's Book Stores, 1972), 179. The classic account of this history is found in Peter Fryer, *Staying Power: The History of Black People in Britain* (London: Pluto Press, 1984).

5. The Commonwealth Immigrants Act of 1962 was the first of a series of acts that tightened the requirements for immigration from Britain's colonies and former colonies in the Caribbean, Asia, and Africa. For further discussion, see, for instance, Paul Gilroy, *"There Ain't No Black in the Union Jack": The Cultural Politics of Race and Nation* (London: Hutchinson, 1987).

6. See Anne Walmsley, *The Caribbean Artists Movement, 1966–1972: A Literary and Cultural History* (London: New Beacon Books, 1992), for a more extensive listing (and description of) the writers and artists who came to Great Britain after World War II, a group that also includes authors who began publishing books much later, such as James Berry and E. A. Markham. The remainder of her book provides an excellent account of the Caribbean Artists Movement, the aesthetic movement that serves as the most obvious successor to the Windrush writers.

7. Edward (Kamau) Brathwaite, "The New West Indian Novelists—I," *Bim* 8, no. 31 (1960): 204. On the revolutionizing impact of Windrush writers, see also John Clement Ball, *Imagining London: Postcolonial Fiction and the Transnational Metropolis* (Toronto: University of Toronto Press, 2004); John McLeod, *Postcolonial London: Rewriting the Metropolis* (London: Routledge, 2004); Sukhdev Sandhu, *London Calling: How Black and Asian Writers Imagined a City* (London: Harper Perennial, 2004).

8. George Lamming, *The Pleasures of Exile* (1960; repr., Ann Arbor: University of Michigan Press, 1992), 38.

9. Searches of the MLA database give a sense of which authors from the Windrush period have maintained critical prestige. The English-speaking region's two Nobel Prize winners, Naipaul and Walcott, are by far the most canonized: the former has 667 articles and book chapters devoted to his work, while the latter has 691 (their only apparent competitor being Jean Rhys, who wrote both before and after the period, but not during it: she has 560). Other canonical Anglophone Caribbean writers from the Windrush generation have received consistent attention but at a markedly lower level: Harris comes in at 261, Brathwaite at 183, Lamming at 175, and Selvon at 124. There is far less scholarship recorded

in the standard US and UK databases on their contemporaries—Roger Mais has 24, Andrew Salkey 16, John Hearne 14, and Edgar Mittelholzer 11—despite the fact that they were considered influential members of the Windrush generation at the time. MLA International Bibliography Ebsco Host search conducted March 19, 2013.

10. Selwyn R. Cudjoe, *Beyond Boundaries: The Intellectual Tradition of Trinidad and Tobago in the Nineteenth Century* (Wellesley, Mass.: Calaloux Publications, 2003); Alison Donnell, *Twentieth-Century Caribbean Literature: Critical Moments in Anglophone Literary History* (London: Routledge, 2006); Evelyn O'Callaghan, *Women Writing the West Indies: "A Hot Place Belonging to Us"* (London: Routledge, 2003); Leah Reade Rosenberg, *Nationalism and the Formation of Caribbean Literature* (New York: Palgrave Macmillan, 2007); Faith Smith, *Creole Recitations: John Jacob Thomas and Colonial Formation in the Late Nineteenth-Century Caribbean* (Charlottesville: University of Virginia Press, 2002). Also, of course, Reinhard Sander, *The Trinidad Awakening: West Indian Literature of the Nineteen-Thirties* (New York: Greenwood Press, 1988), offers an account of pre-Windrush literary activity, albeit one that prefigures the later generation's narrative of national self-realization.

11. Belinda Edmondson, *Making Men: Gender, Literary Authority, and Women's Writing in Caribbean Narrative* (Durham, N.C.: Duke University Press, 1999); Belinda Edmondson, *Caribbean Middlebrow: Leisure Culture and the Middle Class* (Ithaca, N.Y.: Cornell University Press, 2009).

12. Patricia Joan Saunders, *Alien-nation and Repatriation: Translating Identity in Anglophone Caribbean Literature* (Lanham, Md.: Lexington Books, 2007); Kezia Page, *Transnational Negotiations in Caribbean Diasporic Literature: Remitting the Text* (New York: Routledge, 2011); Raphael Dalleo, *Caribbean Literature and the Public Sphere: From the Plantation to the Postcolonial* (Charlottesville: University of Virginia Press, 2011); Michael Niblett, *The Caribbean Novel since 1945: Cultural Practice, Form, and the Nation-State* (Jackson: University Press of Mississippi, 2012).

13. Donnell, *Twentieth-Century Caribbean Literature*, 72.

14. For the most famous example of Windrush's influence on Anglophone African writing, see Ngũgĩ wa Thiong'o, *Homecoming: Essays on African and Caribbean Literature, Culture, and Politics* (London: Heinemann, 1972), which pays particular attention to Lamming as an inspirational force. For a broad, detailed account of the synergistic establishment of Anglophone African and Caribbean literature, see Gail Low, *Publishing the Postcolonial: Anglophone West African and Caribbean Writing in the U.K., 1948–1968* (New York: Routledge, 2011).

15. Lamming, *Pleasures of Exile*, 36.

16. For critical assessments of the significance of the folk in Anglophone Caribbean literature, see Gordon Rohlehr, "Literature and the Folk," in *My Strangled City and Other Essays* (Port of Spain: Longman, Trinidad, 1992), 52–85; and Christian Campbell, "The Politics of the 'the Folk' in Caribbean Discourse: 'Folking' up the Criticism," in *The Routledge Companion to Anglophone Caribbean Literature*, ed. Michael A. Bucknor and Alison Donnell (London: Routledge, 2011), 383–392.

17. Lamming, *Pleasures of Exile*, 26.

18. G. R. Coulthard, ed., *Caribbean Literature: An Anthology* (London: University of London Press, 1966), 9.

19. Bruce King, ed., *West Indian Literature* (Hamden, Conn.: Archon Books, 1979), 3.

20. Sandra Pouchet Paquet, "The Fifties," in King, *West Indian Literature*, 64.

21. Norval Edwards, "The Foundational Generation: From *The Beacon* to *Savacou*," in Bucknor and Donnell, *Routledge Companion to Anglophone Caribbean Literature*, 111.

22. Sylvia Wynter, "We Must Learn to Sit Down Together and Discuss a Little Culture," Parts I and II, *Jamaica Journal* 2, no. 4 (1968): 24–32, and 3, no. 1 (1969): 27–42; Louis James, introduction to *The Islands In Between: Essays on West Indian Literature*, ed. Louis James (London: Oxford University Press, 1968), 25.

23. Ramchand quoted in Campbell, "Politics of the 'the Folk,'" 389; Ramchand quoted in Edwards, "Foundational Generation," 111.

24. Kenneth Ramchand, ed. and intro., *West Indian Narrative: An Introductory Anthology* (London: Nelson, 1966), 3. In his most recent work on the canon, Ramchand reveals his long-standing investment in the cultural nationalist role of literature, explaining that his objective in centering the curriculum of the University of the West Indies around West Indian literature was to "loosen the grip of what the [British] canon implied about other cultures and peoples"—namely that it made it difficult to "find . . . or make . . . the true self in a colonized context." See Kenneth Ramchand, "Canons, Curriculums, and Critics," in Bucknor and Donnell, *Routledge Companion to Anglophone Caribbean Literature*, 357.

25. Kenneth Ramchand, *The West Indian Novel and Its Background*, 2nd ed. (London: Heinemann, 1983), 63. The wording Ramchand employs suggests, in fact, that this observation holds true even in 1970, when his study was first published.

26. Lamming, *Pleasures of Exile*, 42.

27. Edward (Kamau) Brathwaite, "Roots," in *Roots* (Ann Arbor: University of Michigan Press, 1993), 42. The essay was originally published in 1963 in *Bim*. Not long after this, of course, Brathwaite would turn to Windrush expatriate Mais (author of the archetypically exilic "Why I Love and Leave Jamaica") as his primary exemplar of a properly Caribbean prose writer.

28. Ramchand, *West Indian Novel*, 74.

29. For prominent meditations on the dangers of the region's literary predilection for exile, see ibid., 13–14; O. R. Dathorne, *Caribbean Narrative: An Anthology of West Indian Writing* (London: Heinemann Educational Books, 1966), 6; Edward (Kamau) Brathwaite, "The New West Indian Novelists—I," *Bim* 8, no. 31 (1960): 201–202.

30. Dalleo, *Caribbean Literature and the Public Sphere*, viii. Edwards, too, traces this trope back to the Windrush era, observing that "the major critical interventions of the 1950s were thus made by critics extrapolating the conjunctural contingencies of Caribbean exile into a teleological axiom and foundational category of West Indian writing" (Edwards, "Foundational Generation," 115).

31. Numerous feminist critics could be cited here, including many already mentioned above (Donnell, Edmondson, O'Callaghan, and Saunders). Pertinently, Curdella Forbes has provided an enlightening reading of gender in the works of two of the most prominent Windrush writers, Lamming and Selvon. See Curdella Forbes, *From Nation to Diaspora: Samuel Selvon, George Lamming and the Cultural Performance of Gender* (Kingston: University of the West Indies Press, 2005).

32. Rhonda Cobham, "Women in Jamaican Literature 1900–1950," in *Out of the Kumbla: Caribbean Women and Literature*, ed. Carole Boyce Davies and Elaine Savory Fido (Trenton, N.J.: Africa World Press, 1990), 215–217.

33. Shirley Toland-Dix, "The Hills of Hebron: Sylvia Wynter's Disruption of the Narrative of the Nation," *Small Axe* 25 (2008): 58. See Davies and Fido, *Out of the Kumbla*; and Evelyn O'Callaghan, *Woman Version: Critical Approaches to West Indian Fiction by Women* (New York: St. Martin's Press, 1993), for crucial early examples of the later emergence of a consolidated feminist Caribbean criticism.

34. Laurence A. Breiner, "The Eighties," in *West Indian Literature*, 2nd ed., ed. Bruce King (London: Macmillan, 1995), 76.

35. Hena Maes-Jelinek and Bénédicte Ledent, "The Novel since 1970," in *A History of Literature in the Caribbean*, ed. A. James Arnold (Amsterdam: John Benjamins, 2001), 2:177.

36. For a further discussion of the implications of seeing Caribbean women writers emerging only in the 1970s, see Donnell, *Twentieth-Century Caribbean Literature*, 11.

37. See Makeda Silvera, "Man Royal and Sodomites: Some Thoughts on the Invisibility of Afro-Caribbean Lesbians," *Feminist Studies* 18, no. 3 (1992): 521–532; and Michelle Cliff, *Abeng* (Trumansburg, N.Y.: Crossing Press, 1984).

38. Lucy Evans, "Introduction," in *The Caribbean Short Story: Critical Perspectives*, ed. Lucy Evans, Mark McWatt, and Emma Smith (Leeds: Peepal Tree Press, 2011), 15, 16. Evans rightfully notes the role of newspapers and small magazines in facilitating this prewar tradition. For a convincing account of these publishing currents in Trinidad specifically, see Kate Quinn, "'I Will Let Down My Bucket Here': Writers and the Conditions of Cultural Production in Post-Independence Trinidad," in *Caribbean Literature after Independence: The Case of Earl Lovelace*, ed. Bill Schwarz (London: Institute for the Study of the Americas, 2008), 21–40.

39. The most famous case of this policing of the literary boundaries is probably Brathwaite's rejection of Rhys as a West Indian author, in Edward (Kamau) Brathwaite, *Contradictory Omens: Cultural Diversity and Integration in the Caribbean* (Mona: Savacou, 1974). See Peter Hulme's evenhanded summary of the disagreement over Rhys in "The Place of *Wide Sargasso Sea*," *Wasafiri* 20 (Autumn 1994): 5–11. This sparked a response from Brathwaite, to which Hulme and several other scholars subsequently responded in the pages of *Wasafiri*. Lamming's dismissal of Hearne for his middle-class focus—discussed in this collection by both Kate Houlden and Kim Robinson-Walcott—stands as an earlier, class-based iteration of this exclusionary logic.

40. Ramchand, *West Indian Novel*, 223–236.

41. For a good contemporary account of the different ideological purposes to which the notion of creolization has been put, see Shalini Puri, *The Caribbean Postcolonial: Social Equality, Post-Nationalism, and Cultural Hybridity* (New York: Palgrave, 2004).

42. Brathwaite, *Contradictory Omens*. Atreyee Phukan's essay in this collection argues that Brathwaite's philosophy of creolization can be read more inclusively.

43. Donnell, *Twentieth-Century Caribbean Literature*, 7.

44. Ibid.

45. It appears that only Barbara Howes's anthology, *From the Green Antilles: Writings of the Caribbean* (London: Granada, 1971), included Indo-Caribbean authors other than Naipaul and Selvon—namely, Ismith Khan and Daniel Samaroo.

46. As noted above, Brathwaite's dismissal of Rhys's claim to recognition as a Caribbean author—and the subsequent literary contretemps—is a later iteration of this debate.

47. Lamming, *Pleasures of Exile*, 45; Wynter, "We Must Learn," Part 2, 35.

48. Besides the Peepal Tree Press series, recently published postwar work includes Lizabeth Paravisini-Gebert, ed., *Love for an Island: The Collected Poems of Phyllis Shand Allfrey* (London: Papillote Press, 2014); Martin Carter, *University of Hunger: Collected Poems & Selected Prose*, ed. Gemma Robinson (Newcastle upon Tyne: Bloodaxe Books, 2006); Joyce Gladwell, *Brown Face, Big Master*, ed. Sandra Courtman (Oxford: Macmillan Caribbean, 2004); Errol John, *Moon on a Rainbow Shawl* (London: Faber and Faber, 2012); Roger Mais, *Brother Man* (Oxford: Macmillan Caribbean, 2004); Elma Napier, *Black and White Sands: A Bohemian Life in the Colonial Caribbean* (London: Papillote Press, 2009); and Eric Walrond, *In Search of Asylum: The Later Writings of Eric Walrond*, ed. Louis J. Parascandola and Carl E. Wade (Gainesville: University of Florida Press, 2011), which contains essays and short stories Walrond published in the 1950s when he was a patient in Roundway Hospital, a psychiatric hospital near Wiltshire, in the United Kingdom.

49. David Scott, "The Sovereignty of the Imagination: An Interview with George Lamming," *Small Axe* 12, no. 3 (2002): 7–200; "The Paradox of Freedom: An Interview with Orlando Patterson," *Small Axe* 17, no. 1 (2013): 96–242; "The Re-Enchantment of Humanism: An Interview with Sylvia Wynter," *Small Axe* 8, no. 3 (2000): 118–207.

50. Laurence A. Breiner, "How Shall the History of West Indian Literature Be Told?" *Journal of West Indian Literature* 11, no. 1 (2002): 42.

Part One

Negotiating National Belonging

Indianness and Nationalism in the Windrush Era

LISA OUTAR

In looking back at the Windrush era and considering its significance for the trajectories that Caribbean discourses of nationalism and cultural identity have taken, we are tossed back into the excitement and complexity of the anti-colonial movement, the trenchant and poignant idea of the empire coming home to roost, optimism about the possibilities of nationalism, and a sense of the tricky road to new forms of political and cultural identity shaped via vexed concepts of home/away, insider/outsider, citizen/migrant. To assess the Windrush era through the lens of little-known Caribbean Indian voices who were addressing questions of belonging and the limits of prevailing narratives of political and social identity at the time is both to foreground a gap in our thinking about that era and to uncover some of the anxieties of the period that were often projected onto this group of relatively recent migrants. Indians—who were in the process of defining their place both within Caribbean societies and within larger frameworks of British and Indian colonial identity—as well as the region's non-Indians, were trying to figure out what role Indianness should play in the new national formations being imagined. The pre- and post–World War II period was a particularly intriguing time for Caribbean Indians, coinciding as it did with the hundredth anniversary of the Indian presence in the region and the movement of Indian nationalism on the subcontinent, which was nearing its key goal of independence, achieved in 1947. It was thus a moment of reflection about what had been achieved in the time since the arrival of Indians, what desires were for the time ahead, and what sorts of relationships with the political and cultural influences of the subcontinent should be pursued.

As we know, it is not that Caribbean Indian voices are absent in our thinking about this period. In fact, V. S. Naipaul and Samuel Selvon are celebrated as part of that breakthrough generation who brought Caribbean literature into a fertile new international era. However, they are rarely examined in terms of their relationships to other forms of Caribbean Indian writing at the time, and the representation of Indianness in the work of the rest of the Windrush writers is almost never examined. While novels like George Lamming's 1958 *Of Age and Innocence* express deep fears of what Indian instinctive behavior might mean for the future of nationalism in the region, a review of Indian journals and literary publications of the era suggests that the presumption of unified action or thinking on the part of this community was erroneous indeed. In *Finding a Place: Indo-Trinidadian Literature*, Kris Rampersad tracks what was going on with Indian writing from the 1850s to the 1950s in Trinidad and suggests that there was an active debate within the Indian community that was being ignored by dominant discourses of nationalism at the time. She argues that "while to others they appeared to be united, internal divisions were strong and festering, and widened as the stakes in the society became higher, to climax into a clear rift on the eve of independence."[1] In this chapter, I select George Lamming and Edgar Mittelholzer as representatives of two particular strands of Windrush-era thinking about nationalism and examine them as writers who were in fact actively trying to imagine spaces for Indians within new national collectives. However, I contend that despite these authors' aspirational rhetoric of common creole identity, they ended up portraying Indo-Caribbeans as a potential threat to Caribbean nationalism.

Further, I argue that their depictions seriously misrepresented the commitment to Caribbean nationalism that we see in the work of Indo-Caribbean writers and intellectuals of the period. The work of two journals in particular, the *Observer* and the *Spectator*, while evidencing key disagreements about choices for Indians in the region, was united in its complex understanding of nationalism's relationship to ethnic memory and cultural exploration: both journals rejected the notion that the retention of Indian cultural identity meant a betrayal of nationalist ideals. I argue that the *Observer* and the *Spectator* end up invoking what Arjun Appadurai has called "trojan nationalisms." Containing as they did "transnational, subnational links and, more generally, nonnational identities and aspirations," the conceptions of citizenship that Indo-Caribbeans demarcated for themselves offered key challenges to emerging norms of nationalist rhetoric that emphasized affective loyalty to only the Caribbean as homeland.[2] Shaped within a context of Indian cultural identity and an awareness of the subcontinent's own anticolonial struggle and emergence into independence, these unique expressions of Caribbean nationalism imagined new possibilities of alliances that encompassed the subcontinent, the Caribbean, and Britain.

While the plural society model has long been discarded in our considerations of how Caribbean cultural and political formations have taken shape, it is useful to revisit it for what it has to say about Indians in this era, especially since it coincided with popular thinking of the time. In 1965 M. G. Smith tried to theorize why, in the British Caribbean, "nationalism has been slow to develop, and separatism is as pronounced within the colonies as between them."[3] Smith chalked the situation up to the fact that most of these societies were multiracial, laying particular blame at the feet of Indo-Caribbeans: "Little research has yet been done on these substantial East Indian populations, but it is known that Hindustani is spoken among them, and that the majority of these East Indians remain loyal to Indian culture and Indian nationalism. These loyalties are related to the slow growth of a Caribbean national sentiment."[4] For Smith, the retention of Indian languages and a continued sense of themselves as Indian citizens are characteristics that serve to place this group outside any sense of Caribbean affiliation. Though Smith's rhetoric thus sounds initially contradictory to George Lamming's in *The Pleasures of Exile*, in which Lamming praises Selvon's peasant sensibility (presumably derived from his Indianness) as key for the formation of an anticolonial nationalism, their common ground, as revealed in *Of Age and Innocence*, is the sense of Indo-Caribbean people as somehow being too authentically Indian to be loyal Caribbean subjects.

Lamming's novel, while committed to the vision of a multiethnic Caribbean, reveals a profound, stereotypical fear of Indian clannishness, or, to use Édouard Glissant's term, the group's propensity for "filiation."[5] In large part, the figure of the Indian emerges in *Of Age and Innocence* as the foil against which the celebrated nationalist body is defined. The novel reveals the author's own conflicted and fearful views of Caribbean shortcomings more so than it does a confident vision of the possibilities of a postcolonial Caribbean. In his consideration of how a multiracial society, in its struggle toward independence, negotiates difference, Lamming depicts the spectacular failure of a promising political alliance due to the action of an Indian character, Baboo, who assassinates the popular black leader, Shephard, thinking he is clearing the way for someone more like himself to gain power. As he plaintively relates to Singh, the Indo-Trinidadian politician to whom his murderous act was devoted, it "was only for you I do it . . . from infancy I dream to see someone like myself, some Indian with your achievement rule San Cristobal."[6] Through one of its climactic moments, the novel thus signals a fear that the Indo-Caribbean is incapable of the selflessness necessary to sustain the sort of coalition effort it would take to lead the Caribbean to freedom from colonial rule. In this fictional world, the authenticity of one's claim of belonging to the nation is ranked according to pain and sacrifice, and the Indian is shown to be incapable of sacrifice in service of the nation. *Of Age and Innocence* thus plays into the persistent idea that those descended from slavery suffered most in the Caribbean's history and so were most deserving of inheriting the reins of power from colonial authorities.

In the depiction of Baboo as narcissistic (seeking to have a version of him-self in power), untrustworthy, and primarily motivated by greed, we see that Lamming's disappointment in the shortcomings of Caribbean nationalist movements ends up fitting easily into available stereotypes of the Indo-Carib-bean as clannish and continually seduced by the lure of money at the expense of other human and moral connections. Baboo and the other silently hovering Indians he presumably speaks for are set up as immature citizens who need to be taught how to be a part of a multiethnic collective; they are rendered in Lamming's novel as people for whom the abstract ideals of nationalism—loyalty outside the bonds of blood kinship—did not come naturally. In his later comments on the writing of the novel, we find Lamming supporting this idea of citizenship that has to be cultivated and taught. Framing *Of Age and Innocence* as his reflections on the possibilities for cooperation across ethnic lines in Guyana in the 1950s, Lamming argues that human solidarity "requires a kind of educational work, a kind of indoctrination, a reciprocal sharing of cultural histories, which has never been at the center of our political agendas in the Caribbean."[7] However, because the character who betrays the solidarity movement is an Indian who desires an Indian leader, the novel suggests that it is Indians especially who must be taught these reciprocal values. Without these values—those found lacking most of all in the Indian characters—Lam-ming implies that San Cristobal may not be competent for self-rule.[8]

Like Lamming, Mittelholzer was committed to the depiction of a multi-ethnic Caribbean that included Indians, yet his 1950 *A Morning at the Office* also projects onto Indians deep anxieties about Caribbean claims of measur-ing up to its colonizers and, consequently, about the region's readiness for self-rule. This novel is particularly important for assessing Mittelholzer's vision of ethnicity and national belonging because it presents the multiethnic staff in a corporate office as a microcosm of Trinidadian society and thus illustrates Trinidad's figurative cohesiveness as a nation and its readiness to rule. In a letter to the Guyanese poet A. J. Seymour, Mittelholzer writes: "There is much need in England and America of a true representation of the coloured mid-dle-class element in British Guiana and the West Indies. We've been looked upon too long as 'natives' and for once and all I want to have the truth out. I want the English and the Americans to realize that there are coloured natives out here who can be just as educated and refined as they can be."[9] What I note in Mittelholzer's comments here and in *A Morning at the Office* in general are the intertwined racial and class connotations of this creative undertak-ing. If it is the Caribbean middle class who can hold their own against the English and Americans, then there ensues a particular kind of disavowal of the non-middle-class member of Caribbean society that falls more heavily on some racialized bodies than others. My argument here is that in *A Morning at the Office*, the figure of the Indian comes to represent the peasant body: that which needs to be rejected by the modern state and citizen. Importantly, Mittelholzer thus disagreed with one popular nationalist trend in efforts to counter charges of cultural inferiority—the celebration of the idea of the authentic peasant. In fact, Mittelholzer's 1950 novel, while accepting of Indians as an incontrovertible part of a multiethnic landscape, shows them most prominently as a shameful reminder of a peasant past.

Scrambling at the bottom of the racial and class hierarchy that Mittelholzer sets up in the novel is the Indian Jagabir. He is a profoundly disturbing presence to the other characters, who are shown as more capable of social mobility, albeit with limitations based on skin color and class origin. While Jagabir's mocking of the office boy's crush, combined with his endless snooping, seems cause enough for him to be an object of dislike, the intensity of feeling expressed toward him in the text demands our closer attention to this character. At various points people in the office describe their feelings for him in terms of "contempt," "disgust," "detesting," and "hate." Jagabir is described as a "cheap coolie" and "the nasty dog," with the word "coolie" being tossed about most often. Some of the complex reasons for the contempt that Jagabir inspires are revealed by the colored Miss Henery's assessment of him. Describing a "deep contempt and disgust" inspired by "his ingratiating, yet at the same time nagging and accusatory, voice," she goes on to argue that her upbringing led her to feel that "East Indians were inferior, contemptible people" and "dirty coolies."[10] Particularly interesting to me is her description of Jagabir as "nagging and accusatory." Why does she experience him as nagging? What is the nature of his accusation? The language of her description of him indicates that Jagabir bothers her, that Indians bother her in general (regardless of whatever liking she may express for the other Indian character, Miss Bisnauth), because they remind her of ungenteel origins. Her insistence that her grandparents had been "respectable," "educated," and "well-bred" when "coolies" were still laboring in the fields is an important one.[11] It is by disavowing the presumed Indian qualities of dirtiness and inferiority that Miss Henery can establish her own respectability.

Miss Henery's rejection of the Indian is a repudiation of her own connection to this history of hard work, a refusal of the memory that her family members were once slaves working in dire conditions of poverty and prey to many of the same accusations she hurls at Jagabir and Indians in general. For Miss Henery, whose family has struggled up to the standards of European middle-class respectability from the cane fields, part of the discomfort of having Jagabir in the office is having to deal with the reminder he brings (which she experiences as "accusatory") of humbler origins. In this vein, the Indian's fault is not that he or she is poor or a peasant, but that he or she is belated. He or she comes late to the development of the nation and makes evident a facet of its past his or her predecessors would prefer to forget.

Moreover, in this iteration of Windrush writing, attainment of middle-class status does not help liberate the Indo-Caribbean from the weight of these expectations of backwardness and self-interestedness. The middle-class Bisnauth family, described as "thoroughly Christian and western in outlook, like their parents before them," is nevertheless depicted as hampered by a "clannish" Indian mentality.[12] The Bisnauths speak no Indian language, seem to practice no Indian rituals, and embrace European and American cultural practices. In the world the novel creates, where everyone is striving for middle-class respectability as shaped by European norms, this failure to cling to tradition is not a tragedy. What is presented as resistant to the logic of creolization and national belonging, however, is their clannishness. This trait is described as an instinct, as something that "continued subconsciously in them from the seed of their forebears."[13] As with Singh and Baboo from *Of Age and Innocence*, there is no rational justification of this feeling. It is a matter of deep instinct that comes from the body: "They just felt so; they could offer no explanation of the matter."[14] Miss Bisnauth's plan to marry the mixed-race Arthur (with its implications of Caribbean unity) is cast into grave doubt under the weight of this allegedly instinctive behavior, as the novel points an accusatory finger at Indian ethnic exclusivity as a disruptor of national togetherness.

In differing ways, then, we see these leading writers of the Windrush generation portraying Indo-Caribbeans as a potential threat to Caribbean nationalism. Neither in Lamming's celebration of the folk nor in Mittelholzer's interest in the more elite classes as the basis for national identity do we see productive spaces assigned to Indo-Caribbeans. Relatedly, the forms of nationalism that *did* emerge from Indo-Caribbean communities at the time have often been perceived as inherently dangerous and racist. Tony Martin's description of the trajectories of African and Indian nationalism in the Caribbean, where he primarily associates Indian nationalist expressions with quests for separatism and political domination, is a particularly vivid example of this.[15] He emphasizes ways in which Indian political movements worked against Afro-Caribbean goals, arguing that "Indian communalism in politics could on occasion be used as a weapon to frustrate or delay constitutional advance sought by Africans."[16] While the racism and other discourses of exclusion that circulate in Caribbean Indian communities are generally glossed over in the work of Indo-Caribbean scholars, it remains true that perceptions such as Martin's are often based on the voices of a few influential Indians such as Trinidad's H. P. Singh, considered the father of Indo-Trinidadian nationalism (and, interestingly, a member of the same India Club the Bisnauths belonged to in *A Morning at the Office*). In this way, Caribbean intellectuals often fail to take into account the variety of voices that arose from the Indian community in the postwar era on questions of belonging, cultural identity, and citizenship.

Part of the reason for this suspicion of Indian nationalist discourse may lie in the fact that such discourses often contained the seeds for transnational approaches to the idea of nation that did not necessarily align with the Windrush goals of an anticolonial (regional) nationalism. The anticolonial movement in India in the 1930s and 1940s and the bloody achievement of independence in 1947 made Indo-Caribbeans keenly aware, and proud, of their identities as Indians, while also inspiring concern about discourses of group identity that might result in violence against those considered minorities. The forms of cultural and national identity that several Indo-Caribbean thinkers promoted called upon British and Indian facets of their Caribbean identities as well as links to the United States and to other colonial sites. Paradoxically, we have to return to the local in order to perceive the more global perspective that Indian writings promoted. Rampersad argues that in order to bring the wide array of Indo-Caribbean contributions to literature and to discourses on nationalism into view, it is important to shift focus onto national literature rather than regional, the latter being the view that the Windrush movement often encouraged. Rampersad turns attention to local traditions of writing in Trinidad, to the little-celebrated institutional forms that supported and nurtured the writers who went on to greater fame in the United Kingdom and elsewhere. She rightly argues that Indian works are generally not included in the histories of publications in the region. Nevertheless, the many and often short-lived publications that she assesses, like the *Indian Koh-i-Noor Gazette, East Indian Herald,* and *East Indian Weekly* (often the output of literary and cultural organizations), did not make efforts to establish separate Indian political parties but remained invested in the larger society. I argue, in fact, that in the period's Indo-Trinidadian writings we see an insistence on alternate models of nationalism emerging, ones that encompassed a connection to the subcontinent while also embracing Caribbean identity and nationalism.

Invocations of India and things Indian were a delicate matter in the midst of the bourgeoning nationalist movement and were clearly a sore point for those like Eric Williams, who famously argued: "There can be no Mother India for those whose ancestors came from India. . . . There can be no Mother Africa for those of African origins. . . . There can be no Mother England

and no dual loyalties. . . . A nation, like an individual, can have only one Mother. The only Mother we recognize is Mother Trinidad and Tobago and a Mother cannot discriminate between her children."[17] What would it mean for Caribbean Indians to be interested in India and in themselves as people of Indian origin? Many suspected that it might constitute what the Francophone Caribbean creoliste writers would later call "exterior vision" (which they describe as anchoring oneself to mythical shores when afraid of the Caribbean's uncomfortable muddle of histories).[18] Most certainly there was the presumption that glances in the direction of the subcontinent denied the idea of the Caribbean as home and showed a clear preference for India in that affective role. The writings by Indians of the period, however, reveal a more complicated account.

The two publications that I am particularly interested in are Trinidadian ones: the *Observer*, published from 1941 to 1960 and headed by H. P. Singh, who took over as editor in 1946; and the *Spectator*, published from 1948 to 1965, founded and edited by Dennis Mahabir. They were magazines that stood at the intersection of the literary and the journalistic. Both were addressing larger issues facing Indians in the society, such as high rates of illiteracy and poverty, at the same time as they were introducing and fostering an appreciation of literature and culture. To be sure, these were middle-class publications, but from the ads and the letters to the editor that appear within them, they seem to have circulated throughout Trinidad and, especially in the case of the *Spectator*, abroad to Guyana and sites of the Caribbean diaspora in Toronto and London. There are interesting links between the two publications in that Mahabir and Singh belonged to the same literary clubs—the Minerva Club and then the India Club (which replaced the Minerva Club in 1945)—and also in that Mahabir was in fact a coeditor of the *Observer* before leaving Trinidad for England in 1945 to study law. Moreover, both men worked on the Minerva Club's *Minerva Review*, which was published from 1941 to 1944 and was specifically dedicated to publishing original book reviews, poetry, and short stories (and in fact included work by Selvon and Seepersad Naipaul).[19] The editorial work of both men thus emerged from a vibrant local tradition that encouraged intellectual pursuits that cut across ethnic lines and associated them with the advancement of the larger national society.

Singh was on the ideological side of the spectrum urging protection of Indian interests in the colony. As he is considered the father of Indian nationalism in Trinidad, it is important to consider exactly what sort of nationalism he and the *Observer* were espousing. The *Observer's* debut editorial declared: "We are not advocates of any narrow nationalism or racial segregation seeking rights and privileges to the exclusion of others . . . [which] have no useful place in our cosmopolitan community. We Indians are Trinidadians first of all but we are Indian Trinidadians and, conditions being what they are, we shall have to meet problems from this standpoint for many years to come."[20] In a later moment, we find Singh, who published several pamphlets around the time of independence and emerged as one of the most vociferous as well as controversial figures of the period, arguing that it was natural to turn to India for inspiration, while at the same time soundly claiming belonging in Trinidad. The first loyalty of the Indians of the colony, he argued,

> is to the country where they live, do business, raise their families and have social and other ties.... But [they] have come from an ancient land which has now awakened to seek its rightful place among the great nations of the world, and its [sic] would be equally unnatural were they not drawn by bonds of affection and pride to the land of their origin. If others find that they are not so fortunate then the fault surely is not ours! ... We serve notice to all that in this land which is very much our own we shall be as loyal as anyone, as strong as anyone and as jealous of our interests as anyone.[21]

This layered rhetoric of loyalty to one's homeland, political force, and pursuit of ethnic interests is striking in its invocations of multiple forms of belonging. We see here the important ways in which Indians were not only claiming the Caribbean as home, rather than a site of temporary settlement, but also challenging the available narratives of nationalism, arguing that pride in India and continued connection to it did not constitute betrayal of national goals. Singh's rhetoric is also notable here for its problematic echoing of a contemporary British perspective that India was a noble civilization as compared to other sites of British colonization. As Faith Smith has shown, such claims were subject to radical reversal and repositioning as the British attempted to control their black and Indian labor forces, but in this period we find scholars like Max Muller exploring the origins of Aryanism and connections between British and Indian languages. This was going on at the same time as coverage of the Indian independence movement, which evoked images of Indian strength and nobility, especially in the figure of Gandhi.

In Trinidad, the stereotypes of the coolie prevalent in Mittelholzer's novel were very much on the mind of these local Indian writers, and, as we see in the passage above, those like Singh were invoking scholarship by Indologists and the successful Indian independence movement to push back against the charges of coolie status and degraded identity leveled at Caribbean Indians by some from the Caribbean and indeed from India itself. Yet we also find discomfort with applying the versions of nationalism emerging in India to the

Caribbean. While he was using images of noble India to demonstrate respectability and legitimacy (in fact, the front covers of the *Observer* were often of Nehru, Gandhi, and Tagore), even the conservative Singh was critical of the religious and caste strife to be found there. In particular, we find his uneasiness with the divisions between Muslims and Hindus on the subcontinent as he was arguing for the need for Indian unity in Trinidad.[22] Early writings by those like Peter Ruhomon proudly proclaimed the virtues of Indian culture in the Caribbean for having broken from caste and religious divisions.[23]

While Singh was calling for the acknowledgment of "bonds of affection and pride" to India, Mahabir, in the *Spectator*, was calling in 1948 for a "centripetal" approach to Trinidad and for a "centrifugal" one to India, declaring that "the *Spectator* will always maintain that we should be Trinidadians first, Negroes, Chinese, Indians, second, Catholics, Mohammedans or Atheists third."[24] In particular, Mahabir was drawing attention to the irrevocable rupture between India and the Caribbean in the form of a generational divide reflected in contemporary Caribbean Indian leaders, calling for a "competent and unselfish leadership"[25] instead of "irresponsible Indians who have long outlived their days of usefulness" and "can do nothing but cause Indians to be a suspected people in the West Indies."[26] His strong language in 1948 about "incompetent old fossils"[27] was directed against Singh and others like him—people who, notably, did not pursue higher education and for the most part had not lived outside the colony as Mahabir had. Mahabir was particularly invested in broadening the perspectives of the large masses of the uneducated and illiterate (at least in English) Indians who remained primarily in the agricultural sectors of the country, an effort he thought necessary to head off what he saw as views dangerous to emerging national and regional projects of solidarity. Like Mittelholzer in some ways, he was arguing for the pursuit of middle-class status by Indo-Caribbeans: "The people must be educated and they should know that 'remaining an agricultural people promises no reward, new fields of activity must be sought.'"[28] In this vein, his coverage of the outside world was not limited to India, but extended all over the world (the *Spectator* featured correspondents from the United Kingdom and the United States as well as from within Trinidad).

The ambitiousness of the goal of these magazines to bring a local Indian intellectual tradition into being in Trinidad is perhaps best illuminated by the fact that three-fifths of the Indian population were illiterate in English. Nevertheless, these publications seemed to have been disseminated and invoked responses far and wide within the society. Our attention to them, as I have been arguing, is critical to understanding the limitations of dominant discourses of nationalism during the Windrush era and the new transnational possibilities they offered. Yet we have serious challenges of access due to both their ephemeral nature and inadequate archiving and an even greater issue of the ideological bias of those who attempt to recuperate such lesser-known writers. In *The Mystic Masseur*, V. S. Naipaul presents these early journals in which his father's work appeared in a particularly satirical light, mocking and distorting their actual concerns with India and Indianness.

The writings of H. P. Singh are also filtered through some very polemical eyes. The 1993 republishers of Singh's major writings read his work and the whole atmosphere of the preindependence region through the lens of a failure of that early community to be politicized enough. In it, Singh's most controversial statements are presented as prescient responses to overt racism against Indians. In their foreword, we find the editors condemning people like Adrian Cola Rienzi, who sided with C. L. R. James to form the Workers and Farmers Party in 1965, as "compromising his Indian-ness" and promoting "an ideology for genocide for Indians."[29] They also lament "the tendency for Indian nationalism in Trinidad not to move in the direction of political organization" as "an error the Indian community will pay for in the future."[30] While most Indian thinkers and writers of the period were not rabidly violent and racist, as Martin's analysis of Indian nationalism would suggest, neither were they merely the put-upon victims of racism that the editors of the Indian Review Press perceive. Above all, it is imperative that we fight the presumption that there was a monolithic identity for this group at this time. This brief look at the Indian magazines of the time reveals the heterogeneity and conflicts within the community, thereby allowing us to see the more complex narratives of national and cultural identity that emerged in this period and that were persistently, then and now, misrepresented.

In *Sovereignty of the Imagination*, we find Lamming calling for "an *authentic civic nationalism* that will embrace and recreolize all ethnic types in Caribbean society."[31] I would argue that in such a statement and in *Of Age and Innocence*, he fails to see the multiple forms of nationalism that were emerging in the region and thus fails to recognize that one such type was not going to be sufficient to encompass the ethnic diversity of the region. In her more recent considerations of Indo-Caribbean musical production, the Indian scholar Tejaswini Niranjana argues:

> Instead of asking for a place in the dominant narrative of nationhood in India on the terms of Indian nationalism, East Indians might emphasize the specificity of their genealogy and attempt to link this emphasis to questions about the composition of the "Indian" being raised by different subaltern groups in India. Such a rearticulation of the East Indian claim on India might eventually also change the way Indianness is claimed in the Caribbean.[32]

This is precisely what was starting to happen in the early Indian publications, where the writers were juggling the pull of multiple allegiances—as Indian, as British colonial subjects, as Trinidadians, and as global citizens—and articulating alternative forms of nationalism that did not rely simply on anticolonial rhetoric of solidarity or exilic longing, but explored local specificity in relation to connections to India and to other sites of imagined modernity. As we saw with Lamming's and Mittelholzer's novels, respectively, stereotypes about clannishness and a distaste for "coolieness" and its reminders of past shame often stood in the way of perceiving such developments. In our contemporary context, we find the Trinidadian singer Drupatee Ramgoonai describing what she was wearing when performing the indigenous Caribbean genre of chutney soca as "something indianish."³³ I like thinking of what these magazines were shaping in relation to this term, which to me suggests the rich and ever fluid possibilities for new and complex articulations of ethnic and national identity in that fertile postwar period.

Notes

1. Kris Rampersad, *Finding a Place: Indo-Trinidadian Literature* (Kingston: Ian Randle, 2002), 6.

2. Arjun Appadurai, *Modernity at Large: Cultural Dimensions of Globalization* (Minneapolis: University of Minnesota Press, 2003), 165.

3. M. G. Smith, *The Plural Society in the British West Indies* (Berkeley: University of California Press, 1965), 10.

4. Ibid., 12.

5. See Édouard Glissant, *Poetics of Relation*, trans. Betsy Wing (Ann Arbor: University of Michigan Press, 1997).

6. George Lamming, *Of Age and Innocence* (London: Allison and Busby, 1958), 384.

7. George Lamming, *Sovereignty of the Imagination: Conversations III* (Philipsburg, St. Martin: House of Nehesi, 2009), 66–67.

8. In his pamphlet *West Indians of East Indian Descent*, (Port of Spain: IBIS, 1965), we find C. L. R. James arguing to the contrary that "East Indians have proved their capacity to be first-class West Indians," but he too raises the issue of teaching Indians: "Now, I haven't to tell the youthful West Indians of Indian descent that they have to Act. We can give them some help; and some guidance. But they know what they want—and being young, they are not afraid. They do not want an East Indian party. They know that that has failed. It isolates the East Indian minority and creates more disharmony, disorder, suspicion, more hatred than ever before. They want a united party, Indians and Negroes united. They are politically a splendid body of young people. I meet them every day. In spirit they are politically the most advanced people in the country: they want to finish with the old ways." The rhetoric of Indians as those who need to be prepared for the responsibilities of citizenship echo here

again with the notable difference that training appears to be possible, that the turn to clannishness is not instinctive and unbreakable.

9. Cited in Frances Williams, "Colonial Literature or Caribbean Orature: *Creole Chips* by Edgar Mittelholzer," in *Telling Stories: Postcolonial Short Fiction in English*, ed. Jacqueline Bardolph (Amsterdam: Rodopi, 2001), 130.

10. Edgar Mittelholzer, *A Morning at the Office* (London: Hogarth Press, 1950), 55.

11. Ibid.

12. Ibid., 75.

13. Ibid.

14. Ibid.

15. See his chapter "African and Indian Consciousness," in *UNESCO General History of the Caribbean*, Vol. 5, *The Caribbean in the Twentieth Century*, ed. Bridget Brereton (London: Palgrave Macmillan, 2007), 257–312.

16. Ibid., 291.

17. Eric Williams, *History of the People of Trinidad and Tobago* (Port of Spain: PNM, 1962), 281.

18. *Jean Bernabé, Patrick Chamoiseau, and Raphaël Confiant, Éloge de la Créolité (In Praise of Creoleness)*, trans. M. B. Taleb-Khyar (Baltimore: Johns Hopkins University Press, 1990), 88.

19. The *Minerva Review* was also notable for eliciting work by non-Indians and for its refusal to adhere to principles of ethnic exclusion. As one of its editorials declared: "It is our aim to confine our paper to things literary, and since party politics will not creep into our columns, our magazine may be read without prejudice by every section of the community.... The *Minerva Review* is the emanation of that integral portion of any civilized community—the literary club, an organisation which has done much to mould the minds of many of our well-known public figures, men and women who now inevitably have the spotlight focused upon them, partly because they themselves in youth helped to bear the torch of the literary club." From Rampersad, *Finding a Place*, 195–196.

20. Ibid., 213.

21. H. P. Singh, *The Indian Struggle for Justice and Equality against Black Racism in Trinidad and Tobago 1956–1962* (Chaguanas, Trinidad and Tobago: India Review Press, 1993), xxx–xxxi

22. Ibid., xxxiii.

23. See Lisa Outar, "Tropical Longing: The Quest for India in the Early Twentieth-Century Caribbean," *South Asian History and Culture* 2, no. 4 (2011): 464–481; and Peter Ruhomon, "The Building of Greater India," in *They Came in Ships: An Anthology of Indo-Guyanese Prose and Poetry*, ed. Joel Benjamin et al. (Leeds: Peepal Tree Press, 1998), 64–65.

24. Rampersad, *Finding a Place*, 227.

25. Ibid.

26. Ibid., 228.

27. Ibid.

28. Ibid., 217.

29. Singh, *Indian Struggle*, xxxviii.

30. Ibid., xxx.

31. Lamming, *Sovereignty of the Imagination*, 65.

32. Tejaswini Niranjana, *Mobilizing India: Women, Music and Migration between India and Trinidad* (Durham, N.C.: Duke University Press, 2006), 53.

33. Ibid., 236.

Contradictory Omens: Repatriation and Resistance in Ismith Khan's *The Jumbie Bird*

ATREYEE PHUKAN

The East Indian, looking to India, becomes Indo-Caribbean.
—Edward (Kamau) Brathwaite, *Contradictory Omens*

Despite the diverse range of literature on the inherent complexities and con-tradictions in creolization movements, a black, Afrocentric vision was preem-inent in Caribbean anticolonial writings of the post–World War II decades. For the Windrush generation, the birth of a new literary undertaking made possible the reinvention of West Indian identity. In literature, theory, and popular culture of the period, mainstream constructs of "creole" (as in native) identity allude to Africanized strategies of belonging, which position Indian-ized (as in Indo-Caribbean) forms at the periphery of, or exterior to, the con-struct "West Indian." Literally and literarily, for the first time, so-called New World writers were finding themselves anew in Europe precisely as Caribbe-ans in exile. The unmitigated newness of their circumstance made this group of men and women, in George Lamming's view, the "most cosmopolitan" in the world because of the inherent heterogeneity brought over from the Caribbean—"no Indian from India, no European, no African can adjust with greater ease and naturalness to situations than the West Indian," for whom "racial integration is the background" of his or her life.[1] Simultaneously dem-onstrating the radical newness and heterogeneity of this new literary subject and subjectivity, Lamming's popularized configuration of the "West Indian" centered on inclusivity and variability as positive markers of identity and resistance for postcolonial writers.

Whereas it is commonplace to view the 1950s and 1960s as a period of liberation, the political climate during decolonization did not in fact offer Indo-Caribbeans equal or automatic access to the rewards of postcolonial res-toration and restitution. In the same period, efforts made by Indo-Caribbeans to theorize and fictionalize belongingness to include historical and cultural indentureship have been, inadvertently or not, overshadowed. While newness and heterogeneity are equally central to the political consciousness of Indian writers, their configuration of the newness of the "West Indian" from an Indo-Caribbean perspective has too often been received as a separate endeavor. The latter view in particular reinforces the misleading perception that constructs of Indo-Caribbean identity developed separately from, rather than in collaboration with, the West Indian. As this essay endeavors to show, a postcolonial Caribbean aesthetics that has from its inception privileged inclusivity, interraciality, and resistance against Old World colonial orders requires taking into account Indo-Caribbean writers and their reimagining of Indianness. Their contributions would shed light on alternative narratives of hybridity, in which a poetic resistance against the (differently) Old World order of India marks the entry, rather than strangeness, of Indo-Caribbean symbology into the burgeoning West Indian literary canon.

Published on the eve of Trinidad's independence in 1962, Ismith Khan's *The Jumbie Bird* offers a complex rendering of Indianness during decolonization. While positing the rebirth and resistance of a newly forming Trinidad nation as the critical foundation for the growing political consciousness of Indo-Trinidadians, Khan engages in the act of "looking to India" as a way to imagine the East Indian *becoming* Indo-Caribbean. Overlooked within the Caribbean canon in general, Khan also has been overshadowed by the prominence of his Indo-Trinidadian contemporaries V. S. Naipaul and Samuel Selvon. Quite differently from both, Khan's thematic attention to Indianness, indentureship, and Indo-Trinidadianness includes the cultural hybridization of Trinidad's minority Muslim Pathan community (a nomadic warrior group) and depicts this process using the language and vocabulary of Afro-Caribbean mythology. Furthermore, Khan's juxtapositioning of Trinidad's future with the imprint of independence in South Asia, while peculiar in the Caribbean literary canon, even among other Indo-Caribbean novelists, strategically includes ancestral India in order to present nostalgia for the motherland as an obstacle to envisioning an inclusive Caribbean space. To this point, the novel portrays repatriation (a contractual guarantee after the end of indentureship in 1917) as a debilitating desire that parallels the violent fragmentation of the Indian subcontinent after independence in 1947. Positing "Hindustan," the hallowed ancestral land of indentured Indians, as a contradictory sign, *The Jumbie Bird* unmoors Indianness from the subcontinent to establish its presence in a newly forming Caribbean.

The circuitous construction of Indianness being suggested here is analyzed for its profound affinity with the poetics of contradiction and relation espoused in the works of pan-Caribbean writers Edward (Kamau) Brathwaite and Édouard Glissant, who, though writing contemporaneously, are not typically viewed as Khan's creative models. The search for Indo-Trinidadian rootedness in *The Jumbie Bird* can be read in dialogue with Glissant's poetics of "Relation" and Brathwaite's creolization in order to uncover parallels between the novel's examination of Indo-Caribbean identity and the writers' shared meditation on the centrality of an open-ended, inclusive creolization to anticolonial discourse. In this vein, Khan attempts a fusion of African and Indian folklore by associating the figure of the mythological jumbie bird with the Muslim festival of Hussay. In figurative terms, this cultural synthesis revises the failure of repatriation as a positive reality so that Trinidad, rather than India, is presented as the rightful site of belongingness for Indo-Trinidadians. The death of the protagonist, Kale Khan, whose raging desire to return to India literally breaks his heart, demonstrates conclusively the novel's examination of the urgent need of a free and plural Trinidad for Indian identity. Subverting its association with bad luck in Caribbean mythology, the bird's ominous calling here signals the inauguration of a new, culturally heterogeneous future.

Khan's novel has more typically been read as an autobiographical footnote or as a critique of the maltreatment of Indians during racial riots that marked the 1950s and 1960s in Trinidad. Such analyses, while valid, devalue the novel's radical effort of employing an Indo-Caribbean perspective to theorize an inclusive creolization. Indeed, Khan's fusion of Afro-Indian mythology is something unfamiliar in mainstream West Indian literature of the period, which may explain why much of the scholarship on the novel focuses on its Indian elements while ignoring its titular subject, the African mythological jumbie bird. The tumultuous interethnic politics of the time when Khan's novel appears may make it difficult for readers to discern the promise of creolization in *The Jumbie Bird*'s unique representation of interraciality and resistance. While Khan's treatment of the relationship between hybridity and becomingness is unprecedented in *Indo*-Caribbean writing, these ideological tenets are in fact in close alliance with Glissant's and Brathwaite's definitions of anticolonial resistance as a signifying process of ceaseless discovery through interculturation, or creolization.

Glissant's and Brathwaite's pioneering texts themselves make clear that competing definitions of creolization plagued the theorization of the concept from the outset. To the extent that these authors' methodology and style appeared contentious to their peers, Khan's own interpretation of creolization must have appeared equally strange and deviant, perhaps even more so since his work predates theirs. In the preface to *Contradictory Omens: Cultural Diversity and Integration in the Caribbean*, published in 1970, Brathwaite opens by admitting that his vision of creolization will frustrate easy categorization, a useful reminder of the inherent complexity of his theory.

Playfully, Brathwaite cautions that his statements be spared from seeming to come from a dazed and "raptured West Indian . . . dripping with the tropical sun."[2] He clarifies that the seamless "sharing and inter-lapping" of Caribbean geography (a clear precursor to Antonio Benítez-Rojo's "repeating island") make necessary his vision of the theory as thoroughly contradictory, so as to distinguish creolization from more familiar concepts that pertained to "African or North American notions of cultural diversity and integration."[3]

Perhaps as a way to stress the importance of creolization as process, *Contradictory Omens* ends with four words and a missing punctuation mark: "The unity is submarine."[4] The absence of the period, as the final sign of the text, lays accent on his discussion of creolization as an incomplete process, "not a product," which combines the difficulty of "ac/culturation" with the spontaneity of "inter/culturation."[5] While the former refers to the forceful "yoking" of the "slave/African to the European," the latter was an "unplanned, unstructured but osmotic relationship" that followed out of the acculturation between African/European. The binaries Brathwaite employs here help explain why his work is known for its contention that the twentieth-century Caribbean is predominantly caught between "white" and "black" cultural contexts. However, Brathwaite's argument advances the idea that the "truly creole form" will continue to shift and change such that this too will be "assaulted by (or called upon to respond to) new waves of cultural incursion: the Chinese and East Indians."[6] While Brathwaite acknowledges that cultural diversity in the Caribbean is mainly "black rooted or oriented," he suggests that this may be "accidental . . . a trend, fashion or opportunity rather than an offered norm."[7] The inherent complexity and contradictoriness of the process of interculturation, then, directly confront the ways in which different minorities in the Caribbean do or do not creolize. Of these groups, Brathwaite says that "East Indians" are unique, particularly in places where their populations are large (for example, Guyana, Trinidad, and Jamaica), because interaction between peasant Indians and the "black masses [has] contributed to new configurations of creole."[8] The indentured Indians' closer connection to ancestral culture, which was absent and/or forbidden to slaves, allowed Indian groups to resist adopting new cultural models in the Caribbean and to preserve those transported from India. Since complete resistance was impossible as a matter of survival, Brathwaite views "Indo-creole" identity as a singular product of "selective creolization" because it combined old and new cultural practices.[9] Thus, for Brathwaite, by "looking to India" Indo-Caribbean culture opens itself to assimilation with Afro-Caribbean culture while at the same time importing and processing Indianness for its redefinition in the Caribbean.

These contiguous forms of contact, in Brathwaite's model, are the most accurate way to unite the legacies of slavery and indentureship as part of a single evolution that both cracks and connects continents. The arrival of Chinese and East Indians can thus be seen as a complementary, rather than aberrant, stage that leads to emancipation. Insofar as unpredictability is the goal, any cultural norm associated with the Caribbean will be productively "cracked, fragmented, ambivalent, not sure of itself, subject to shifting lights and pressures."[10] Expectation of anything else would result in a hardening process for which Brathwaite pointedly uses the imperial symbols of "crown: jewel: diamond."[11] Indeed, Brathwaite lays emphasis on seeing the "cultural incompleteness" of *all* of postcolonial Caribbean society: "we remain part creole, part colonial, seeking many-ancestoried conclusions," and this becomes an "ultimately co-operative" endeavor for all cultural groups in the Caribbean who are joined in the exercise of self-determination.[12] For Brathwaite, remembrance that leads to nostalgia, especially one that provokes a desire to return to the ancestral land, perpetuates a negative consciousness whose source lies in colonial oppression/suppression. Alternatively, the act of looking toward the imagined collective past, be it in Africa, Syria, China, or India, is a first step in the creolized individual's realization that only the Caribbean can be his or her true home.[13]

The element of cooperation stressed here develops Brathwaite's definition of creolization as not only a contradictory but also a contingent practice since "it [creolization] will depend too on the kind of influence their [Chinese and Indian] ancestral cultures can and wish to exert . . . and their response, too, to the existing submerged mother of the creole system, Africa."[14] Thus, for Brathwaite, any notion of Caribbean "wholeness" depends on perceiving an intercultural whole constantly subjected to interruptions and irruptions—and, importantly, one that will require *both* the "original 'mulatto' capability" and the "'new' groups" to respond to each other's cultural impulses.[15] While acknowledging that political and cultural confrontations between races exist, Brathwaite sees hope in the forms of resistance and difference that come out of this conflict, forms that continue the Caribbean's equally important legacy of "maroonage"—a "kind of partial/ambiguous separateness."[16] The postcolonial migrant recognizes the present habitus as a positive form of maroonage that allows traditional identities and practices to break free of earlier constraints. If not always explicitly emphasized in Brathwaite's conception of creolization, the Indo-Caribbean nevertheless fits readily into his theory's structure, in which the "knowledge of ancestral cultures" can be practiced in new spaces that "take us forward" in the present, toward the future.[17]

For his part, Glissant begins the chapter "For Opacity" in *The Poetics of Relation* by acknowledging that his statements were originally, in the 1970s, ill-received and viewed as a type of "barbarism" because they appeared to renounce the principles of visibility and agency deemed essential to postcolonial identity in the Caribbean.[18] Glissant's undermining of the transparent is commonly interpreted as being a mistrust of the hypervisible (that is, colonial), a quality Brathwaite symbolizes in the bejeweled imperial crown. For Glissant, postcolonial subjectivity required a new ontology based on opacity, a beingness wholly impenetrable and uncontainable by the panoptic gaze of authority. As a truly freeing principle, the "right to opacity" was a defiance of the politics of exclusion exercised by the dominant power.[19] If all people practiced and believed in their right to opacity, they would freely "coexist and converge, weaving fabrics" without fear of surveillance.[20] In essence, prior imposed divisions would collapse as humans finally engage in "discover(ing) what lies at the bottom of [all] natures.... This-here is the weave, and it weaves no boundaries."[21] In Glissant's hopeful view, the fabric of this submarine unity is "the real foundation of Relation," uniting all migrants to the Caribbean, and the coincidence of their arrival from multiple points of departure creates the "this-here," new societies created by postcolonial migrants.

For Glissant, the unstoppable mixing of cultures, like Brathwaite's "osmosis," performs the unpredictable weaving process that connects geographical spaces in defiance of political state boundaries. Brathwaite's particularization of creolization as an unfinishable and unpredictable process, an extension of Caribbean maroonage, closely parallels Glissant's view of anticolonial resistance as "Relation." The latter is a form of creolization based on an anarchic weaving process driven by the "imaginary," which Glissant defines as "thinking thought [that] spaces itself out into the world."[22] To Brathwaite's model of spontaneous and perpetual movement, Glissant adds the anarchy of rhizomatic, nomadic thinking that allows people to take the "risk" in new ways of seeing and being. Within this regional debate, therefore, Khan's own representation of creolization as an anarchic, contradictory heterogeneity is extremely relevant. Khan explores how the act of "looking east" engenders a form of rhizomatic thinking that displaces the hegemonic presence of India—the great unknown for second- and third-generation Indo-Trinidadians—and gives birth to unpredictable forms of Indianness in a new Trinidad.

In essence, both Brathwaite and Glissant imbricate the psychology of contradiction at the center of rebuilding identity, community, and nation to highlight the complications that come from contact between colonial others historically kept in antagonism. Khan's interrogation of creolization and decolonization is similarly involved in an exercise of contradiction in its assertion that Indianness is organic to Trinidad. The contradictory and unexpected valences in creolization offered in Brathwaite's and Glissant's critical frameworks help to contextualize Khan's depiction of the clash between different constructs of Indianness arising out of India and Trinidad.

Importantly, the reward of a nationalized and local form of interculturation is critical to the novel's optimistic conclusion that new generations in Trinidad can embrace the incompleteness of the decolonization period as a positive sign, and the setting of the novel on the cusp of national independence reinforces the point that a cooperative creolization is essential to the future of the country. Combining the political with the personal, *The Jumbie Bird* concentrates equally on conflicts pressing the nation and those in the Khan household. When we first meet Kale Khan, he is an indomitable figure who lives, his daughter-in-law mocks, to keep the 1857 revolt[23] alive, as if "the Sepoy barracks outside the door [and he is] keeping himself in shape in case of a skirmish."[24] Embittered by the realization that Rahim, his son, will never be a Pathan like his forefathers, Kale Khan pins all his desires and ambitions on his grandson, Jamini. Rather than have Jamini grow up as a social outcast like most other ex-indentured Indo-Trinidadians, Kale Khan wishes to give his progeny a lasting gift by taking him back to India. Once there, they could grow strong together, he thinks, "wrestling with the elements side by side with the hill tribes of Hindustan, dwelling in the mysterious valleys of the Pathans, the last outposts that prevailed against all the invaders who swept past the centuries in Hindustan."[25]

Kale Khan's pride comes from the fact that he belongs to Trinidad's minority Muslim Pathan community, which he claims as being the only free migrants to the islands (specifically, as unemployed soldiers), unlike most other first-generation Indians who came as indentured laborers. He habitually reminds Jamini that as a rare class of free migrants to Trinidad, the family's value-system is based on the bravery and honor of Pathans and is in every way superior to the contracted, lower-caste sugar plantation workers. He includes in his diatribe a warning that Jamini is already partially contaminated by his mother, who is of indenture ancestry, and uses this to convince the impressionable twelve-year-old that returning to India will serve as a purification process necessary for his real destiny as a Pathan warrior.

Trinidad's search for a new order, it could be said, echoes the younger Khan's need to break free from Kale Khan, whose domination of family (based on his meteoric rise as a rebel leader) is presented as repressive and counterproductive. A legendary island hero in his forties when he fought against the British in the 1884 Hussay riots, Kale Khan shows clear signs of dementia at eighty in his last efforts to rally for the repatriation of Indians, and as the family's patriarch, he ultimately does more to sever kinship ties than sustain them. Most indicatively, he decides on the banishment of his own wife, Binti, because she refuses to support him in his endeavors to plan for a return to India. The novel makes clear, however, that Binti is in fact a figure of tremendous love and industry who sneaks visits to her family between numerous jobs in the city. Moreover, it is she who ultimately preserves the family, since it is her thrift that provides them with a home after all is lost when her husband dies. Thus the novel clearly portrays the need for a form of order different than the aggressive, patriarchal purism of Kale Khan.

The novel's overt portrayal of a nation undergoing decolonization highlights similarities between a colony's need to rebel against imperial power and the ways in which sons must fight against, without destructively superseding, their fathers. The difficult search for freedom and independence lies in the hands of the son, Rahim, and grandson, Jamini—the new generation. The story as such traces the new generation's troubled entry out from the shadow of an oppressive presence of the family's octogenarian grand patriarch and the inflexible demands he places on them as his male descendants. Contradictorily, the family tradition of filigree, which Rahim learns from his father, becomes that which marks their differing positions on belongingness in Trinidad. As Kale Khan becomes intent on returning to India, he abandons the craft and revives his identity as a sepoy (soldier) ready to fight his way back to the motherland. Rahim, on the other hand, treasures the skill and sees it as a virtuous practice that is his source of pride and livelihood. Kale Khan's death, therefore, is emancipatory in that it allows Rahim and Jamini to move beyond his crippling dreams of repatriation to India and envision a larger map of Indianness that includes their hybridization as Trinidadians.

Khan's representation of the complex coming-together of old and new cultural identities and practices echoes Brathwaite's specific definition of creolization as being both process and pressure for minority groups. While Khan explicitly shows that Rahim and Jamini must creolize in order to belong as Trinidadians—because their biggest hurdle is imposed by an insider (Kale Khan)—their self-creolization is problematized by their need to navigate beyond the selective practices they have been taught in the family. In the novel, the symbology of filigree jewelry making is the most powerful presentation of self-creolization as a complex coalescing process. Remarkably similar in design to Glissant's image of the rhizome—an "enmeshed root system"—filigree becomes the metaphorical gateway by which the younger generation look backs in order to move forward.[26] As a practical skill passed from father to son, jewelry making ultimately affords the next generation a professional future in Trinidad outside of the doctrine of Pathan warriorhood espoused by Kale Khan. In this sense, mastery in jewelry making fosters the attitude of an inclusive transnational consciousness that Rahim, the son, inherits from his forefathers but personally develops and alters for his own success in Trinidad. Once Rahim asserts his identity as both Indian and Trinidadian, this collocation becomes impossible to disentangle, just as his completed works of jewelry combine tradition and originality. The act of *looking* back represented by Rahim's unwavering devotion to the art of filigree goes beyond merely supplanting his father's call for an actual physical return. In its stead he begins a productive "weaving" process that transposes his ancestral inheritance and affirms his belongingness in the present.

Closely paralleling the ideology asserted by Brathwaite and Glissant, Khan's novel insists on a poetics of relation as necessary for the creation of a hybrid narrative that opens itself equally to the Afro-Caribbean mythology of the jumbie bird and Indo-Trinidadian Hussay. Thus relationality between forms of Caribbeanness takes precedence over differences in Indian identities (as will be shown later). This unprecedented convergence builds toward the novel's establishment of Trinidad as the "this-here" of interculturation that issues from the efforts of new generations who can begin to see themselves as heterogeneous—that is, Trinidadians—by bringing together previously segregated cultural contexts. In this sense, the titular jumbie bird signals not so much the doom of Indo-Trinidadians who cannot repatriate, but rather the end of a colonial world order represented by Kale Khan.

Subverting the jumbie's association with bad luck in Afro-Caribbean mythology, Khan uses the bird to celebrate death as a baptism. Similar to "duppy," the jumbie bird is traditionally a malevolent spirit. Appearing mostly in Afro-Guyanese tales, the jumbie is often described as a black bird nesting in the "devil's tree" and identified by its cry. While the jumbie bird is typically heard but never seen, its role in the novel as a visionary agent is made clear by its appearance to Jamini on the morning of Kale Khan's death, which coincides with the last day of Hussay, when mausoleums (colorful replicas of the tomb of Hosein and Hassan) in honor of the prophet Mohammed's grandsons are offered to the sea. Kale Khan's death, therefore, shares in a celebration of the self-sacrifice martyrs take upon themselves for the greater good. The bird's self-revelation, on this specific date, symbolically performs an Afro-Indian fusion, translating the imagery of death from Afro-Caribbean mythology with that of rejuvenation from an Indo-Trinidadian festival commemorating the martyrdom of the prophet's male descendants. The bird thus signifies the possibility of creolization as enlightenment and, specifically as a symbolic messenger to the grandson Jamini, promises the youngest generation release from a stigmatized past.

In this light, it is meaningful that Hussay plays conflicting roles that book-end Kale Khan's youth and old age on the island. The festival's heterogeneous nature (traditionally Muslim Indian, it integrated Hinduism and aspects from the Afro-Caribbean carnival) in fact frames the complex cultural hybridization of the novel's most anti-Trinidadian character. In the 1880s Kale Khan rises to legendary status for his role in the historic Hussay riots of 1884, during which he single-handedly shoots down six colonial officers. In the 1950s he again rises to fame as the voice of Indians demanding repatriation in protest against the government's maltreatment of the community. He writes numerous letters to the government of India detailing the plight of the Indians and appealing to the ancestral motherland for help. When a commissioner from India does arrive, everyone believes Kale Khan to have orchestrated the visit to coincide with the annual Hussay celebration, even though he alone has to bear the burden of the commissioner's rejection of their pleas.

During his visit, it becomes clear that the commissioner has, in fact, come to correct Kale Khan's misunderstanding that he has come to rescue Indians or take them back home. The answer to Kale Khan's call for repatriation is supplied, ironically in this case, by another Indian who frames the displacement felt by first-generation Indo-Trinidadians as an outcome of India's postcoloniality. As the commissioner would have Kale Khan understand, India views Indo-Trinidadians as citizens of a long-ago forgotten time and place, and the commissioner asks, "How many people in India know of your existence?"[27] The commissioner's suggestion that Kale Khan and his contemporaries are trapped in an anachronism is amplified by the latter's use of "Hindustan," rather than "India," which highlights their remove from dramatic political changes in modern India. The word itself, "Hindustan," achieved currency during the Mughal era (1300–1854) to distinguish the religious difference between colonizer (Islamic Mughal) and colonized (Hindu). Even the writing of the constitution of modern "India" in 1948 is at pains to give the new country its own name and chooses the indigenous "Bharat" from "Bharatvarsha," referring to the empire of the mythological hero Bharata found in Hindu and Jain scriptures.[28] The arrival of the commissioner thus strategically makes clear that Kale Khan, having left Hindustan in the late nineteenth century, cannot hope to imagine or comprehend partition's role in the fracturing of the continent and the deracination of Pathans, his own ethnic group, across three nations in the subcontinent (modern-day Pakistan, Afghanistan, and India).

The double betrayal felt by Indians is framed by the novel's temporal outline, which connects major turning points in Trinidad's colonial history, the Hussay riots, repatriation, and impending independence. Pivoting on the repatriation of Indians in the Caribbean during the 1950s, *The Jumbie Bird* documents a crisis specific to the preindependence years referred to as the "East Indian problem"—a phrase used by the colonial overseas office on the issue of repatriation for postindentured East Indians across the Caribbean. While the return of postindentured Indians did occur in small measure from some islands, principally Jamaica, at the behest of the British Parliament, the initiative stopped suddenly without notice, leaving thousands, mainly in Guyana and Trinidad, waiting in vain for ships that never arrived. Thus the repatriation of Indo-Caribbeans was a delicate issue that played out in a convoluted way. For one, modern India insisted that it was the responsibility of the British to solve the complications it had left dangling with their departure. The British government, however, was unwilling to make compensation for indentureship, officially holding the view that it was a product of the greed of merchants and traders and thus not a state responsibility. Ultimately, India and Britain agreed amicably to forgive and forget past transgressions, leaving Indians of the Caribbean to realize slowly the uselessness of labor contracts that promised return passage. In this context, Kale Khan's appeal to the Indian government to rectify a colonial fracture (specifically, indentureship) is seen as an anomalous irrelevance by the commissioner, who is the novel's spokesperson of modern India.

Ironically, whereas Hussay is the vehicle by which Kale Khan becomes visible as a national hero, it is also the event at which a fatal blow to the head coincides with his realization that he will never return to India. While standing in the middle of the road amid a battery of floats, Kale Khan's epiphany comes like a death wish, and he jumps to join a traditional stick-fight against an opponent whose power he knows he will be unable to withstand. Ducking from the arc of the other's *lathi*, Kale Khan pulls in and out of the crowd in a frenzy. In his disorientation, the crowd appears to him to be an angry mob set to kill him. Delirious, "his mind slipped once more," and all he can hear is the "commissioner's voice telling him that he had done wrong by inciting his people to rebellion, by sowing discontent among them, by promising them that they would go back home . . . that he should have tried to help them make this place their home rather than set them against it."[29] A fatal blow by a young stick-fighter strikes him at the same moment that the crowd becomes a vast "watery expanse," and he even fails to recognize his son Rahim, the only one to rush in and save him.[30] In his head ring the commissioner's words of the previous night, relating that "he was not sent to Trinidad to revive old quarrels, that the past was dead and over, that India was no longer at odds with the British, and that India wished that they would settle here and try to make this place their home."[31] At that moment, Kale Khan remembers how "a horrifying loneliness seize[d] him ... there was no home, no land peopled by men among whom he could walk and feel that it was his world, his home, a world that did not leave him alien and a stranger in the streets."[32]

The commissioner visits Kale Khan at his deathbed the next evening and tries to explain to Binti that he had not come to Trinidad as a fellow Indian but "as a stranger" who knew "nothing of our people abroad" because India has had "too many things" happening of their own.[33] While acknowledging an ethnic connection, the commissioner nevertheless denies Indo-Trinidadians status and citizenship in his India. In referring to the trauma of partition— what he obliquely describes as "too many other things"—the commissioner recalls the immediacy of displacement on Indian soil from which occurrences in the Caribbean appear distant and alien. Even as an Indian in the company of Indo-Caribbeans like Kale Khan, the commissioner regards himself as a "stranger" among the Indian diaspora, making explicit his view that they are outsiders to the modern, independent Indian nation.

Hussay, then, captures not only the pride and joy of the Indian community but also their suffering. Shalini Puri notes Khan's exceptional treatment of Hussay, which she reads as the "site of struggle" for national identity jointly shaped by Africans and Indians during colonialism.[34] The festival, involving stick-fighting and floats, evolved in Trinidad as an interracial celebration that included African drummers, dancers, and other participants no longer allowed to celebrate Carnival publicly after a colonial ban issued in 1881.[35] Especially historically, Puri shows that Hussay offered "Islam [as] a common point of reference for people of African and Indian descent" and did not enter the public realm as rigidly Indian but as a "secularized assertion of *pan-Indian* cultural nationalism and pride [and] an emergent *Trinidadian* cross-racial cultural and class solidarity ... auguring the possibility of joint black and Indian opposition to government."[36] Similarly, Hena Maes-Jelinek sees an important element of religious hybridization in Khan's novel. Rightly highlighting Khan's focus on East Indian Muslim celebrations, Maes-Jelinek views the Hussay festival as the locus of Khan's creation of a pan-Indianness. Thus the "festival of Hussay, . . . creolized or assimilated to festivals in other religions (Hindu and Christian)," represents the "three stages in the West Indian experience: a deep sense of exile, at once nourished and resisted by the hope of returning to the country of origin; the disorientation of a second generation caught between two worlds; and the difficulties of the growing body in the third generation."[37]

The exclusion felt by Kale Khan and others, however, makes clear that some models of pan-Indianness are debilitating, in particular those that situate India at the center. It is clear, therefore, that Ismith Khan utilizes an

Afro-Indian fusion to claim a new diasporic identity for his Indian characters. Theirs is firmly embedded in Trinidad, the only geopolitical space in which they can claim their version of a transnational Indianness. Though the commissioner positions those like Kale Khan on the periphery of his Indian diasporic map, the novel realigns the cartography to suggest something quite different. It does much more than construct a pan-Indian identity (Puri) or attempt a fusion of Hinduism and Christianity (Maes-Jelinek). I would go further and argue that the novel's use of religious syncretism via Hussay and the jumbie bird positions Trinidad as the center and source of Indo-Caribbean identity, with India merely haunting the periphery. Historical specificity provides a subtle but meaningful analysis: the modern, independent India Kale Khan imagines that can rescue the masses of poor and wretched Indo-Trinidadians is itself shown to be ideologically founded on the trauma of othering and displacement within its own territory. Strategically, then, Khan uses the commissioner's remarks about a partition marked by religious segregation to make even more urgent the need for Indo-Caribbeans to reassess their ties to modern India, rather than merely relying on ancestral memory. Syncretism (religious or otherwise) appears more possible in Trinidad, a newly imagined international space, especially for future generations of Indo-Caribbeans. As a type of "opacity," Ismith Khan's alternative form of Indianness, outside but not exclusive of India, is a writerly exercise that deliberately robs our ability to see, know, or even imagine the kinds of identity the new generations represented by Rahim and Jamini are in the process of forming.

The real tragedy lies in Kale Khan's version of Indianness and vision of repatriation, both of which depend on a memory of India that blinds him to possibilities in Trinidad and even the impracticality of his return to an altered India. The idea of India as aporia, literally impassable, is perhaps most acutely felt by Kale Khan himself, for he hates the "Trinidad to which he had come to find a new life" but also the "India from which he had fled."[38] Presciently, Jamini's feelings when his grandfather promises to take him to their ancestral land are mixed. He is initially mesmerized by the prospect of being carried on Kale Khan's shoulders all the way to Hindustan and excited by the prospect of an adventure into unknown territory, which it is for him. At the same time, he cannot help but think that they would make a very lonely twosome. He inherently trusts "Dada," who vows to carry him personally, but he also predicts a sadness in the prospect of "never com[ing] back to Trinidad." Kale Khan is unable to answer him when he asks, "Dada, we goin' back . . . only you and me . . . you think we can carry anybody else when go back to India?"[39] While the young boy trusts in his grandfather's strength to carry him over, he also views the elder's version of return as an obstacle to an inclusive worldview that makes no accommodation for others to be a part of the imagined future. This provocative scene does much to characterize Kale Khan. For the old man, his shoulders figuratively represent the Pathan traditions he believes are Jamini's true inheritance. For the young boy, however, this act of shouldering includes the connotation that his grandfather's back is firmly turned against both Trinidad and (much of) India, by which he senses the flaws in Kale Khan's grand claims.

It is the language and imagery of the text that steers free of the paradoxes and flaws in logic to which so many of the characters fall prey. The narrative itself, therefore, is the space in which we can most clearly discern the author's attempt to stress the inevitable but convoluted "osmosis" of Indians in their path to becoming Trinidadian. Interestingly, Kale Khan's language and symbology very often betray a creolization he himself is unaware of or indifferent to. His creolized vision can be seen in his explanation of why he is altogether a different type of Pathan. The fact that Kale Khan sees himself as black amplifies his susceptibility to altering his Pathan identity in regionally specific terms. Unlike the famous Pathans legendary for skin as fair as the snow-capped mountain range of their homes, so white that "one could see the swallow of the betel juice as it coursed through their throats," he is "black ... dark," as is the meaning of his name, "Kale."[40] Furthermore, he uses Afro-Creole symbology in order to explain his view of a government system whose sole purpose is to rob people of their cultural history and cultural knowledge. Evoking the language of obeah, Kale Khan understands colonial government as a powerful malevolent force that in accumulating unsuspecting followers has become "a stronger 'Obeah' than anything we have."[41] Using the term "obeah" to evoke spirit-possession, Kale Khan betrays his own creolization (never openly acknowledged) using an Afro-Caribbean touchstone to define his perception of cultural and political corruption. Significantly, Ismith Khan points to both sides of the cultural associations of obeah in Kale Khan's political analogy: it appears as both a native healing source and as a purportedly malevolent force outlawed by the colonizer. Kale Khan rants about the English obeah that has possessed the minds of young Indo-Trinidadian returnees who "laffin' and laffin' at they own poopah an' moomah; they t'ink is a shame to eat wid their hand, and they settin' up their face when they see Indian food."[42] Although defending traditional practices, the old man's evocation of an "Indian obeah" as a possible corrective against a stronger colonial one suggests his own imbrication in the discourse of resistant creolization.

Kale Khan's swift death on the final morning of Hussay suggests his martyrdom to what is ultimately presented as a hopeless and misguided cause. Though he dies after having fought unsuccessfully for the political rights of postindentureship Indians, his death is the first step in a rite of passage for Jamini. Early on the same day, the jumbie bird finally shows itself to the young boy. No longer an ominous calling from the calabash tree, the bird is now visible and clearly "perched in a tree." Jamini sees the "bright yellow of [the bird's] breast, the light brown of its back and tail, and when it opened its beak to call again, he could see the pink of its throat, and its little pointed tongue."[43] The boy's sudden vision of the bird in its minutest details is an important contradictory omen—he will be heartbroken to find out that his grandfather is dying, but he will also soon begin to heal relations with his own father. He will no longer need to believe blindly in a past that has never been his and can instead start to explore the land of his father, Rahim, which he can eventually come to view as his own.

Rahim does not attempt to determine Jamini's future as Kale Khan does his. Rahim's confusion as a second-generation Indo-Trinidadian is the right kind of ambiguity that gives him the courage to help his own son search for meaning in Trinidad. It also stems from the conflicting role of jewelry making, a profession in which Kale Khan teaches Rahim to excel. In his old age, however, Kale Khan rejects every trace of the profession he learned after migration. His tools then lie abandoned and gathering dust from disuse. This is a far cry from the man who originally offered his own handiwork as a token of his undying love for Binti. To honor and respect her abandonment of family and home to follow him to Trinidad, Kale Khan had promised "one day [to] make [her] a necklace of filigree that even the spider in his web will envy."[44] In his later years, however, he abandons his devotion to both the trade and Binti, viewing filigree jewelry as a useless commercial activity learned out of a necessity to survive after migration to Trinidad. It becomes a tainted compromise incomparable to the codes he once honored as a Pathan warrior.

For Rahim, however, the art of filigree is akin to a mode of thinking, a delicate tracery that teaches him the sophisticated psychology he needs to resist the militant warriorhood espoused by his father. Filigree, as a metaphor of being and belongingness, is thus an intertwining process wherein a single connective thread suffices to bind together a collective, whose shape and boundaries are indeterminable and thus inextricable. Perhaps as once his father did, Rahim understands how to appreciate the strength of filigree as one of balance, the line "fine, fine, fine" as "spider web" but finally "strong . . . like iron."[45] As he sits alone in their shop on Woodford Square, Rahim comes to realizations of his own while gazing at a brooch he is working on. He sees the finished product as physical evidence of his knowledge and skill in making jewelry, but he also finds in it a powerful metaphor of the contradictory impulses that he views as shaping his belongingness: "how much it meant to him to have

each of its minute dots of metal shaped into perfect spheres, each sphere sol-
dered on to a frame so that in the end, the intricate mass held together with
the strength of a single bar of solid metal."[46] For him, it is the unity of the
woven-together "perfect spheres" that holds promise. Kale Khan, on the other
hand, sees only disconnected spheres: a perfect "Hindustan" versus an imper-
fect Trinidad. With Kale Khan's death marking the end of an old order, the son
begins to weave his future onto Trinidad, the ultimate "this-here" where India
is only one among many spheres connected to a larger network.

An altogether different type of father, Rahim is thrilled by the prospect of
Jamini attending a private school that will open opportunities inaccessible to
any other male in their family history. Rahim welcomes the unknowable as
the best future for his son, perhaps to stem the cycle of burdensome dreams
and desires transmitted by Kale Khan, from which he himself cannot ever
be freed. At the novel's end, Rahim encourages his son to let go, in a way
neither were able to when Kale Khan was alive. The last image of father and
son sees them on a bridge. Though they spend this moment sharing dark and
disturbing thoughts of Kale Khan's death and the uncertainty of their future,
Jamini makes his father proud and happy simply by agreeing that he will
search relentlessly for "that something that the world have [sic] for you to do,"
whatever that may be.[47] There, they make a secret pact to set themselves adrift
and to plunge toward a "lust [that] called from the unknown."[48] As such, the
anarchic space of decolonization has throughout framed and foreshadowed
the end of an ideological era with the death of Kale Khan. On the threshold of
a wholly new, albeit unpredictable, future, Rahim and Jamini no longer view
themselves as exiled or displaced from India but as active agents who join in
the birthing pangs of their true home, Trinidad.

Kale Khan's legacy does live on, resurfacing in the life of his son, for whom
jewelry making is more than a mere profession. Filigree becomes an alternative form of warriorhood in that its aesthetic principles provide Rahim with
the kind of militant strength needed to begin the delicate work of rebuilding selfhood. Because filigree is a handmade trade that must compete against
machine-made, mass-produced jewelry, Rahim's effort to save a dying craft
from extinction comes from a fighter's instinct that revises his father's version
of resistance and rebellion. Rahim also achieves his own moment of glory
when a wealthy American man seeks him out personally to commission
"the finest work from this area."[49] Having lost home and workshop after Kale
Khan's death, the arrival of a stranger who trusts him with a generous cash
bonus validates Rahim's decision to continue the craft as a means of livelihood for his family, re-creating a new yet still unsettled version of his father's
life as the novel closes. *The Jumbie Bird* thus exemplifies Ismith Khan's efforts
to include an Indo-Caribbean perspective in the discourse of anticolonial

creolization that was preoccupying many writers of the independence generation. Khan's fictionalized version of creolization, which asserts Trinidad's centrality to Indo-Trinidadian cultural identity, is open-ended, inclusive, and, finally, transnational in a way that shifts the significance of Indianness outside of its conventional borders. Trinidad's imminent independence, as the novel suggests, is a time of crossover that weaves India onto the Caribbean, Kale Khan's prerogatives into those of his son and grandson. More than autobiography or social documentary, therefore, the novel is a metaphysical meditation on incompleteness that refuses to project a predictable ending to the stories of the next generation of Indo-Trinidadians.

Brathwaite's insistence on a "folk/maroon" interpretation of creolization is ultimately a call to read signs of change such as decolonization as a hybrid encounter between forces of hegemony and their resistance. This imperative is echoed in Glissant's definition of heterogeneity as a spontaneous and perpetual movement characterized by the transformative power in rhizomatic thinking. Indeed, the "folk/maroon" rhizomatic potential in *The Jumbie Bird* is found by tracing the merging and translation of "Hussay" and "jumbie." This complex mix foregrounds a dialogic narrative wherein the Indo- and Afro-Caribbean contexts are mutually indispensable in producing a collective, collaborative imaginary. Both are mythologies that, through migration, transform unexpectedly in the Caribbean; as parts of a new whole in Khan's literary text, they foreground Trinidad's symbolic place as the center and source of a burgeoning national consciousness that is interracial. The imagined nation is stylized as hybrid, and nationhood, like osmosis, is depicted as a slow process in which old hegemonies gradually open up to new identities, practices, and traditions. Importantly, this construct of hybridity demonstrates the productive possibilities in the merging of conventionally opposed cultural contexts without predicting an end product. The Afro-Indian symbology of the novel is a rebellious hybrid, as each part translates the other to suggest a bold new outlook for Rahim and Jamini, whose destinies nevertheless remain unpredictable. For them, looking to India is a weaving exercise that is not an anachronism, but the discovery of a new Trinidad without boundaries.

Notes

1. George Lamming, *The Pleasures of Exile* (1960; repr., Ann Arbor: University of Michigan Press, 1992), 37.

2. Edward Brathwaite, *Contradictory Omens: Cultural Diversity and Integration in the Caribbean* (Mona: Savacou, 1974), 5.

3. Ibid.

4. Ibid., 64.

5. Ibid., 6.

6. Ibid.

7. Ibid., 55.

8. Ibid., 53. As examples, Brathwaite says that spirit possession by Indian Hindu gods is not uncommon in Jamaica, while in Trinidad the Hosein festival has become "integrated into the creole imagination" (ibid.). Contrarily, Indians have demonstrated kinship with obeah practices and are even in some cases obeah practioners.

9. Ibid., 54.

10. Ibid.

11. Ibid., 58.

12. Ibid., 55.

13. Ibid., 57.

14. Ibid., 6.

15. Ibid.

16. Ibid., 62, 64.

17. Ibid., 61.

18. Glissant, *Poetics of Relation*, 189.

19. Ibid., 190-191.

20. Ibid., 190.

21. Ibid.

22. Ibid., 3.

23. The 1857 Sepoy Rebellion in India is considered to be the first, before 1947, indigenous battle for colonial independence.

24. Ismith Khan, *The Jumbie Bird* (Trinidad and Jamaica: Longman, 1974), 2.

25. Ibid., 89.

26. Glissant, *Poetics of Relation*, 11.

27. Khan, *Jumbie Bird*, 170.

28. Ranbir Vohra, *The Making of India: A Historical Survey* (1997; repr., New York: M. E. Sharpe, 2001), 13–14.

29. Khan, *Jumbie Bird*, 169–170.

30. Ibid., 168.

31. Ibid., 69.

32. Ibid.

33. Ibid., 178.

34. Shalini Puri, *The Caribbean Postcolonial: Social Equality, Post-Nationalism, and Cultural Hybridity* (New York: Palgrave Macmillan, 2004), 178.

35. Importantly, Hussay itself was a translation of the Afro-Caribbean Carnival. For instance, the highly sarcastic and performative nature of the Indian carnival borrows from the Afro-Trinidadian "social commentary" calypsos and the African-style mask Carnival, such as *mas*, which were parodies of stock colonial figures. A typical Indian parody would reenact the allotment of land to Indians by portraying a khaki-outfitted character using a measuring tape. The Carnival itself was "introduced by French planters, popularized by poor Black creoles, and by 1950s [was] a part of urban Indian and Chinese life as well." Roger

Sanjek, "Conceptualizing Caribbean Asians: Race, Acculturation, Créolization," in *Caribbean Asians: Chinese, Indian, and Japanese Experiences in Trinidad and the Dominican Republic*, ed. Roger Sanjek (Flushing, N.Y.: Asian American Centre at Queens College, SUNY, 1990), 116.

36. Puri, *Caribbean Postcolonial*, 177.

37. Hena Maes-Jelinek, *A History of Literature in the Caribbean: English and Dutch-Speaking Countries*, ed. Albert James Arnold (Amsterdam: John Benjamin, 2001), 137.

38. Khan, *Jumbie Bird*, 2.

39. Ibid., 4, 6.

40. Ibid., 3.

41. Ibid., 90.

42. Ibid., 91.

43. Ibid., 163–164.

44. Ibid., 172.

45. Ibid., 55.

46. Ibid., 118.

47. Ibid., 190.

48. Ibid., 188.

49. Ibid., 185.

Between Windrush and Wolfenden: Class Crossings and Queer Desire in Andrew Salkey's Postwar London

NADIA ELLIS

"The name's Sobert. Johnnie Sobert. Jamaican. R.C. Middle class. Or so I've been made to think."[1] So begins Andrew Salkey's *Escape to an Autumn Pavement*, with all the identity markers—class, nationality, religion—and all the uncertainty necessary to inaugurate a comedy of manners. Salkey's decision to begin his novel with a list of his main character's sociological markings is not incidental. Throughout the course of *Escape*, the reader is subjected to Johnnie's fine-grained impressions of other characters' differences, as much as to Johnnie's obsessive ruminations about his own personality, status, and decisions. What makes Salkey's second novel—published in 1960 and only recently rediscovered—such an apt text to reexamine critical narratives of the Windrush era is that it is one the few Anglophone Caribbean novels of the period that presents the conundrum of migration from the perspective of the West Indian bourgeoisie. Alone, this representation of the Jamaican middle class may not appear remarkable—though, as I discuss momentarily, it is. But the fascination of Salkey's eccentric book is that it positions middle-class Jamaican identity in relation to British narratives of class and sexuality, so that in it we have one of the first occasions to examine the relationship between Windrush and Wolfenden—the debates that led to the legalization of homosexual acts between consenting adult men in 1967.

Escape to an Autumn Pavement presents two dramas of homosocial sociality, both starring our class-bound, neurotic hero Johnnie Sobert, a middle-class Jamaican who has migrated to London and is working in the rather disreputable occupation of a waiter at a bar. Both these narratives are legible and dramatic only because of Salkey's clear delineation of the class dynamics among the characters involved. As I go on to show, the relationship between Johnnie and Dick Snape, a genteel chauffeur with whom he ends up living momentarily, describes a form of middle-class companionate queer cohabitation most legible in the wake of the Wolfenden debates, which enshrined a "respectable" form of bourgeois male homosexuality. On the other hand,

Johnnie's hostile relationship with his working-class neighbor Gerald Trado, mediated by Trado's girlfriend, Fiona, displays all the erotic frisson his relationship with Dick lacks, a frisson present in large part because of the class differences between the two men. It is the fraught relationship between Johnnie and Trado that makes visible the problematic spectacle of the Caribbean middle-class migrant to London during the Windrush era. Educated heir to English letters and yet colonial subaltern, Johnnie represents a figure unassimilable to the more familiar image of the working-class black migrant. The instability of his race and class markings makes him both irritant and object of desire to those around him in his London rooming house, setting the stage for a form of homosocial *ressentiment* between two men that is inflected by race and coloniality.[2]

The prominence of his books for children notwithstanding, Salkey has mostly been overlooked in the development of a canon of modern Caribbean literature—overshadowed, it would seem, by peers more stentorian (V. S. Naipaul, George Lamming) and more accessible (Samuel Selvon).[3] And yet he was absolutely central to the community of West Indian writers in London during the mid-twentieth century: he wrote prolifically and also made considerable contributions to several important archives, including those related to the Caribbean Artists Movement and Bogle-L'Ouverture Press. Aspects of his early novels, especially, have greater salience now than ever. *Escape to an Autumn Pavement* offers one of the first fictional representations of a protagonist coming to terms with his queer desire by an Anglophone Caribbean writer, and several of Salkey's later novels, equally overlooked and in some ways just as fascinating, use sex to think about a complex of issues relating to class, race, and national belonging. In this way, Salkey's work anticipates many of the issues that are in play in contemporary debates about identity, including the politics of competing localities and the tensions of nationalist narratives with certain genders and sexualities.

His novels also help us to see that alongside popular discourses against homosexuality and literary tropes of heterosexuality engendering the nation, there is a separate, distinct tradition of homosociality in Caribbean culture.[4] Salkey's *Escape to an Autumn Pavement, The Late Emancipation of Jerry Stover* (1968), and *The Adventures of Catullus Kelly* (1969) all betray a deep skepticism about the pleasures and possibilities of male-female "companionate love."[5] In these works, the society of men is privileged: ties between men are sturdier and more appealing by a large degree than the heterosexual relationships portrayed. Indeed, the heterosexual structure—considered by race relations scholars of the era such as Sheila Patterson to be the apex of sociosexual hygiene—is almost invariably marked in Salkey's novels by tawdriness or

anaesthetized compulsion.[6] Given that in the first waves of migration to England, men from the colonies outnumbered women to a great degree, Salkey's
representation of a fraught and energized male world (not unlike that found
in Selvon's more well known novels) illustrates the gendered demographic
realities of Windrush migration in a fascinatingly contemporary light.

In the Dick and Johnnie storyline of *Escape*, two political plotlines converge—Wolfenden and Windrush—in ways not found elsewhere at the time.
The sexual and gender landscape Salkey felt compelled to represent places
his work at a slight remove from that of his contemporaries, and this fictional
eccentricity was only compounded by his preoccupation with the peculiari-
ties of the Caribbean bourgeoisie.[7] Salkey wrote from the perspective of the
educated middle-class colonial in Britain. The cynicism and torpor of his fictional heroes demonstrate the insecurity of a certain kind of middle-class
man: groomed for power, but uncertain of his place in the nation—displaced
in migrancy and displaced, too, in a rapidly changing homeland. Indeed, back
in heady, newly independent Jamaica, Salkey's novels were raising "awkward
questions," to borrow from the title of Arthur Drayton's paper on a 1969
University of the West Indies panel at which Salkey was asked to defend
his portrayal of middle-class characters.[8] He was being asked to explain his
habit of putting the Caribbean's chattering classes out for public view, particularly since his characters were in the habit of chattering far more than
they acted. There was a sense that representing Jamaica's best and bright-
est as ambivalent drifters was a betrayal of the mandate of the West Indian
writer abroad. If we recall Lamming's early and now famous claim that "it is
the West Indian novel that has restored the West Indian peasant to his true
and original status of personality," we remember that many of the fictions of
the 1950s West Indian literary renaissance—and certainly the ones that are
still read and taught widely today—feature poor or rural characters, often in
extremis.[9] West Indian novelists, reckoning with the legacies of colonialism
and concerned to discover the unique aesthetic contribution of the islands,
understandably focused on representing the denigrated creolized forms of
the working-class black and Asian majorities of the region. This made historical and aesthetic sense, though it did have some problematic effects at the
level of reception, creating an almost uniform impression of the class position of the "West Indian migrant." The only Caribbean colonial relationship
to the metropole worth exploring, it seemed, was that of the working-class
male migrant, not his politically dubious, bourgeois kin. Salkey has remained
an outlier in foundational West Indian fiction, arguably, because he was concerned not just with the poor Jamaican worker (as in his first novel, *A Quality
of Violence*, published in 1959) but also with the confusions and motivations

of a privileged class of men who found themselves abashed and confounded by their ambivalent relationship to the motherland (and, especially, its male denizens).[10]

Escape to an Autumn Pavement presents a figure of Jamaican masculinity situated at the junction of three currents: a newly emerging British homosexuality (primarily white), the trope of the sexually rapacious black immigrant to London (primarily straight), and the imperative of the educated, middle-class West Indian to go home and build the new nation. The figure asked to stand at this impossible crossroads, *Escape*'s Johnnie Sobert, is impotently enraged by his untenable position, and Johnnie's travails reveal the erotic implications both of British attempts to make sense of its shifting social structure in the wake of mass immigration from the West Indies and of West Indians' struggles to construct national identities in the midst of migrancy and decolonization. The volatility of masculine sexual desire in this historical and political context mirrors the instability of identity during this period, when things were both falling apart and coming into being. Salkey's determination to have his narrative play out unstably, to keep our baffling hero perpetually in flux, is therefore of a piece with the dynamic historical context in which he lived. At the end of the novel, having received a note from Dick saying he must make up his mind between him and Fiona, Johnnie escapes to the sidewalks of London "heading nowhere in particular."[11] "I had a choice of lives before me," Johnnie thinks:

> A choice of loves. . . .
>> Fiona was waiting.
>> Dick was waiting.
>> And in another way, London also was. And so was I. I knew I had to wait. For the truth about Dick, about Fiona, about myself.[12]

To end a novel with a character in suspension about fundamental aspects of his identity is to urge upon readers a form of identity politics characterized by deferment and interrogation, a politics not necessarily associated with the polarizing discourses of Windrush migration. This was a moment in British and West Indian history, after all, when popular representations of black migrant masculinity veered between images of malingering dockworkers or (in liberal discourses meant to explain and recuperate "race relations") erudite men possessed of unerring gentility.[13] In such a context, Salkey's presentation of a malingering hipster, resolutely and by choice *not* a credit to his race, is a risky and fascinating counterpoint to established narratives of identity at the time.

I have alluded to two separate homosocial narratives of class, affection, and belonging in the novel, the details of which I will now fill in. The first, and in some senses more prominent, narrative involves Johnnie struggling with his conflicted attraction to his presumably gay neighbor, Dick. When Dick is first introduced early in the novel, Johnnie describes him using the class-based terms he used to introduce himself on the novel's opening page. In describing Dick, Johnnie notes: "Long fingers with manicured nails. Third-class citizen with a first-class citizen's grammar and accent."[14] Though in retrospect the novel has laid the foundation early on for Dick and Johnnie's amorousness—they initially keep meeting in the rooming house bathroom, and at one point early on Johnnie wonders to himself whether Dick is "*that way*, really?"—it is still something of a surprise when Johnnie and Dick take a flat together, living as domestic partners would.[15] In part this sense of surprise results because the novel narrates this subplot so elusively: Johnnie goes from being friendly with Dick in the rooming house, to listening to him sharing a confidence about his female boss's sexual overture, to wondering "why I like him as much as I do," to feeling, suddenly, as if he is "with Dick."[16] The progression of their relationship plays out in a choppy, elliptical, and largely unelaborated way, mirroring the muddle this relationship causes for Johnnie. What we know for certain is that by the middle of the novel, when Johnnie gives in to the overtures of one of his other neighbors, Fiona (the woman who mediates the novel's other homosocial plot), he is explicit about where his affections actually lie. As Johnnie and Fiona kiss he thinks, "She's calling the wrong boy. . . . Doesn't she feel it? Doesn't she understand her defeat. Doesn't she understand Dick's victory. Dick's supremacy. Dick's gift of freedom to me?"[17] The layering of that juvenile double-entendre ("dick's supremacy") with the first genuine expression of amorous fealty to his male friend is characteristic of the novel's ambivalence. The pun is also the closest we get to any actual representation of sex in Johnnie and Dick's relationship—which is to say that we do not get very close at all. When Johnnie says that "Dick's on the brain, again," as Fiona first approaches him, we are encouraged to smirk, and we also learn that, for Johnnie, the silence around homosexual love in his Jamaican milieu will give his own experience of it a rather slanted and mediated aspect.[18]

Johnnie does choose, at least momentarily, to be with Dick and not Fiona, and they have a period of comfort together. I read in this first narrative of queer desire features of the historical moment of which *Escape to an Autumn Pavement* was a part. In 1954 the Departmental Committee on Homosexual Offences and Prostitution, known as the Wolfenden Committee, was charged with the task of rethinking the laws that criminalized certain sexual acts, in part because several high-profile arrests of prominent men for "sexual indecency" rendered increasingly insupportable the separation between Englishness (indeed, "decency") and homosexuality. The release of the Wolfenden Report in 1957 initiated widespread national discussions of the committee's recommendation that adult male homosexual acts be decriminalized (the law doing so, the Sexual Offences Act, was eventually passed in 1967). As Matt Houlbrook has argued, the presentation of a certain kind of gay man—pedigreed, educated, settled, white—helped pave the way for legal inclusion.[19] The image of men living companionably together in arrangements not unlike heterosexual marriages varied from images of male queerness that often gathered around the theatrical, the outlandish, and the outlawed. Johnnie's trajectory toward a settled domestic arrangement with Dick, one in which sex between the men is never portrayed, thus mirrors the political trajectory of a certain form of male legal inclusion in Britain at the time.[20]

The second narrative of male affection involves Johnnie's intense relationship with his other neighbor, the working-class Englishman Gerald Trado. The two men identify with each other and are repelled by each other in equal measure. Hostile and interested, each is fearful that the other might compromise his claims to Englishness. Paradoxes of masculinity and class are worked out most fully in the intense dynamic between Johnnie and Trado, a dynamic of homosocial anxiety that is particularly well defined because it is laid alongside the narrative with Dick, from which it is distinguished. Indeed, if *Escape* is one of the first novels by a Caribbean writer to narrativize male same-sex desire, it is fair to ask whether this is done more clearly through Dick, whom Johnnie loves, or Trado, whom Johnnie hates, and whose wife he decides to bed. The novel appears to set up a choice for Johnnie quite starkly between "heterosexuality"—an affair with Trado's wife, Fiona, that is described always in terms of a suffocating, pathological enclosure—and "homosexuality," portrayed as a settled, contented domestic arrangement with Dick. However, neither of these plotlines actually provides any true moment of crisis or narrative drama in the novel. Instead, Johnnie's feelings for Trado prove to be the most fertile ground for understanding the formation of Johnnie's masculinity and its relationship to Englishness and class. In the romantic triangle of Johnnie, Trado, and Fiona, Johnnie's greatest intensity of emotion is reserved, by far, for his nemesis Trado. Between Johnnie and Trado is all the class-based eros that the black colonial arrival in England stirred up during the middle of the twentieth century.

Johnnie's psychosexual ménage à trois forms in the wake of a heated and telling encounter with Trado surrounding Trado's books. Early in the novel, when Trado summons Johnnie to his room to berate him about late rent, Johnnie coolly sizes up his collection of little magazines and novels. His apparently casual assessment of Trado's tastes is meant to contrast with Trado's effortful acquisition of culture and to mark out a crucial class and culture difference between the two men:

> Sexy boy Trado is sprawling in an armchair. Quite obviously reading *The Observer*. Quotes Ken Tynan the way a Jamaican peasant quotes the Bible.... Carpet by mantlepiece [*sic*] a trifle threadbare; just the spot where jolly Trado takes his stand after a hard night at the pub and lays down the law on anything *The Observer* had already made clear to him the Sunday before.
>
> In the left-hand corner, a delightful tortoise-shell cat, curled protectively against the thick Sunday-newspaper atmosphere. Multicoloured cushions. Ubiquitous Penguins, little reviews, Thomas Manns, Evelyn Waughs, and precious back numbers of *Horizon*....
>
> All protective colouring. All that keeping up with the dead literary Joneses—museum bait.[21]

"Sexy boy Trado" sprawled in his armchair is simultaneously a figure of scorn and passion for Johnnie. He knows that Trado is engaged in a project of self-improvement, acquiring culture as a step toward class mobility. The phrase "protective colouring" applies equally to both men: Johnnie disguises his pain at cultural exclusion with nonchalance, while Trado redresses his social inferiority with books. The analogy Johnnie draws between Trado and a Jamaican peasant is telling. In England, Johnnie is finding, his race and colonial background place him in a much more complicated relationship to workers, like Trado, above whom he has always presumed himself to be educated. All Trado's conspicuous learning is supposed to be pitiable to Johnnie, who, effortlessly bright, need not show off. (He is of course, as a narrator, showing off to us.)

When Trado tries to racially humiliate Johnnie, insinuating he might run off without paying the rent, Johnnie's normally distant, ironic self-commentary explodes into one of the only scenes of real passion in the novel, no less intense for it occurring entirely within Johnnie's mind. At first he admonishes himself: "Ignore him. He's lonely. He's anxious. He's insecure. He's bisexual. He's unhappy. He's anything. For God's sake, just don't do anything stupid. Hold on, boy!"[22] However, in the next moment Johnnie is recanting:

> Can't let his jackass get away with all this! Might as well jump him and be over with it. Surely, it's the only way to deal with a crap hound like Trado. Of course, there's no use in behaving like a *civilized chap*. No use behaving the way my mother would want me to, responsibly and politely; the way she would be proud

of; the way a *little gentleman* is brought up to behave; the way up to the bloody stars! I'll just mess his face about a bit; and as I'm about it, I might as well smash his little library-cum-castle of a room. Won't touch Mrs. Trado though. Wouldn't do to—[23]

The appeal to middle-class colonial values as a safeguard against violence shows how closely Johnnie's class identity plays into his physical and sexual repression.

All this intense feeling around books is one of the most distinctive aspects of the hostility between British working-class and colonial characters in the postwar era. White workers sometimes found themselves striving for an Englishness that properly educated black and brown colonials already felt at ease in having. In a novel published not long after Salkey's, Alexander Baron's *The Lowlife* (1963), the main character, Harryboy Boas, is a working-class autodidact musing upon the fate of his neighborhood given the new, respectable brown neighbors who have moved in. When he happens upon another lonely reader in the local library, Harryboy muses:

> Among the uneducated (which frankly is what you would call the general population where I live) the serious reader is a lonely person. He goes about among the crowds with his thoughts stuffed in him. He probably dare not even mention them to his nearest pals for fear of being thought a schmo. There's a hunger in his eyes for someone to talk to. He watches, and from time to time when he sees someone likely, he makes his signals. His situation is very much like that of the nancyboy.[24]

Baron's extended riff on similarities he perceives between the bookish boy and the "homosexual" resonates with Salkey's novel of a few years earlier. Johnnie Sobert would recognize the sense of lonesome singularity that comes from having "thoughts stuffed in him," working his way through the crowds of London streets looking for someone likely. And Gerald Trado would recognize the loneliness of the serious reader among those less educated. What is telling about Salkey's novel is that Johnnie and Trado do not, like Vic and Harryboy in *The Lowlife*, bond over their shared love of books. There is no meeting of the minds in Salkey's novel, only an intensely felt, subterranean, and violent desire, enacted primarily through Fiona. The difference is racial. Trado does not feel that he can afford to bond with Johnnie, insecure as his own class status is. And Johnnie has used his presumed intellectual superiority over Trado to guard against the racist slights he suffers from him. Intellectual bonding would eliminate Johnnie's sense of academic security, the only inheritance of his colonial upbringing that he is certain has had some positive effect.

Johnnie both represents and is at odds with a particular Caribbean figure: the man who emerged at the turn of the twentieth century out of the exhibition prizes to West Indian high schools reserved for the few. Gaining a scholarship to Queen's Royal College in Trinidad, say, meant that a boy could move from a poor rural or working-class family into the intellectual culture of the colonial and brown elite within the space of a few years.[25] The abruptness of this class shift, and the perennial specter of working-class roots, is part of what makes Johnnie's ilk so determinedly conventional, at least in Johnnie's own reading. "You mustn't get Jamaica's middle class wrong," he tells Fiona at one point: "They have the necessary trappings, the deceitfulness, the narrowness, the smugness, the holier-than-thou attitudes—all this plus a deep-rooted working-class mentality. As far as I can see, working-class and slave-class skeletons-in-the-cupboard add up to the most ridiculous situation in the Caribbean Area."[26] Johnnie's mockery of his own class position points to a crucial context: unlike the English scholarship boys of the postwar period, who faced a similar disorientation and brittleness of class position, West Indian scholarship boys and members of the recent middle class such as Johnnie Sobert had behind them the expectation that their personal success would lead to large-scale social change. Class shifts in the Caribbean bore the weight of history, a history that, for Johnnie, a self-described "drifter," both lends him heft and burdens him.[27]

As Ivar Oxaal argues, people like Johnnie were considered "exemplary figures in a society which otherwise provided very limited opportunities for the vast majority of its citizens," symbols of an "embryo meritocracy" whose mettle was tested in the fires of English examinations.[28] Narratives by famous examples of these men such as C. L. R. James and Eric Williams emphasize not their alienation from a lost family or class culture but rather their mastery of an entirely new one. Meanwhile, in Britain, increased access to education created class fractures within families, with British scholarship boys off to grammar school and university developing different expectations and terms of reference than the rest of their family. In Richard Hoggart's important study of this phenomenon, *The Uses of Literacy* (1957), the anxious working-class striver appears as an entirely different figure from the confident West Indian man who proceeded into the English landscape with a social mandate from home and a sense of being a deserving inheritor of its intellectual tradition.[29] C. L. R. James in *Beyond a Boundary* (1963), for instance, represents no necessary correlation between brains and physical weakness. On the contrary, James presents an ideal of the new class of black leader, who combined the physical grace of the cricketer with the intellectual prowess of the scholar. For James, this new class was to be a vigorous generation of men who would take the nascent island nations into independence.

Meanwhile, Britain in the wake of World War II was experiencing its own set of shifts around gender and class, appending to the demands of heroic masculinity the somewhat contradictory necessity for masculine domesticity. The model man on the home front during wartime combined elements of the public school code—fair play, "decency"—with the physical vigor of sportsmanship, thus creating a composite of emotional reserve and bodily strength that could be mandated for middle-class as well as working-class men.[30] Hoggart's sense of the implications of economic improvement for working-class masculinity connects with these new masculine imperatives. Hoggart writes that "the valuable social changes of the last fifty years" are accompanied by cultural changes that "are not always an improvement but in some of the more important instances a worsening."[31] He is focusing mainly on the undoing of the family structure and the deleterious effects of "new mass culture," but he also spares a thought for what he calls "the uprooted and the anxious"—those working-class scholarship boys and self-made men who move into greater literacy without an accompanying sense of social ease or prestige. The similarities between Hoggart's nervous working-class reader and Johnnie's perception of Gerald Trado are striking. Hoggart talks about the "ostentatious adoption of protective colouring" that some middle-class aspirants take on as recompense for lacking either the poise of the securely middle class or the brio of the brilliant and earnest working man.[32] Hoggart describes a situation of feminization that mirrors Johnnie's attempt to pyschologize Trado's sexuality ("he's bisexual") when he writes of the smart working-class boy being separated from "the lads" and his tendency to be "closer to the women of the house than to the men."[33] Hoggart writes: "Such a scholarship boy has lost some of the resilience and some of the vitality of his cousins who are still knocking about the streets. . . . His sexual growth is perhaps delayed."[34] For men like Trado, who never made it to grammar school but who nevertheless strive for intellectual improvement, Hoggart sees a person who "cannot face squarely his own working-class," is sometimes "ashamed of his origins," and consequently "provides himself with a mantle of defensive attitudes": "He tries to read all the good books, but they do not give him that power of speech and command over experience which he seeks. He is as gauche there as he is with the craftsman's tools."[35] For such a man, the easeful colonial middle-class subject, seemingly already familiar with the genteel cultures to which he, the British working-man was only now gaining access, could become a symbol for all the barriers that still stood his way, a social fact reflected in Trado's anxious relations with Johnnie in *Escape*.[36]

There is a passage in Hoggart's almost anthropological description of the working-class reader that sounds uncannily like Johnnie Sobert's eagle-eyed assessment of Trado's reading habits. Summing up the naive reading choices of the self-taught worker, Hoggart writes:

> I have in mind the reading of cultural publications which is from one aspect improper, which is inspired by too strong and too vague an expectation. It is my impression that this kind of interest in serious publications is more common than is generally thought. . . .
>
> For some people the late *John O'London's Weekly* obviously met a strong felt need, one stronger, I think, than it could have legitimately claimed to meet. Others are proud of reading J. B. Priestly and writers such as him, because they are "serious writers with a message." Others have learned that Mr. Priestly is a "middlebrow" and only mention him in tones of deprecation. They tend to read bitterly ironic or anguished literature—Waugh, Huxley, Kafka and Greene. They own the Penguin selection from Eliot, as well as some other Penguins and Pelicans; they used to take *Penguin New Writing* and now subscribe to *Encounter*. They know a little, but often only from reviews and short articles, about Frazer and Marx; they probably own a copy of the Pelican edition of Freud's *Psychopathology of Everyday Life*. They sometimes listen to talks on the Third Programme with titles like, "The Cult of Evil in Contemporary Literature."[37]

That a character in a middle-class West Indian writer's novel would make assessments about the striving of a working-class intellectual similar to those of a British-born academic drawn from the ranks of those he analyzed is in itself fascinating. Such a convergence only amplifies the sense that shifts in working-class culture were visible as anxieties as much as improvements, a sense registered in all its complexity in Salkey's novel.[38]

Returning to the rooming house in *Escape to an Autumn Pavement*, there is one last, silent eruption from Johnnie after Trado insults him again:

> Hit him! Hit him murderously hard and be done with it. Bash whatever little brains he has left and feel like a man afterwards. There's only one way to get out of this with any satisfaction, and it is done with a touch of violence. Not enough to land in prison. Just enough to restore the balance of power. That's all. Drive him a nice one in the mouth, and two swift ones in the guts.[39]

Having, of course, not done any of these things, Johnnie climbs the stairs to his room, where he has the following elliptical thoughts: "Door knob feels like Trado's head. Cold. Round. Easily destroyed. Wrenched off and discarded at the back of the house."[40] When Johnnie sleeps with Fiona (a classic homosocial substitution for beating Trado to a pulp) their assignations are strikingly disembodied, in contrast to the imagined feel of Trado's skull, the squash of his guts. Fiona's body is never imagined, and it is not even really felt. When they first make love on Hampstead Heath, Johnnie recites poetry to himself in order to mimic the rhythms of sex: he drowns Fiona out with words. To the extent that Johnnie can engage with Fiona's femininity at all, he is repulsed by it. Her perfume is overwhelming; her speech is likened to "albumen" exploding over everything. When he does eventually end the affair, Johnnie tells her it is "to be rid of your overpowering passion and depressing sexuality."[41]

The battle Johnnie has with Trado approaches what Eve Kosofsky Sedgwick describes in *Between Men* as "murderous ressentiment."[42] By fantasizing about "jumping" Trado, Johnnie can imagine breaking out of the confines of middle-class colonial respectability—experienced here as a feminized, ersatz version of robust English masculinity. Johnnie is understandably enraged and confused: this is a fairly complicated reversal of the expectations of colonial British masculinity. Trado is an irritant because no one else makes Johnnie feel as feminized and with no one else are his claims to Britishness as compromised. But Johnnie also identifies with Trado's ambivalent relationship to Englishness. The modern ideal of gentlemanly English conduct, forged along with empire in the eighteenth century, has a difficult relationship to the masculine body. On the one hand, a proper English man is vigorous, exercising control and intellectual mastery over his body. Deviations from this ideal—whether into unmanly foppery or creole sexual licentiousness—deeply complicated a man's relationship to his Englishness, and there was always the danger that attention to the physical ideal could veer into the unsafe territory of vanity. A further complication occurred when this ideal was transplanted to the black colonial. As the novel makes clear, Johnnie's school and his overbearing mother trained him to aspire to a modern, bourgeois version of the English gentleman. But in an island colony where class distinctions must be closely guarded and, as Johnnie is always reminding Fiona, where there is little actual capital ("Surely it takes much more than a hundred and twenty-eight years after the Abolition of Slavery for a middle class to evolve?" Johnnie says to Fiona), Johnnie has also been taught to distinguish himself from those who work.[43] This is the conundrum Johnnie faces: having been trained to contain physical expressions of rage, he has also been trained out of one of the most obvious expressions he could use to demonstrate superiority over Trado. It is little wonder the pounding Johnnie (almost) delivers takes on the force and frustration of unconsummated sex: identification is often soluble with desire.

We do not ever know for sure whether Johnnie's relationship with Dick is sexual, though there is a moment when Fiona asks for a clear answer on this very point, and Johnnie denies it—a little too strongly, he admits. Even without this doth-protest-too-much denial, I want to distinguish Dick and Johnnie's relationship from the more ambiguous feelings Johnnie has for Trado, and indeed from something like the affectionate relationship Jerry has with Bashra in the later novel *The Late Emancipation of Jerry Stover*. Dick's relationship with Johnnie is clearly in the lineage of homosexuality as identity, which is why Dick forces Johnnie to make a choice between him and Fiona, urging him to "make up his mind" about himself. There is never any question that Dick is gay—though no words beyond "that way" are ever used to name Dick's sexual orientation.[44] Whether Johnnie will finally identify as gay or not, we know that he has deep emotional ties to Dick that he has to no one else. When he sleeps with Fiona after moving in with Dick, he feels he has cheated on Dick. And when he goes to his Jamaican barber friend, Larry, to ask for advice, Larry asks him first if he has woman trouble, and Johnnie has to correct him to say his relationship trouble is with a man. Larry is taken aback, but then asks straightforwardly, "You happier that way [in his shared flat with Dick] than with a woman?," to which Johnnie answers unhesitatingly, "I'm sure of it!"[45] Larry later tells Johnnie that he has sought out his relationship with Dick because he is in search of a nation: "You want an identity like. You want to feel that you have a nation behind you, a nation that you call your own."[46] His coworker Biddy's voice tells Johnnie that now that he's living with another man, apparently loving another man, he is "finished as a man."[47] In these voices, Johnnie hears the conjunction of masculinity and nationality, and he wonders whether his two friends might be right, that he is not manly enough, not grounded enough to know his way in London. Johnnie feels both unmanned and deracinated, and it is tempting to see those two things finding their fullest expression in Johnnie's being gay. This interpretation is clearly in play—not just in this novel, but in Caribbean cultures where legal and social injunctions against homosexuality circumscribe national boundaries and create sexual out-groups. What I am suggesting with my reading of *Escape to an Autumn Pavement*, however, is that in this novel the most potent pressure point in the nexus of class and sexual identity is not at the homosexual, but at an even less straightforward, less easily defined point in the relations between two men—what I have been calling here the homosocial (which also lies within the capacious critical category of queer). It is at that place where desire and identification are not sexual per se, but intense, hostile, and evocative of sexual intimacy. In Johnnie's case, it is at those moments—when envy and resentment flare into violence and anger with Trado, or when the comfort of Dick's identifiably middle-class mores combine with his preferred masculinity to lead to a sense of domestic "freedom"—that we have the fullest, most generative sense of Caribbean migrant identity in productive formation. By enabling us to read between Windrush and Wolfenden, that is, Salkey's novel makes available different narratives of class and sexuality, narratives that disrupt the assertive certainties of gender and nationalism commonly attributed to this period at empire's end.

Notes

1. Andrew Salkey, *Escape to an Autumn Pavement* (London: Hutchinson, 1960), 11.

2. For the foundational theoretical discussion of such homosociality, see Eve Kosofsky Sedgwick, *Between Men* (New York: Columbia University Press, 1985).

3. His novel *Hurricane* has been a classic for young readers in the Caribbean for decades.

4. As will be seen in my reading of *Escape to an Autumn Pavement*, the novel is a veritable model of Sedgwick's idea of the erotic frisson of nonconsummated male friendship and desire. Variations of this structure are to be found in Selvon's *The Lonely Londoners*, in C. L. R. James's ravishing attention to cricketers, and in many other aspects of the political culture of early Caribbean nationalisms.

5. Andrew Salkey, *The Late Emancipation of Jerry Stover* (London: Hutchinson, 1968); Andrew Salkey, *The Adventures of Catullus Kelly* (London: Hutchinson, 1969). One notable exception is the marriage of Erasmus and Bridget in *The Adventures of Catullus Kelly*, which is portrayed with warmth and humor. Needless to say, they are not the main focus of the novel. Among the lettered and bored Kingston set in *The Late Emancipation* and in swinging London with *Catullus Kelly*, Salkey portrays male-female relationships that are strikingly at odds with the settled and relaxed affections of male alliances.

6. See Sheila Patterson, *Dark Strangers: A Sociological Study of the Absorption of a Recent West Indian Migrant Group in Brixton, South London* (London: Tavistock, 1963), a foundational text for the formation of the study of race relations in the United Kingdom.

7. Belinda Edmonson's recent *Caribbean Middlebrow: Leisure, Culture, and the Middle Class* (Ithaca, N.Y.: Cornell University Press, 2009) is an intriguing examination of the cultural tastes and procedures of the West Indian middle class.

8. Arthur Drayton, "Awkward Questions for Jamaicans," *Journal of Commonwealth Literature* 7 (1969): 125–127. In this, Salkey's critical plight is similar to that of John Hearne, as discussed elsewhere in this collection by Kate Houlden and Kim Robinson-Walcott.

9. George Lamming, *The Pleasures of Exile* (1960; repr., Ann Arbor: University of Michigan Press, 1992), 39.

10. Andrew Salkey, *A Quality of Violence* (London: Hutchinson, 1959).

11. Salkey, *Escape*, 208.

12. Ibid.

13. Perhaps the most famous example of this is Sidney Poitier's character in the 1967 film *To Sir, With Love*, which is based on E. R. Brathwaite's 1959 memoir of the same name. See also Earl Cameron's roles in various midcentury "issue films," including *Pool of London* (1951) and *Sapphire* (1959).

14. Salkey, *Escape*, 15.

15. Ibid., 16.

16. Ibid., 95, 107.

17. Ibid., 106–107.

18. Ibid., 101.

19. Matt Houlbrook, *Queer London: Perils and Pleasures in the Sexual Metropolis, 1918–1957* (Chicago: University of Chicago Press, 2005).

20. The twist, of course, is that Johnnie is black, a migrant, a figure who was at the center of the *other* heated political debate of the 1950s and 1960s around colonial immigration.

21. Salkey, *Escape*, 19.

22. Ibid., 20.

23. Ibid.

24. Alexander Baron, *The Lowlife* (London: Collins, 1963), 60–61. "Nancyboy" is a slang term for a homosexual male.

25. Lamming, of course, is one of the most famous examples of such a move among the era's literary figures.

26. Salkey, *Escape*, 47.

27. Ibid.

28. Ivar Oxaal, *Black Intellectuals Come to Power: The Rise of Creole Nationalism in Trinidad and Tobago* (Cambridge, Mass.: Schenkman, 1968), 59.

29. Richard Hoggart, *The Uses of Literacy* (London: Chatto and Windus, 1957).

30. Martin Francis, "The Domestication of the Male? Recent Research on Nineteenth- and Twentieth-Century British Masculinity," *Historical Journal* 45, no. 3 (2002): 644.

31. Hoggart, *Literacy*, 260.

32. Ibid., 239.

33. Ibid., 241–242.

34. Ibid., 244.

35. Salkey, *Escape*, 246.

36. This is complicated, of course: there was plenty of imagery to go around where black male migrants were concerned, and as much as the educated West Indian was a threatening figure, so too was the supposedly shiftless black worker. Marcus Collins's account of the perceptions around West Indian men in Britain during the postwar era works through the sociological and autobiographical literature of the period and describes the contradictory associations around West Indian men during this period. See Marcus Collins, "Pride and Prejudice: West Indian Men in Mid-Twentieth-Century Britain," *Journal of British Studies* 40, no. 3 (2001): 391–418.

37. Hoggart, *Literacy*, 252–253.

38. While it is beyond the scope of this essay, it bears noting that the convergence of West Indian fiction with British cultural studies is visible at its very inception in *The Uses of Literacy*. The shared concern of writers from abroad and British intellectuals developing new models for questioning British culture is fascinating in its implications, and it is not accidental that Stuart Hall, a Jamaican migrant, joined Birmingham's Center for Contemporary Cultural Studies at Hoggart's urging and took over as director in 1968.

39. Salkey, *Escape*, 21.

40. Ibid., 22.
41. Ibid., 135.
42. Sedgwick, *Between Men*, 102.
43. Salkey, *Escape*, 47.
44. Ibid., 16, 175.
45. Ibid., 175.
46. Ibid., 199.
47. Ibid., 201.

Genre and Gender

Rescripting Anglophone Caribbean Women's Literary History: Gender, Genre, and Lost Caribbean Voices

ALISON DONNELL

The recent acceleration of critical interest in Anglophone Caribbean women's literary voices that have been variously lost, abandoned, or neglected over the last century has revealed a reach and range of literary cultures and women's writings within the region that remained routinely unseen under the Windrush lens of diasporic male writings. New editions of works by Frieda Cassin, Una Marson, and Elma Napier, along with careful analyses of these and other "early" women writers, have significantly enriched our appreciation of the region's literary history.[1] This essay continues this restorative task by drawing on the women's short stories from the BBC *Caribbean Voices* radio program, broadcast from London to up to ninety thousand radio sets in the Anglophone Caribbean between 1943 and 1958. Not only does this archive of broadcast scripts offer an important resource for recovery research, but the established cultural phenomenon of *Caribbean Voices* as a launchpad for male West Indian literary careers affords a useful case study for thinking through the distillation of writers and writings into a post-Windrush canon.

The link between *Caribbean Voices* and the making of West Indian male literary authorship has been well established, and yet the role of this radio program within a narrative of women's literary history from this region is still close to unknown.[2] Virtually all of the women writers whose work it broadcast remain unfamiliar to readers and even researchers of Caribbean literature today. What follows is an attempt to consider the causes for the rapid disappearance of this body of work from any platform for critical or creative commentary. This essay thus provides the first steps and foundation for retrieving an Anglophone women's literary history of the Windrush era by examining women's role as writers on *Caribbean Voices* and in locally published magazines, newspapers, and anthologies. Attention to these women makes it clear that an alternative West Indian women's literary history existed alongside the canonical male Windrush writings. Yet during the 1950s a mixed and broad hub of assorted literary activity was reshaped into a narrow pathway for professional male authorship and the attention-grabbing phenomenon of the boom of the West Indian novel. It would seem that the focalizing spotlight on those men who wrote novels in the metropolis cast women writers into a shadow of obscurity from which they have yet to emerge. Although gender is pronounced in its effect, inasmuch as we can easily note the absence of women writers before 1970 in most literary histories of the region, it has remained largely uninterrogated as a factor guiding the successes of authorship. My focus on these women and their works aims to identify the causes of their subsequent invisibility by foregrounding the bearings of gender upon questions of location, production, genre, and reception. Asking the question as to why so few of these women became West Indian writers that we know of today is crucial to the task of restoring a longer, fuller history of women's writing from the region. It is also central to the task of understanding how the idea of a West Indian writer took shape in the profoundly formative post-Windrush moment.

Before going on to talk specifically about the *Caribbean Voices* program and women's writings, it is important to address the major factors governing literary production and reception for Anglophone Caribbean writers, circumstances that gave rise to a historical legacy dominated by prominent male authors. In her landmark 1929 essay *A Room of One's Own*, Virginia Woolf talks about the topic of women and writing to demonstrate the layers of external and internal impediments that must be peeled back in order to glimpse the conditions of possibility for a woman's achievement of professional authorship.[3] Writing back to a time period not that distant to Woolf's in terms of women's literary possibilities, my own discussion of Anglophone Caribbean women's writing, like Woolf's, cannot approach the question of female authorship in the postwar period without framing the conditions of their material and creative lives and the gendered expectations of literary achievement that primed their vulnerability to obscurity.

A crucial factor dictating the demonstrably gendered nature of the pathway from "creative writing" to professional authorship for Caribbean writers was migration patterns. Female migration to the metropolis was not a defining feature of this period, and consequently, the presence of women who wrote was not registered or felt in the same way as the active nucleus of male writers who settled in London and frequented the BBC freelancers' room at the Langham Hotel. The strongly gendered socioeconomic pressures and attachments that Caribbean women had to manage at home—often taking a primary role in child care while securing the financial viability of their families—meant that women did not migrate in the same numbers (and when they did, they typically worked as domestics, nurses, or teachers). Moreover, while women generated a significant portion of the remittance economy of this period, they did not find equal prominence in cultural spheres, with few having access to cultural networks or likely even to material resources such as expensive typewriters, paper, and pens.

The gendering of literary vocation, although harder to quantify, should also not be dismissed. Professional authorship was already the objective of George Lamming and Sam Selvon, who shared an Imperial typewriter on the Atlantic crossing. It has always been the pride of V. S. Naipaul, whose Penguin author information strikingly declares he "began to write, in London, in 1954. He has followed no other profession."[4] For women, the vocation of writer seems less defining.[5] Una Marson, one of the few women writers who did migrate, had already published two collections of poetry and seen her first play successfully staged in Jamaica before she left for Britain. Yet in London, despite staging her play and writing another, she also took on a range of jobs as secretary and assistant, and there is every indication that her writing career slowed. She wrote only a handful of poems in England, although crucially she was able to build a profile across theater, journalism, and broadcasting that became instrumental to the writing opportunities of other Caribbean women.

In trying to reconfigure the literary milieu of this period, it seems not insignificant that the conjunction of migration and writing, as well as a certain masculinity associated with the daring of both endeavors, is seen as defining for Roger Mais. Just before he died in 1955, Mais described the Caribbean writer as "essentially a travelling, 'gambling' man with a manuscript or two in his bag and a big dream of contributing to contemporary English literature."[6] Mais himself was a good fit with this description, having migrated from Jamaica to the United Kingdom in 1952 with two short story volumes to his name. In London, his authorship status was firmly established by the publication of three novels with Jonathan Cape in as many years: *The Hills Were Joyful Together* (1953), *Brother Man* (1954), and *Black Lightning* (1955).

The issue of literary genre, though not commonly subjected to analysis, was arguably an equally important factor to migration in terms of gendering writerly recognition. Women's commitment to the short story form increasingly marginalized their literary standing during this formative period, when the rise of the novel became the defining development in West Indian literary culture. The arrival in England of a number of significant male novelists (Edgar Mittelholzer, Mais, Vic Reid, John Hearne, Andrew Salkey, as well as the soon towering figures of Naipaul, Lamming, Wilson Harris, and Selvon) was, by the 1960s, to form a defining template for the West Indian canon. The relatively swift transformation of the West Indian literary scene that took place across the 1950s—from an abundance of lively small-scale activities scattered across the region in venues such as newspapers, little magazines, yearbooks of poetry leagues, and anthologies for schools into an established group of West Indian male novelists based in the United Kingdom is such a well-established fact that very often the abundance and variety of what came before the customary canon simply remain unseen.

In Lamming's often-quoted tribute to the *Caribbean Voices'* editor Henry Swanzy, he argues that "no comprehensive account of writing in the British Caribbean during the last decade [1950s] could be written without considering his whole achievement and his role in the emergence of the West Indian novel."[7] At first glance, Swanzy may seem like an unlikely catalyst for the rise of the Anglophone Caribbean novel, given that he edited a radio program that broadcast short fiction and poetry. *Caribbean Voices* was outside of print culture and did not directly publish the works that it broadcast at all until a modest anthology of poems appeared in 1966, edited by John Figueroa. Although there was a reciprocal arrangement with Frank Collymore, the editor of the Barbados-based little magazine *Bim*—with Collymore sending work and his critique to Swanzy in London—*Bim* was also an outlet for short fiction. Yet Lamming was not mistaken in his homage. What Lamming recognizes and affirms in his praise of Swanzy is an alternative and highly influential cultural economy that bridged the *Caribbean Voices* program and a UK publishing career in which respect, friendship, contacts, and advice were traded among male writers and editors in the cause of the West Indian novel.[8]

In fact, the *Caribbean Voices* program came into being at the hands of Una Marson, a Jamaican woman writer who first traveled to London in 1932 and became the first black woman employed by the BBC in March 1941. As a full-time program assistant for *Calling the West Indies*, which was primarily designed to relay "morale-boosting" messages from servicemen based in the United Kingdom back home to the Caribbean, Marson was also involved in the prestigious BBC poetry program *Caribbean Voices*. Always keen to think laterally and creatively, Marson starting weaving readings of published works by Caribbean writers and reports of cultural events into her broadcasts, and the success of this format provided support for her idea for *Caribbean Voices*, unique in BBC overseas programming. Although women like June Grimble and Mary Treadgold remained active in the program's production, Marson's 1946 departure as primary editor changed the gender dynamics of the show's programming considerably.

While the program retained its upper management in the person of John Grenfell Williams (Director of African Services), Henry Swanzy took up the position of editor, supporting and shaping the literary agenda of the program and arguably of West Indian literature as it is now known and cherished. All the subsequent gatekeepers were men, with Naipaul, Mittelholzer, and Salkey acting in editorial roles at various points. Although Gladys Lindo was appointed as the program's West Indian representative in Jamaica, there is strong evidence that her husband, Cedric, actually selected scripts for Swanzy in London. For Swanzy, an Irishman, *Caribbean Voices* was crucially about creating an opportunity for cultural immersion, and he favored West Indian tales that declared their locatedness through reference to the local, the distinctive, and the oral. He wanted listeners to feel that they had "sat with the fishermen hefting sea-eggs, gone with the pork-knockers in to Guyana jungles, followed the saga-boys and the whe-whe players, heard the riddles, the digging songs, the proverbs, the ghost stories, duppies, La Diablesse, Soukivans, zombies, maljo, obeah, voodoo, shango."[9]

Importantly, there is no indication of gender preference in either Marson's desire to weave literary achievements and distinctions into an overseas broadcast program or in Swanzy's explicitly culturalist preference. All the same, gender does seem to weigh in the mediation, production, and internal reception of works broadcast on *Caribbean Voices*. Somewhat ironically, given her own feminist agendas as a writer and journalist, Marson's project of building a literary platform in the metropolis successfully serviced the careers of budding metropolitan-based male novelists while leaving women historically silenced. Although for Swanzy cultural difference was far more operative as a literary category, his vision seems to have accrued complicatedly gendered expectations around women's authentic experience and their intimate connection to the lives and voices of the folk—a view possibly affirmed by the fact that the women writers generally remained part of their home communities. Unsurprisingly too, in the context of the male-dominated environment that structured the program after Marson left, it is possible to find signs that the expectations of a normatively masculinist culture went largely unchallenged.

Like early poetry and short story collections published in the Caribbean that featured both male and female writers (although not often in equal numbers), the weekly *Caribbean Voices* shows also comprised a wonderfully assorted medley of literary work from an astonishingly broad constituency of writers. Of the program's 372 contributors, 71 were women. Yet only Louise Bennett's and Sylvia Wynter's names can be found in canonical accounts of Anglophone Caribbean literary history alongside those men whose literary careers the program is known to have helped advance: Michael Anthony, Edward (Kamau) Brathwaite, Lamming, Mais, Mittelholzer, Naipaul, Selvon, and Salkey. Talented writers such as Eula Redhead, Inez Sibley, Marjorie Brown, and Edwina Melville remain, by and large, unremarked upon. The very fact that Sibley and Melville went on to publish story collections of their own is unacknowledged, even seventy years after the program began. Indeed, the dominant historical legacy of the program, its personalities, and its era did indeed come, as Lamming implies, with the male writers' move into the novel form (always the genre accorded more status and prestige). It was also this shift that most dramatically demarcated the gender divide of literary reputation and recognition for Anglophone Caribbean writers in the post-war period.

The story behind Naipaul's literary launch at Andre Deutsch is an instructive, if not entirely happy, example of this transition. Introduced by Salkey, with whom he worked on *Caribbean Voices*, to Diana Athill, an editor at Deutsch, Naipaul handed her the manuscript for *Miguel Street*. Yet despite the fact that both Athill and Francis Wyndham were enthusiastic about it, "Andre Deutsch, the Hungarian-born impresario behind the company, thought a book of short stories about Trinidad by an unpublished author was unlikely to sell."[10] Recalling this event much later, Naipaul tells Patrick French, "He said stories don't sell, and of course *Miguel Street* has never been out of print since it was published. It has not been out of print. He tormented me in that way. So I had to write a novel, and I did the *Mystic Masseur* with great unhappiness."[11] In this example and others, *Caribbean Voices* acted as a congregation point for West Indian writers and provided a contact zone with British and other Commonwealth writers. While Lamming had been encouraged to write by his teacher Collymore and had published short stories and poems in *Bim*, after he arrived in London in 1950 and started working at the BBC in 1951, there was a shift in his chosen genre, and he published four novels between 1953 and 1960. Lamming's tribute to Swanzy shows that he recognized the link. For Selvon, whose short stories remain among the finest in the Anglophone Caribbean tradition, his place in canonical history was similarly assured by his novelistic rendition of immigrant life, *The Lonely Londoners* (1956).

Thus, while the literary culture of *Caribbean Voices* remained gender inclusive and diverse in terms of its own programming, the literary networks of the BBC corridors were beginning to shape a different West Indian literary tradition that would leave hardly a trace of the breadth and variety of the writers whose work it broadcast. A striking reminder of just how swiftly and persuasively this transition took place can be found in Salkey's "Introduction" to his 1960 anthology, *West Indian Stories*, which gathered some wonderful short prose fiction by the new generation of noted novelists and was published by Faber and Faber in London. Already by this date, just two years after *Caribbean Voices* stopped broadcasting, Salkey, who was himself involved with the program and part of its writerly grouping, had accepted the idea that the West

Indian novel was the tradition's dominant genre. Here he needs to correct himself, and his readers, with a brief literary history lesson:

> On reflection, though, I think I was wrong. Established novelists like V. S. Reid, Roger Mais (now dead), George Lamming, Samuel Selvon, Jan Carew, and Neville Dawes were first of all noticed as short story writers . . . by successive producers and editors in the B.B.C.'s Caribbean and Colonial Service (Miss Una Marson, Henry Swanzy, E. R. Edmett, V. S. Naipaul, Edgar Mittelholzer, and now Miss Mary Treadgold) and by editors of West Indian literary reviews (Frank A Collymore and W. Therold Barnes of *Bim*, A. J. Seymour of *Kyk-Over-Al*, and Mrs Edna Manley of *Focus*).
>
> It is nearer the truth to say that the West Indian short story and its logical development, the West Indian novel, have had dissimilar yet complementary midwives and guardians, at home and in exile.[12]

From today's perspective, however, even Salkey's corrected account remains flawed. Those editors and mentors based in the Caribbean whom he mentions here did not act as "midwives and guardians" to the novel form for the many women writers who were broadcast on the BBC's Caribbean Service or published in the pages of local literary reviews. While the men who traveled and networked may have found a home away from home, the women staying in the Caribbean were soon in literary exile.

For most women writers, the failed crossing from the short story to the novel, as well as from the West Indies to England, left them without any place in literary history. The sense of this loss is palpable. If we consider *Bim*, whose stated mission was "experiment and encouragement," we can look back to a publication where barely a single page in its impressive index of writings from 1942 to 1972 does not list one or two women writers.[13] The cataloging of a literary culture in which women actively participated is demonstrable, and yet their names are now almost uniformly unfamiliar—Elizabeth Walcott, Ursula Walcott, Flora Squires, Yvonne Padmore, Millicent Payne, Marion Marsh, Jeanette Layne, Ellice Honychurch, among many others. In relation to *Focus*, the progressive annual little magazine published in Jamaica at irregular intervals (1943, 1948, 1956, and 1960), apart from Edna Manley, who was editor and is retained in memory as Prime Minister Norman Manley's wife, the women writers associated with this publication have now also descended into literary obscurity: Vera Bell, Barbara Ferland, Dorothy Whitfield, and Michele Edwards.

How then might we restore a fuller version of Anglophone Caribbean literary history in the 1950s against this selective tradition that emerged so powerfully and persistently? Research on women writers in *Caribbean Voices* suggests that there exists an alternative literary history of women's writing that begins with small magazine and newspaper publishing in the region, flourishes through the BBC program, and then continues in short fiction anthologies and educational publications. When Marson left the *Caribbean Voices* program and returned to Jamaica in 1946, she took up editorship of the newly founded Pioneer Press, the book-publishing arm of the *Gleaner* newspaper. This press was clearly one outlet for the ambitions of cultural nationalism in Jamaica that were riding high at this time, and, in contrast to the strongly homosocial environs at the BBC, women, as well as men, were central to the cultural scene. The Pioneer Press published books by male writers, including Claude McKay and Tom Redcam, but it was demonstrably active in its support of women's writing and became an important venue for publishing work by the Jamaicans also broadcast by the BBC. Its 1950 anthology, *14 Jamaican Short Stories*, included stories by Vera Bell, Terry Burke, and three by Ethel Rovere. In the same year, the press published Laurice Bird's *Maxie Mongoose and Other Animal Stories for Children* and Louise Bennett's *Anancy Stories and Dialect Verse* (republished in 1957), both also broadcast by the BBC. Its 1953 collection, *Caribbean Anthology of Short Stories*, by Ernest Carr and others, published work by Vera Bell, Lucille Iremonger, and Ethel Rovere.

A number of other women across the region whose work appeared on the *Caribbean Voices* program also went on to publish volumes of short fiction. These include the Guyanese writer Edwina Melville, whose *This Is the Rupununi: A Simple Story Book of the Savannah Lands of the Rupununi District, British Guiana* was published by the Government Information Service in British Guiana; Jamaican Inez Knibb Sibley, whose collection *Quashie's Reflections: In Jamaican Creole* was published in 1968 by the Bolivar Press in Jamaica; and Grenadian Monica Skeete, whose *Time Out* collection was published by Nelson in England in 1978 as part of the expanding educational market. The short stories of Skeete and other *Caribbean Voices* writers also enjoyed something of an afterlife on account of this educational market. Works by Skeete, Flora Squires, Elizabeth Walcott, and Dorothy Lovell were reprinted from *Bim* in a 1969 Nelson anthology, *Response: A Course in Narrative Comprehension and Composition for Caribbean Secondary Schools*, and later revived in 1982 under the title *Wavelengths*. Barbadian Undine Giuseppe also edited a collection, *Backfire: A Collection of Caribbean Short Stories*, published by Macmillan in 1973, and also aimed at secondary schools. In this collection, too, women's short fiction is well represented, with works by Shirley Tappin, Ida Ramesar, Joy Moore, Joy Clarke, Flora Spencer, Ninnie Seereeram, and Undine Giuseppe herself.

In contrast to the predominantly locally published literary activity by women in the West Indies in the post-Windrush period, the literary tradition of male novelists was being consolidated in the English metropolis by a number of field-defining anthologies. Tellingly, in Salkey's introduction to his *West Indian Stories*, he had listed Ada Quayle as the only woman in "a remarkable upsurge of new writing from the West Indies."[14] Quayle's novel *The Mistress*, published by MacGibbon & Kee in 1957, made her the closest companion in terms of genre, although she has now long been an obscured figure. The only work by a woman actually included in Salkey's anthology is "Arise, My Love" by the English-born Jan Williams, whose stories had been broadcast on *Caribbean Voices* and published in *Bim*. Salkey's later edited collections, *Stories from the Caribbean* (Elek Press, 1965) and *Caribbean Prose* (Evans Bros., 1967), presented a more standard West Indian literary canon that would tenaciously hold critical and publishing attention for decades to come—with no women's writings at all. These and the three fiction anthologies published in 1966—Kenneth Ramchand's *West Indian Narrative*, Barbara Howes's *From the Green Antilles*, and O. R. Dathorne's *Caribbean Narrative*—while slightly different in their remit and reach, all confirmed the centrality of Naipaul, Reid, Mais, Lamming, Selvon, and the now lesser-known Jamaican novelist John Hearne, whose *Voices under the Window* was published by Faber and Faber in 1955.

Bringing the genre divide of ongoing authorship by women in the West Indies back into view alongside the canonization processes for male novelists allows an important observation concerning the gendered division of literary reputations and fortunes that takes place in the 1960s. Not only is there a demonstrable geographical separation of male novelists from women short story writers, but there is also a sense in which literary value is mapped onto the former group by their entry into UK literary fiction publication venues, and cultural and educational value onto the latter as educational publishing becomes the dominant market in the Caribbean.[15]

So far, I have focused on the factors around the *Caribbean Voices* program that influenced its role as a hub for professional male literary authorship. I turn now to the expectations and configurations of the literary within *Caribbean Voices* that may also have impacted the gendered channeling of a narrow history of literary accomplishment from a broad base of literary activity. While the volume of women's writing that was broadcast testifies to the support afforded to all Caribbean writing, the gendered tastes and assumptions of the program remain traceable. In 1948 Swanzy introduced a more academic element to the program, engaging two critics for special quarterly broadcasts based on a discussion of the literary value of selected works. Both were men: Arthur Calder Marshall, the author of *Glory Dead*, a travel narrative about his time in Trinidad and Tobago in the 1930s, and Roy Fuller, the English poet and a well-regarded literary reviewer of the period (who was also instrumental in making the important publishing connection between Walcott and Jonathan Cape). This male cluster formed by Swanzy—comprising British men who acted as literary critics as well as editors—undoubtedly shared a generosity toward West Indian writers and a commitment to West Indian literature. All the same, the *Caribbean Voices* scripts themselves do reveal conceptions of literary value implicitly informed by masculine norms, no doubt regarded as universal in the 1950s. My argument here is not that the program consciously sought to give preference to male writers or writings but rather that the veloc-ity with which the male migrant writers stepped into the wider British literary scene must have created so much light and heat around their writings that the offerings of the women writers appeared, in comparison, as local and authen-tic in a way that was also prone to embedded gendered perceptions around literary significance and expectations of authorship.

While researching "early" Caribbean women's writing in the 1990s, I enjoyed a correspondence with Swanzy and visited him to discuss women's contributions to the program. In one letter Swanzy pauses from his evalua-tions of various women writers who submitted work to the program to offer the following reflection:

> On reading this reply I am uneasily aware that I might be accused of male chau-vinism. Possibly the same thing might be said of the various links in the chain of communication: Cedric Lindo, Frank Collymore, A. J. Seymour. I always think it sad odd that I never even heard of Jean Rhys.[16]

Recognizing that women writers were not connected to the group he worked with, even those based in the metropolis such as Rhys, Swanzy reconfigures the male-dominated "chain" across which women's writing had to pass and hints at the almost inevitable, if not intentional, gendering of perceptions. In the same letter, thinking back through the women writers, Swanzy also seems to indicate that there were unrealized female talents he had encoun-tered according to his own rubric of the West Indian writer.

> I should perhaps add "a proper black girl" called Marjorie Brown who seemed promising. Then there was someone called Inez Sibley, much more gifted than most, I thought, and more closely linked with Jamaican life. Although she wrote mainly prose, she had a remarkable feeling for words and recounting legends from the maroon country, above all "Terror Bill and the Taint Song."[17]

Swanzy's memory of these women writers confirms the impression of an editor who was alert to and cherished literary talent. However, there is a suggested gendering of such talent that surfaces in the framing of women's writing as connected to authenticity, affect, and intimacy. This framing can be linked to a subtle politics of gender that also informs the internal reception of women's writing on the program.

With attention to a selection of women's stories, I offer an analysis of these works that also discusses the gendering of reception marked through the paratextual remarks that frame the broadcast events. One focus for a discussion of this archive is to examine those writers whose works can be described as folklore. We know that folklore was affirmed as culturally meaningful within *Caribbean Voices* and that there was a "Folklore of Jamaica" section that announced this preference quite directly. The idea of an authentic folk "voice" was particularly strong in relation to the Jamaican Louise Bennett. Bennett was one of the very few West Indian women who migrated to London and who took employment with the BBC—first in 1945 during her British Council scholarship to the Royal Academy of Dramatic Art and later when she returned in 1950 to host *West Indian Guest Night*. The BBC file specifies that Bennett was employed for her "recitation of Jamaican dialect rhyme," and it is clear she was valued especially for having an authentic West Indian voice.[18] This sense of her work being of cultural rather than literary value appears to be a more general index for characterizing and discriminating men's writing from women's at this time. In January 1952 Bennett read "Anancy and Monkey" (the first story from *Anancy Stories and Dialect Verse*, published in Jamaica in 1950) for *Caribbean Voices*. The story follows a typical format for this genre of Jamaican folktale, with Anancy the spider trickster figure setting out to survive dismal conditions through his cunning and quick-wittedness. Set in hard times, when "tings was bad wid everybody," Anancy lures Brodda Goat, Brodda Sheep, and Brodda Hog to the makeshift tree house he and his Muma assemble from stolen scraps of wood and metal with the promise of food. Of course, what the guests do not know is that it is they who are the food. The twist in the tale, and where it hybridizes with the animal fable genre, is when Monkey eludes this trap with a "Ki Ki Ki Ki Ki Ki Ki," and, as the story concludes, "From dat day to today Monkey dah laugh after Anancy an any time you see Monkey running up an down tree an laughing is Anancy him remember. Jack Mandora me no choose none."[19]

A "Critique" by Calder Marshall was broadcast immediately following the story, although its opening premise forecloses any serious opportunity for literary analysis:

That story was called Anancy and Monkey and it was told by Louise Bennett. You
notice I omit to add that it was written by her, as well; because that isn't important. This may be A.D. 1952 but that story or rather stories like it were being told
in B.C. 1952 [*sic*] and from the moment that man had developed speech and language. . . . It was a beautiful performance and because the teller and the tale were
inseparable, it was perfect radio.[20]

Although Marshall's point about the origins of Anancy stories in oral culture is valid, his dismissal of Bennett's work from both contemporary scribal
culture and from historical time proper is problematic. Marshall seems to
read the story's traditional ending, "Jack Mandora me no choose none," quite
literally as an affirmation that the story is in no way authored by its teller and
that the teller absolves himself or herself from its message. In fact, this appeal
to the guardian at heaven's door is part of the narrative form and a continuation of Anancy's own thematic of empowering the powerless. The denial of
responsibility is what Jamaicans might call "play fool fi catch wise"—that is,
claiming that the story is not yours and that you are ignorant of its impact
when you are actually responsible for and completely aware of the narrative
meaning. Given that Bennett was a rare female presence within the cluster
of male West Indian authors in London, the relegation of her from writer
to performer, from wordsmith to ventriloquist, offers a rather disheartening
glimpse into the cultural and gendered politics that she must have encountered. While Bennett was clearly validated as an authentic voice, the idea that
she was part of the growing scene of West Indian literature was not enter-
tained. In this, she is pointedly unlike Selvon, whose literary creole, though
put under question, did not prevent the program from promoting his credentials as a serious writer. Certainly there is no sense in which Marshall was able
to recognize how Bennett "took the poetic use of Jamaican Creole and folk-
proletarian material to a degree of subtlety and sustained endeavour (albeit in
purely comic mode), that could not have been predicted from earlier attempts
with dialect."[21]

The direct dismissal of Bennett from the category of literary authorship
is prefigured more subtly in the 1948 broadcast of Grenadian Eula Redhead's
"Czien and the Turtle" (later published in *Bim*). Ten of Redhead's stories were
broadcast on *Caribbean Voices*, an exceptionally high number for a woman
writer, so her work was evidently seen as both fitting for radio as well as
appropriate to the program's rubric of cultural authenticity. Compre Czien
(Brother Spider) is the name for Anancy in St. Lucia and Grenada, and Redhead's narrative is introduced by the announcer as "an elegant little folk tale."
However, Redhead's version of the genre differs from Bennett's in a number

of interesting ways. Written in Standard English and set in a consciously fairytale world in which not only heterosexual romance but also a Caribbean island-scape is knowingly idealized according to Western eyes, the story begins, "Once upon a time on a palm decked island in the blue Caribbean dwelt a very beautiful princess."[22] The story tells how the "greedy and covetous fellow" Czien plotted to "get rid of Lieutenant Turtle and marry the princess himself," following a template where wit again allows the disempowered to triumph. As Czien's victory and poor Turtle's demise unfolds, Redhead also folds in a Grenadian song that recalls the island's earlier French cultural inheritance, "Marrier O! Marrier O! / Moi ear aller marrier, marrier O!," sung by Turtle in his "rich baritone."[23] The story's deft bridging of cultural worlds—African, French, English—that inform Grenadian culture is effortlessly managed by Redhead at the level of both form and content, with the elements of folk tale, fairy story, repetition, and song all blending fluently. While this creative mélange is now richly recognized by the critical vocabulary of creolization, there is little indication that Redhead's considerable skill as a storywriter is appreciated within the postwar London radio venue of *Caribbean Voices*, even though this tale wears its complexity in a style directly legible to a non-Caribbean audience.

Immediately following this broadcast, the announcer comments:

> And I think that you will agree that that story, "Czien and the Turtle" by Eula Redhead of Grenada, is also a great delicacy, a nice piece of Hors d'oeuvres, before we come to the main dish of the evening, "The Prodigal Daughter" by Richard Brathwaite of Trinidad, read by Gordon Woolford.[24]

The calibration of significance implied by the meal metaphor suggests a manifest gendering of literary taste in which the charming "little folk tale" by the woman writer is a natural appetizer to the more substantial male literary offering. The same assumption that stories based in oral traditions and histories are not fully adequate to the satisfactions of the literary is very possibly at work here; however, despite the strong culturalist prism, this view is also overwritten by notions of feminine creativity as innately of a different scale and substance than its masculine counterpart.

In general, *Caribbean Voices* appears to have shown a clear preference for stories from women that communicate folklore or otherwise culturally specific beliefs. At its most troubling, this inclination toward cultural authenticity can license an almost anthropological downward gaze that probably indicates a real cultural distance. This is the case in Eva Nicholas's "The Ninth Night," which opens with its own explanatory narrative that condescendingly positions folk culture within a class context other than the author's: "The Ninth Night is still an old familiar custom of Jamaican life—or rather death. This Island wake is considered by some to be partly of African, partly of European origin. Among certain poor people it is considered an act of callous indifference towards the dead if Ninth Night celebration is not held—a piece of neglect calculated to cause the corpse to 'turn in the grave.'"[25] The story offers a camera's-eye view on Ninth Night, beginning with the ingenuity and improvisation of members of the community as they construct a venue and muster resources for the wake. Although an affectionate portrait, the tendency to romanticize and authenticate the participants (always "they") cannot be ignored: "Bodies sway, eyes and teeth gleam, the tarpaulin shakes with wild exuberance of song."[26] The cultural distance between writer and subject is further registered and seemingly endorsed by the author's recording of talents that will never reach beyond the community aside from her own description of them: "Benjie of Ninth Night fame, would never be known to the world. This human nightingale with God's own music in his throat! But this matters not a whit to Benjie. He loves the admiration of his humble friends."[27] This sense of a writerly hand that levers the voices of the folk into the world of the literary surfaces again at the story's end, where the rendition of village voices finds closure in the knowingly literary flourish of ekphrasis:

> As the hands of the clock point to half past four, the happy revellers rise and sing with might and main. "Praise God from Whom all Blessings flow"—then with expressions of admiration for the way the Ninth Night has "come off"—"A high class affair!" "Lawd what a night!" "Him please wid him own Ni-Night," the tired, happy people troop off to their respective homes, to meet the care of the coming day, whose heralds are even then, painting rosy pictures in the eastern sky.[28]

The story's maintenance of distance between the folk practices it describes and the literary manner with which they are conveyed to a radio audience strongly suggests that "local color," though desirable, was something aesthetically inferior, a decorative, feminine mode that contrasted with the program's purportedly more robust literary endeavors.

However, at its most creative, a talent for rendering local lives and voices seemed capable of manipulating the program's rubric, as seen in the works of the Barbadian Eve Tyrrel. In Tyrrel's "Old Hyghe," an anti–folk tale, the story that a young woman is in fact the legendarily murderous Old Hyghe turns out to be a jealous rumor motivated by romantic rivalry. In contrast to Nicholas's story, Tyrrel's is composed mainly of dialogue, directly voicing the rumor as it moves from "lip to lip" and is finally revealed to Cordelia Jones by her fiancé, James

Thomas, as the reason to call off their engagement, when he tells her: "We can't have no weddin' Easter Monday again! How that will look to marry a girl dat dey makin' a maskerade sing on, dat she is Ole Hyghe?"[29] Here Tyrrel draws on dialogue to capture both the social density of village life and the ways in which romantic competition can trade off folk suspicions as a means of destroying women's reputations. However, in this story, Cordelia refuses to succumb to gossip and leave the village, instead taunting James with an alternative suitor until he declares, "Don't tell me no dam' foolishness bout Ole Hyghe, again."[30] The story gives its ending over to Cordelia's voice as it sings a reinterpretation of the masquerade song that directly addresses her rival: "You remember, gyul, Ah did tell you so!"[31] Tyrrel's story, rather than passively reflecting an authentic folk culture, actively voices a female self-assurance that refutes the power of folkloric myths of predatory female sexuality and calls attention to women's own rhetorical resources in controlling their romantic lives.

While the story itself plays with listener expectations and arguably subjects the impulse to anthropologize West Indian culture to ironic exploration, the only aspect of this deft and humorous story to be commented on and thereby highlighted within the context of the program itself is that of Old Hyghe. Although the pre- or postbroadcast critique could readily have focused on style, intertextuality, or humor—readings to which it would yield readily and which are often used to support the value of male Windrush writings—the framing of Tyrrel's story returns it to its anthropological content. Before the story was broadcast in October 1948, a note written by the author, presumably for the attention of the metropolitan editors, was read:

> In West Indian folklore, Old Hag or "Hyghe" (hig) is a living person, usually an old man or woman, supposedly possessing the power to take the form of a ball of fire (or light). In this form the hag shoots swiftly through the air or along the ground at night and may enter dwellings in search of a sleeping victim, whose blood it sucks to prolong its own evil life. In some colonies, known as "loup garou," the hag is akin to the European werewolf and vampire.[32]

While this note is superfluous to any comprehension of the story itself, it centers the grounds for its inclusion on its insider's appreciation of folk culture, suggesting, in an echo of the story's own use of folk culture, that Tyrrel was well aware of the modes through which the program was likely to understand her writing.[33]

In this light, it is not difficult to establish that a rich body of female writing has been written out of the canonical history of the region due to demonstrably masculinist protocols of thought and analysis in relation to literary value.

These clearly operated at both the macro level of institutional networks—in the form of assumptions about possibilities for professional authorship and the idea of the novel as the proper vehicle for authorship—as well as the micro level of critical evaluations concerning individual acts of writing. The developmental narrative that Salkey offers from short story to novel—and Lamming's similar version moving from Swanzy to the novel and notoriety—was not, it seems, the pathway available to women writers. Neither did they pack bags and travel to London with the hope of becoming recognized within an English literary tradition, the ambition Mais identifies for himself and the male writers of his day. The attachment of the era's women authors to the short story form (and to remaining in West Indian locations) means that they did not form part of the visible boom in the 1950s. However, they do form part of West Indian literary history. An awareness of the volume and variety of these stories enacts a significant shift in our thinking about the literary scene of this period, if only by forcing us to recognize the number of women who were involved in writing. Although still locked in the gallery of lost West Indian narratives, some of these writings, when differently framed and brought into circulation, surely have the potential to alter significantly the telling of individual national literary histories. For example, the simple gesture of recapturing the folk tales of Eula Redhead brings into view an enticing possibility of telling a Grenadian literary history through Redhead to Merle Collins and Joan Anim-Addo, a female tradition in which the subjects of voice, history, and traditional knowledge have a consistently gendered hue.

In the last decade, the scholarly attention to women's writings and to writings that fall outside of dominant nationalist thematics and chronologies has delivered a collective sense of an Anglophone Caribbean literary history that is more textured, fractional, and scattered—as well as substantially fuller in every sense. Studies by Raphael Dalleo, Belinda Edmondson, Evelyn O'Callaghan, Leah Reade Rosenberg, and, most recently, Michael Niblett have brought to light, and to critical understanding, Caribbean writings that reconfigure the cultural and literary past in a much more inclusive and comprehensive fashion.[34] As this collection of essays also testifies, the conditions for the critical visibility of these works have now been established with the much more open and inquiring pursuit of minor literary figures beyond the canonical frame. While the gendering of literary fortunes may resist clear separation from other factors informing professional authorship, it is a crucial line of inquiry for understanding how Anglophone literary history has been shaped, remembered, and celebrated, and, perhaps most important, for questioning how an alternative to the male-centered, London-based narrative of the Windrush generation may still be open for reconfiguration.

Notes

1. Frieda Cassin, *With Silent Tread: A West Indian Novel*, ed. Evelyn O'Callaghan (Oxford: Macmillan, 2002); Alison Donnell, ed., *Selected Poems of Una Marson* (Leeds: Peepal Tree Press, 2011); Elma Napier, *A Flying Fish Whispered* (Leeds: Peepal Tree Press, 2011).

2. See Glyne A. Griffith's essay in this collection for a different angle on the role this program had in the era's literary production.

3. Virginia Woolf, *A Room of One's Own* (London: Hogarth Press, 1929).

4. V. S. Naipaul, *In a Free State* (1971; repr., London: Penguin Books, 1973). This phrasing appears common to almost all of the Penguin editions, and many of the Picador editions, of Naipaul's work.

5. For further discussion of the gendering of literary vocation in this period, see Alison Donnell, "Heard but Not Seen: Women's Short Stories and the BBC's *Caribbean Voices* Programme," in *The Caribbean Short Story: Critical Perspectives*, ed. Lucy Evans, Mark McWatt, and Emma Smith (Leeds: Peepal Tree Press, 2011), 29–43.

6. Andrew Salkey, ed., *Stories from the Caribbean* (London: Elek Press, 1965), 11–12.

7. George Lamming, *The Pleasures of Exile* (London: Michael Joseph, 1960), 67.

8. For an account of the metropolitan patronage that Swanzy facilitated, see Phillip Nanton, "What Does Mr. Swanzy Want—Shaping or Reflecting? An Assessment of Henry Swanzy's Contribution to the Development of Caribbean Literature," *Caribbean Quarterly* 46, no. 1 (March 2000): 61–72; and Peter Kalliney, "Metropolitan Modernism and Its West Indian Interlocutors: 1950s London and the Emergence of Postcolonial Literature," *PMLA* 122, no. 1 (January 2007): 89–104.

9. Henry Swanzy, "The Literary Situation in the Caribbean," *Books Abroad* 30 (1956): 266–274.

10. Patrick French, *The World Is What It Is: The Authorized Biography of V. S. Naipaul* (New York: Alfred A. Knopf, 2008), 159.

11. Ibid., 160.

12. Andrew Salkey, ed., *West Indian Stories* (London: Faber and Faber, 1960), 10.

13. Frank Collymore, "Notebook," *Bim* 15 (1951): 149.

14. Salkey, *West Indian Stories*, 9.

15. For a fuller account of these dynamics, see Gail Low, *Publishing the Postcolonial: Anglophone West African and Caribbean Writing in the U.K., 1948–1968* (London: Routledge, 2011).

16. Henry Swanzy, private correspondence with author, March 23, 1990.

17. Ibid.

18. BBC file reference number RCont1, BBC Written Archives Center, Reading, England. All further references to program scripts will refer to author, title, and date of broadcast.

19. Louise Bennett, "Anancy and Monkey," BBC *Caribbean Voices* manuscript, January 6, 1952.

20. Ibid.

21. Edward Baugh, "Caribbean Poetry," in *Encyclopedia of Postcolonial Literatures in English*, ed. Eugene Benson and L. W. Conolly (London: Routledge, 2005), 1243.

22. Eula Redhead, "Czien and the Turtle," BBC *Caribbean Voices* manuscript, February 15, 1948.

23. Ibid.

24. Ibid.

25. Eva R. Nicholas, "The Ninth Night," BBC *Caribbean Voices* manuscript, November 21, 1948.

26. Ibid.

27. Ibid.

28. Ibid.

29. Eve Tyrrel, "Old Hyghe," BBC *Caribbean Voices* manuscript, October 24, 1948.

30. Ibid.

31. Ibid.

32. Ibid.

33. A similarly playful reinterpretation of the folklore rubric also informs Jamaican Inez Sibley's "The Great Omission," where the fear of duppies and the obeah man is powerfully narrated, only to be dismissed by the reappearance of a migrant in fully human form. The story was broadcast on September 5, 1948.

34. Raphael Dalleo, *Caribbean Literature and the Public Sphere: From the Plantation to the Postcolonial.* (Charlottesville: University of Virginia Press, 2011); Belinda Edmondson, *Caribbean Middlebrow: Leisure Culture and the Middle Class* (Ithaca, N.Y.: Cornell University Press, 2009); Evelyn O'Callaghan, *"A Hot Place—Belonging to Us": Constructions of the West Indies in Early Narratives by Women, 1804–1939* (London: Routledge, 2004); Leah Reade Rosenberg, *Nationalism and the Formation of Caribbean Literature* (New York: Palgrave, 2007); Michael Niblett, *The Caribbean Novel since 1945: Cultural Practice, Form, and the Nation-State* (Jackson: University Press of Mississippi, 2012).

"Neither Pathological nor Perfect": Joyce Gladwell's Late Autobiographical Challenge to the Windrush Generation

DONETTE FRANCIS

This essay situates the long-neglected West Indian intellectual Joyce Gladwell and her 1969 memoir, *Brown Face, Big Master*, in the genealogy of Windrush writers.[1] Specifically, it adds the nuances of her middle-class sensibility to a Windrush canon comprised largely of novels or travelogues centering on the "hustling male economic migrant" or the disaffected male middle-class civil servant.[2] To the extent that male Windrush writers revealed their own aspirational middle-class life stories, these narratives were in the guise of fiction, what Sandra Pouchet Paquet calls "a blurred genre," and offered oppositional models for addressing racial and colonial injustices.[3] Gladwell, in contrast, strips away the mask of fiction to reveal the vulnerabilities, and stakes, of a middle-class Caribbean woman writing autobiographically about the 1940s through the 1960s. Such a woman writer, asserts Gladwell's memoir, unavoidably has to prove her respectability in terms of moral and social standing; and, for Gladwell, Christianity becomes the mode of articulating that performance. With education, hue, and morality, in this preindependence moment Gladwell embodies the idealized female face of the nation, representing the emergent republic's fitness for self-rule. This quotidian reality is at odds with the more dominant discursive imperative to represent the folk. With its invocation of Frantz Fanon's *Black Skin, White Masks*, Gladwell's title, *Brown Face, Big Master*, not only signals a phenotypical class distinction between black and brown in Jamaican society but also gestures to a relationship between class and religion. Performing a double enunciation, the title at once marks Gladwell's color and class location, and immediately links class and color to Christianity. Thus the book's very cover names Christianity as a signifier through which middle-class respectability is lived and prepares readers for the careful attention Gladwell pays to intimate structural details.

The fact that her autobiography makes public the culture of brownness as a structure Gladwell lives places her in conversation with early anthropological and social psychological work of the period. For example, the memoir

references the work of social psychologist Madeline Kerr, whose 1952 sociological study, *Personality and Conflict in Jamaica*, argues that the clash between
cultures of Africa and Europe produces in West Indians an "insecure type of
personality."[4] That Gladwell is reading a text that focuses on "class and color,"
"sex and marriage," and "The Jamaican Personality" *in Jamaica* before migration not only suggests why she pursues a double major in psychology and
anthropology in England but also why her autobiography explores the social
psychology of race, gender, and class. Such a psychoanalytic sensibility also
puts Gladwell's autobiography in direct dialogue with Fanon's *Black Skin, White
Masks*, another work published in 1952. In fact, the very project of Gladwell's
autobiography is best understood as pursuing Fanon's "critical methodology"
toward making sense of colonial sexualities and female subjectivity, illuminat-
ing in particular how central socialization into appropriate comportment and
affiliation was to making and marking her colonial female subjectivity.[5]

Perhaps one of the most important texts of the period to situate Gladwell's
work in dialogue with is anthropologist Peter Wilson's influential 1969 essay,
"Reputation and Respectability: A Suggestion for Caribbean Ethnology," which
offers the dialectic of reputation and respectability as a general schematic for
understanding the gendered dynamics of Caribbean life.[6] In Wilson's dichoto-
mous frame, reputation belonged to the male-identified working-class world
of the streets, and, conversely, respectability described the female idealiza-
tion of middle-class performance of morality in the church and the domestic spheres. Caribbean feminists have challenged Wilson's reductive frame by
first demonstrating how working-class and peasant women have discarded
the oppressive limits of respectability.[7] But critics have spent less time teasing
out the complexities of middle-class female performances of respectability.[8]
In this way the field unwittingly accepts the presumptions around respectability, and leaves Wilson's gender dichotomy in place.[9] Not surprisingly, this
dichotomy was also present in Fanon's gendered characterization of interracial black desire in *Black Skin, White Masks*. In Fanon's account, recognition,
arguably in terms of respectability, is at stake for the middle-class Caribbean
woman seeking a little reproductive "lactification."[10] Conversely, reputation is
most central to the black male's desire for the white woman as recognition of
his manhood.

Belinda Edmondson's 1999 *Making Men* unsettles this gendered binary
by explicitly connecting the question of male respectability to how the
male "founding fathers" of Anglophone Caribbean writing garnered literary authority.[11] She underscores that in spite of the content of their writings,
their writerly self-fashioning depends on performing English gentlemanli-
ness through citations of canonical English literature.[12] Gladwell's 1969 memoir prompts a parallel consideration about how black women writers of the

Windrush generation navigated that literary landscape and made claims to literary authority.[13] The memoir's title, *Brown Face, Big Master*, references God as the head of her Christian faith. While Gladwell rhetorically calls upon God to enable her literary authority and to write herself into being, she also invites her primary readers into a transnational community of Christians, as Inter-Varsity Christian Press published the autobiography.[14]

In this essay, I argue that Gladwell's memoir marks a feminist disruption of Windrush sensibilities. While male authors writing on exile and racism have become the basis for our understanding of West Indian experience and self-fashioning in the period, Gladwell's memoir reveals that middle-class women had very different experiences of emigration, exile, and racism in the metropole. Most notably, they did not have access to prestigious presses such as Heinemann, Longman, and Jonathan Cape, where their male cohorts published. For example, Beryl Gilroy, Gladwell's fellow Windrush woman writer, waited a decade to garner interest in her autobiography after many editors rejected it for being "too psychological."[15] With an interest in the psychological, these middle-class women writers articulated a different sensibility than their putatively political male counterparts, but they were not merely assimilationists who embodied respectability and thereby supported the colonial project. Instead, Gladwell's autobiography presents her as a difficult figure to assimilate into our received Windrush narratives. On first reading, Gladwell maintains the class and color lines. She seeks community not in the Caribbean or England but in rural Canada, another white settler nation. But, finally, and most important, Gladwell embraces Christianity—if not as a progressive practice, then as a productive strategy and mode of intellectual engagement for negotiating colonialism, racism, and gender-based discrimination. In Christianity, Gladwell finds tools to *recognize and confront* her own discriminatory practices as well as the gendered racial acts of discrimination committed against her. While her memoir is *late* and is even out of synch with Windrush, its sensibility is *early* in our rethinking of revolutionary black social movements and their visions for a more just world. To make sense of the writer and her writings is to unearth a silence in our intellectual genealogies around theorizing the stakes of Caribbean female respectability and of taking Christianity seriously.

Insecurely Brown: Race and the Education of Desire

Rather than the standardized Windrush narrative of metropolitan migration to the United Kingdom and return home, or migration to and settlement in an imperial location, Gladwell's story maps periodic settlement in England, a two-year return to Jamaica, a brief summer stint in the United States (Cambridge, Massachusetts), before she finally settles and—in her words—"secures a place in Canada," where she has resided for the past forty-two years.[16] In a 2007 interview, Gladwell responds to why her family chose Canada as the place to settle: "England was getting crowded . . . and Canada seemed like a place with open spaces and seemed like a good place to raise one's family and seek advancement in work." More specifically, she continues, "I chose to live in a small town in Canada which is largely populated by Mennonites, who are accepting people."[17] Joyce Gladwell (née Nation), along with her twin sister, Faith, was born in Jamaica 1931 to Daisy and Donald Nation. In 1942, at age eleven, Joyce and her sister won scholarships to Saint Hilda's, an Anglican boarding school located on the island's North Coast, "established for the daughters of English clergy, property owners, and overseers."[18] At twenty-two years old, after having taught two years in Jamaica, she migrates to England for college, to University College London. In London, her first metropolitan stop, Joyce Nation meets and later marries the young white British Graham Gladwell—against her in-laws' initial reservations about the challenges of an interracial marriage. The couple has three sons, one of whom is the best-selling author Malcolm Gladwell. Her memoir is published in 1969 after the family moves to Canada for her husband to take up a post as a math professor at the University of Waterloo. For more than a decade, Gladwell dedicates herself to being a stay-at-home mother. In 1980, at age fifty, with her sons out of the house, Gladwell enrolls in a marriage and family therapy course at the University of Guelph, and subsequently becomes a practicing psychotherapist. Today, she contributes regular articles on Christian-centered psychotherapy for the *Presbyterian Record*. She also has a building named in her honor at the Woolwich Counselling Centre in Elmira, Canada. At its 2009 opening she says, "I have secured a place in Canada, in Elmira, which I never imagined, and I'm dumbstruck."[19] As does Michael A. Bucknor elsewhere in this collection, I argue against an exclusive London-based focus in making sense of the Windrush generation, and account instead for the multiple migratory trajectories Gladwell's life story evinces. In this case, Gladwell provides a window into the early settlement of a Caribbean-Canadian Atlantic.

Rendering a nuanced reconstruction of the insecurities attending brownness, the first half of the autobiography depicts Gladwell's early life and the disciplining of desire as a way of performing and maintaining class identity. The second half chronicles how this socialization travels with Gladwell to the heart of the British Empire and the various metropolitan locations to which she migrates. Writing in the tradition of slave narratives and spiritual autobiographies that usually open with details about birth, family, and place,

Gladwell provides mundane yet key details of her life in colonial Jamaica. She carefully discloses the very religious making of her class sentiments to demonstrate how she can at once readily map "an entanglement of sexual pathologies" onto working-class Caribbean womanhood, while herself experiencing an ontological wounding when she is negatively fixed racially and sexually as a black woman—despite her disciplined bodily performances meant to mark her distinction in terms of class, color, and Christianity. Throughout the memoir Gladwell attends to the complexities of the gaze, highlighting that the discriminatory gaze is not always white, and that in this instance it is in fact mostly brown.

The memoir opens with a free verse staging an encounter between Gladwell as a young child and an adult servant woman in order to demonstrate what, for Gladwell, is a multilayered triptych: sexual propriety, religious practice, and brown middle-class Caribbean womanhood. Set on the grounds of a church rectory in rural 1940s colonial Jamaica, the young poetic persona—as omniscient third-person narrator—looks onto a scene of contemplation, where a servant woman sits on the rectory's steps and grapples with what happens to the soul in death if one lives a life in sin. Presuming she is alone, the servant exclaims aloud, "Sin so sweet!" Although still a child, the young Gladwell immediately knows that "the sin" being referred to here is that of cohabitating with a common-law husband. While this is standard practice down in the valley of the servant's working-class black community, in the hills of this middle-class community her nonmarital union is clearly a sin leading to eternal damnation. Gladwell *identifies* with this woman's sense of the oppressive nature of this moral judgment on the most quotidian of practices, stating, "to know that what I did was counted wrong and yet desire led me to it and held me there." But she immediately *disidentifies* with the woman in terms of class, and discloses the expectations of brown middle-class Caribbean womanhood, when she asserts: "I did not share her circumstances. Nor would I. At least I need never know her problem of concubinage" (1). Gladwell's immediate class *disidentification* disavows a past history of concubinage that would be stereotypically and phenotypically marked on her brown body; she suggests instead that marriage and respectability are normative practices for middle-class Caribbean womanhood of the 1940s. Even the spatial markers—hills versus valley—establish a study in contrasts where middle-class life is about learning and performing a Christian-mediated restraint, whereas black working-class womanhood is pathologically constructed around reckless abandon and the pursuit of sexual desire.

This opening scene immediately establishes Gladwell's legitimacy in a colonial Jamaican context, underscoring that she is born in wedlock into the sanctuary of brown middle-class family life. Elsewhere her sister, Faith, remarks that they were proud of the fact that on both sides of their family they could mark three generations of marriages.[20] But the fact that Gladwell dwells on such legitimizing details indicates the memoir's broader political project: to reveal brownness as a diverse and tenuous class location. And for many, this color-based class location is anxiously guarded—in spite of generations of marriage. Her father was a church deacon and head schoolteacher; her mother taught in the school she attended. The family belonged to the Anglican Church, another affiliation that served as a class marker, especially when compared to other religious traditions in the Caribbean such as Baptist or Pentecostal. Therefore, in spite of their modest income, the Nations were received as members of St. Catherine's upper middle class. At every turn— church, school, and home—religious institutions interpolated the girls. To the extent they had access to working-class culture, it was through their household servants and their limited interactions with schoolchildren. In fact, Gladwell recalls that her mother instructed her students "not to pass on these stories to us, 'for my children tell me everything.' She succeeded in silencing them and in isolating us painfully" (59). In this early part of the memoir, readers sense a deep alienation—an unbelonging to her local milieu.

Because brownness metonymically marks class, Gladwell narrates her early socialization in color consciousness and its stakes. Among the social values of her class that Gladwell chronicles is the reproductive investment in whiteness. Again early in the memoir, she narrates her socialization in color consciousness. Her father's fair skin could enable him to pass as white in England, but it does not allow him to do so in Jamaica, underscoring the particular position brownness occupies as a distinction and sociocultural location. Whether passing or not, his near whiteness held both real *and* social capital in Jamaica. Thus her mother, darker in hue—but still of a brown middle class—considered it a "feather in her cap" to have married a "good brown man." Consequently, the girls knew that their mother also expected them to marry someone their color or lighter and to produce children of lighter color to "raise" the family's color: "To marry and produce children of lighter colour than oneself was to 'raise' the colour of the family. To raise the colour of the family was to raise its social status" (68). Her mother's focus on social status, moral standards, and skin color meant an intense policing of her daughters' sexuality. Gladwell exposes the precariousness of their brownness, underscoring that one "wrong" reproductive choice could devalue the family's status. Gladwell's attention to this imbricated class and color anxiety compels a reconsideration of Fanon's ungenerous reading of Mayotte Capecia. The candor expressed in Gladwell's autobiography actually proves Fanon right, even while he should be critiqued for a reductive pathological casting of Capecia, and even further chastised methodologically for deploying a novel and what Omise'eke Natasha Tinsley calls a "pseudo-autobiography" to theorize black women's sexuality.[21] Gladwell's characterizations of everyday socialization practices convey a reproductive investment in whiteness and its centrality to solidifying or enhancing family status. She writes:

Steadily as we grew up [mother] held up before us the goal of marriage as a desirable and good, a precious wonderful relationship. Too anxiously, we thought even then. But understandably so. At school, she knew we would hear a different story—of unions without marriage, one mother bearing children by several different fathers, domestic quarrels and violence, as well as distorted sexual details. (59)

The childhood world Gladwell reconstructs fostered a binaristic (both classed *and* colored) construction of sexuality. The mother's recitation of everyday stories served as cautionary morality tales to ensure the preservation of her daughters' chastity even while attempts to sequester them from their local milieu failed.

If their immediate surroundings offered too much potential to absorb black working-class practices of "sexual looseness," then the Nation sisters welcomed the opportunity to attend an elite boarding school miles away from home among the daughters of white expatriate British settlers. Such an environment would at least provide an opportunity to foster friendships with girls with whom they presumed to share more in common. At Saint Hilda's, however, Gladwell confronts the insecurity of her family's brownness and realizes the layered social distinction between white and brown, and where brown fits vis-à-vis black:

Being brown face, I was both black and white face in one, and more black face than white. I could not change my brown face, but I was pleased only with a white face and wanted to forget the black faces altogether. Here was the seed of trouble. (69)

Effectively, Gladwell here articulates Kerr's "insecure personality" thesis. Rather than classic tragic mulatto musings, Gladwell voices an early articulation of the existential crisis of colonial hybridity. In her school library, she experiences her own ontological othering when she encounters an encyclopedia entry on the "negro" describing his "lower evolutionary" order, his mental inferiority, his sexual insatiability. Putting the book aside, she walks away "wordless and numb. . . . I felt condemned. . . . I was, by virtue of my race, [assumed] inferior in intellect. It became terribly important to me to demonstrate to myself and to other people that this was not true" (100–101). Recognizing the cognitive and epistemic violence that authors of empire have scripted onto the black body, she became determined to prove this stereotype untrue. This demonstration would always be an embodied performance of respectability. Through this experience at Saint Hilda's, Gladwell first learns of scientific racism, and she and her sister become the darker-skinned, less-privileged students whom other students see as inferior. Conceding that brownness gives her distinction in Jamaica's race, class, and color hierarchy, and allows her to perform difference and distancing, Gladwell nonetheless understands herself as a member of the black race. Together these two scenes demonstrate that, even in Jamaica, she realizes blackness as the broader racial category to which she is conscripted. Therefore in spite of class or color distinction, she too suffers the burden of racial representation. Gladwell's recognition of her blackness actually occurs in Jamaica, not London, separating her from many others of the Windrush writers.

This experience of simultaneously identifying herself as black and being aware of her own implication in colonial racism is a critical move in the memoir and a central aspect of the self-development Gladwell charts. Where her male counterparts put forward Marxist, nihilist, and anticolonial nationalist approaches to resistance, it is Christianity, and her struggles to practice an expansive, more inclusive version of Christianity, that both saves and sustains her. And of equal significance, Gladwell's narration seeks to reconcile, rather than overwrite, her socialized desire for white or light partnership. Arguably, grappling with Christianity's vision of freedom is key to her ultimate ability to withstand racism, becoming the spiritual and psychic safe space to which she returns.

The Emotional Color Line

If the first half of the autobiography focuses on discrimination vis-à-vis Jamaica's racial, color, and class hierarchy, the second half engages more with the psychic life of racism as "the emotional color line" that structures black quotidian life in metropolitan locations. Part two effectively opens aboard ship during Gladwell's transatlantic crossing to the metropole, where her experience of racial othering is violently sexed. This ship in movement along the Black Atlantic at once captures the past Gladwell had left behind and the horizon before her. But rather than relaying the excitement of "journeying to an expectation" that her male cohorts chronicle,[22] Gladwell narrates her ship passage by emphasizing the attending dangers for female travelers. For example, unlike Stuart Hall, she traveled alone—he was one year younger and of a similar brown Jamaican middle class, but traveled with his mother.[23] Gladwell does not have the fiscal or physical luxury of parental accompaniment; instead, she forms community among fellow student travelers: "All my savings went to the cost of the boat passage to England. My parents undertook to pay my college fees and boarding expenses and my sister offered to share her scholarship allowance with me for other necessities. It was an adventure in faith" (112).[24]

This faith was tested the first night aboard ship. Flattered to be the only woman sitting at the captain's table, she meets a vacationing British doctor who is also a writer. Rather than an assault by physical stare, she receives his invitation to his cabin later that evening to read his incomplete manuscript as, in fact, an indication that, in spite of her youth, he recognizes her keen intellect. Yet the evening would unfold sexually; and, in recording this shaping experience, Gladwell asserts that for the middle-class female colonial subject, the gaze is not the only way of undoing subjecthood. She narrates the evening's ensuing events as follows:

> I hardly remember looking at his manuscript. For, without much ado he began to make love to me. It was pleasant at first. Only gradually did I realize my predicament. What could I do? *To shout or cry out was out of the question.* Just beyond the porthole on the deck were my companions, the other students of my own age with whom I would be spending the rest of the voyage in constant contact. *They must certainly not know about this.* (111, emphasis added)[25]

Gladwell's narration of this scene raises several questions about autobiographical writing and self-fashioning. She writes and publishes the memoir as a Christian woman in her late thirties reconstructing a younger self. On the one hand, it vividly recaptures the sense of innocence and naïveté, wherein the encounter quickly moves from "making love" to an act of sexual coercion. Yet on the other hand, we also have to ask whether this construction is itself a romance that has to write away this young woman's intimate desire through the language of sexual innocence. Even if we concede an initial interest on her part, Gladwell might reasonably have not expected the extent of the evening's unfolding. In going to his cabin, she has broken a central rule of her classed, Christian gender decorum. Nonetheless, imprisoned in his cabin, she encounters herself as a sexed object. But that this scene also narrates her sense of shame *in addition* to the shock of misrecognition underscores the twinned nature of her experience. Coupled with this ontological undoing is the question of respectability. While she *is* stunned by the sexual encounter, Gladwell immediately worries about her reputation among her peers, as she does not want any of her fellow student travelers to be aware of what transpired. To utter sonic resistance by way of yelling or screaming would be to be found out; she therefore chooses to suffer in silence rather than alert her cohorts of her compromised situation. She continues:

> I dared not make a dash for the door or resist him for fear of arousing him further to violence perhaps. Then I remembered a novel I had read from the sixth-form library in which the hero, finding himself alone with his beloved, was completely put off by her coldness. I could not take you Mary, he said. I proceeded like her to play dead. Quietly but very earnestly I remonstrated. To my astonishment this had no effect. He was completely absorbed in what he was doing and quite indifferent to me. . . . If the resentment and bitterness passed in time, *the sadness still remains.* . . . These were the deepest marks left by that evening's adventure. Physically, I escaped and by the merest accident—because it was an unsuitable time of the month. He had his limits. I think he was also relieved to have a face-saving excuse for calling off the episode as my indifference taxed his ardour. (111, emphasis added)

This scene recalls the "historicity" that precedes and scripts her in an established narrative of black female sexual availability such as she reads in the encyclopedia, and which she herself has been guilty of mapping onto working-class black female bodies. Gladwell nonetheless seeks to navigate this moment of sexual danger through a different text—the Victorian sensibility novel—and the sexual mores she has imbibed from reading such Victorian fiction. Identifying with the novel's heroine, Gladwell assumes that what this protagonist does to attain forbearance in the structure of the romance novel, she can do as well. Unfortunately, however, Gladwell's experience teaches her that her male suitor does not recognize in her an idealized English heroine. Importantly, her citation of a Victorian sensibility novel and path to becoming a woman is not dissimilar to her male counterparts' engagement with Victorian constructions of gentlemanness as Edmondson argues.

This scene in which Gladwell is literally imprisoned in the doctor's cabin genders Fanon's "Look, a Negro!" moment, bringing it into the private rather than public sphere. Similar to Fanon, Gladwell sees herself as a properly disciplined middle-class colonial subject; both, in spite of race, had the expectation that they would be fully recognized as such by white metropolitan subjects. Encountered on the city street, Fanon is shattered into pieces by this epidermal schema. The child who gazed upon Fanon could not see him as a middle-class subject. Gladwell's ship cabin scene reflects a similar mis-recognition, but the shattering takes on a different tenor. Anathema to her self-perception as a middle-class Caribbean Christian young woman, she is simply seen and treated as a potential concubine. The doctor gets the historical moment wrong. If history predisposes him to read her brown body as sexually available, she is indignant that he fails to recognize her as a respectable woman (fully cloaked in three generations of respectable marriage) in the 1950s in the context of imperial decline and impending national sovereignty for which she is the idealized subject. Everything about her self-presentation was designed to make that legible, yet his dominant white male gaze nonetheless sexualizes her brown female body. This encounter, all the more, destroys her at all levels, not just racial. It haunts her, and even as she published in 1969, "the sadness remains" (114).

Throughout the memoir Gladwell painstakingly shows that grappling with the ideals of Christianity enables her to deal with such violent scenes of subjection; yet she is careful to illustrate that Christianity is not a monolithic community of practitioners. There are times when the community most immediately available to her is too conservative, and rather than joining them, she withdraws and seeks "to work out [her] own salvation" (161). For example, once she arrives on the agnostic campus of University College London, Gladwell seeks out a Christian community in an attempt to create an alternative public sphere.[26] In spite of the university's secularism, she integrates Christianity into her intellectual life on campus, noting a sense of "security" in this place where "books, ideas and conversation come first" (143). Nonetheless, inside this faith community she would confront the sexualized racial sentiment of racial difference. She meets Graham Gladwell among this on-campus InterVarsity Christian community. Even while her experience with the doctor on the ship left her harboring resentment toward British men, the practice of Christianity, readers are led to believe, allowed her not to discriminate against the entire population based on one individual's actions. Despite her initial reluctance to form an amorous attachment with Graham Gladwell, their friendship gradually develops into a romance, where race matters centrally. Gladwell first meets her future in-laws in the context of a platonic relationship with their son. And under those conditions, they welcomed her into their home as a part of their international Christian family. But once the friendship blossoms to romance, his parents discourage the union based strictly on her race and the projected problems the couple would encounter with societal acceptance, as well as the complications of having interracial children. By contrast, for Gladwell, raised as she was with the reproductive investment in whiteness as a central value, the possibility of biracial children was not an obstacle but a desire. Graham's parents do not share this sentiment. Gladwell narrates:

> I can guess the reasons for the agony that Graham's parents felt.... I have read enough of the excuses made to justify slavery: that the negro slaves were not fully human but were a kind of advanced ape.... Who would not baulk at the idea of association by marriage with a sub-human species, inferior in intellect, poor in moral discernment and spiritual capacity? And the idea of having grandchildren, *marked with this taint, bearing one's name*, must be intolerable indeed. (147)

Gladwell is nonetheless shocked by their racial rejection.[27] Notably, for the parents the worry is the possibility of reproduction tainting the supposed purity of white bloodlines. Her future parents-in-law raise the historicity of black women's sexual abjection. She escapes the battle between Graham and his parents, which continued for months, by returning to her native Jamaica. While his parents do reconcile with the couple's decision to marry, the inclusion of this story exposes the racial limits of Christianity's liberal democratic values when faced with the possibility of a literal rather than a figurative black member of the Christian family.

Throughout the autobiography, Christianity serves as an interpretative tool that enables Gladwell space for cognition and empathy. The memoir performs a dialectical engagement with discriminatory acts against her as well as her ability to commit discrimination.

In the final scene, Gladwell has to acknowledge that based on her brownness, she too has been guilty of color-based discrimination, and therefore when confronted with racism, she has to reconcile herself with the fact that "as a colored Jamaican," her family "benefited for generations from the hierarchy of race." Therefore she could not "reproach another for the impulse to divide people by the shade of their skin."[28]

> On a Sunday afternoon I stood at my front door waving to Graham and the older children as they set off for a walk ... at that moment a boy went by on a bicycle and shouted at me, "Nigger!" Quickly I glanced at Graham and the children, hoping they had not heard him and then I turned indoors, my heart and mind in turmoil.... A ghost from the past had visited me and I was unprepared and vulnerable. The picture I built up of an accepting community vanished. Once again I lived in an insecure world.... Where was the mastery of myself I thought I had gained—the freedom from concern about colour and race? (178)

Once again, readers encounter Fanon's iconic "Look, a Negro!" moment; but here the doorstep as the entry point into her home is an interstitial space between public and private. This incident sends her to her knees in prayer to which God answers, "Have you not been glad that you are not more colored than you are? Grateful that you are not black?" (163). Again, readers witness the critical self-reflection Gladwell attributes to Christianity. Similar to her male intellectual cohorts, she is concerned with both racism and existential questions. But unlike her male counterparts, rather than repudiate Christianity as empire's handmaiden and embrace purportedly more evolved secular explanations such as Marxism, she actually grapples with the ambivalence of this religious heritage. In Christianity, Gladwell finds tools to recognize and confront her own discriminatory practices. That she goes to Christianity rather than Marxism or nihilism has made her less recoverable in our reconstructions of Windrush-era writings.[29] Certainly wrestling with the ideals *and limits* of her Christian faith would not be viewed as a revolutionary ideological position for Windrush writers;[30] Gladwell, nonetheless, presents it as an alternative to conventional ways of thinking about liberatory politics. In fact, in *Brown Face, Big Master*, Gladwell articulates an independent self-fashioning of brown female subjecthood. In this way, I want to suggest that Gladwell not only departs from the dominant novelistic Windrush sensibility of representing the working-class male rogue, but she is an early progenitor for a modern Caribbean feminist autobiographical tradition—especially one that explicitly writes about sexuality and depression.[31]

Rather than focus on whether the vision of a social movement was realized, the historian Robin D. G. Kelley maintains that it is more instructive to focus on the dreams themselves—since they tell how the actors were transformed and what they hoped and fought to achieve.[32] It is this dream for a new Eden, a new society built on mutual recognition, equality, and respect, that Gladwell's memoir narrates. The Christian fellowship Gladwell imagines and practices provides an alternative, less oppositional model of belonging for a Caribbean social outsider in all the locations in which Gladwell resided—England, the United States, and Canada. Recognizing Christianity as one such alternative model despite its imperfections suggests a wider consideration of the historically available options for addressing the racial injustices shared by the era's migrants, and, for middle-class women especially, how imbricated Christianity was in their strategic wielding of "respectability." Furthermore, if the reflexively oppositional model of the most celebrated Windrush writers now strikes us as overly masculine and tending toward a purist activism destined for failure, excavating these other strategies points to complementary paths taken, paths that could ideally be integrated with the more traditional liberation narratives.

Notes

1. I take the title of this essay from Lisa Thompson's discussion of African American women writers who define this schematic as key to the new black aesthetic. See Lisa Thompson, *Beyond the Black Lady: Sexuality and the New African American Middle Class* (Champaign: University of Illinois Press, 2010). Joyce Gladwell, *Brown Face, Big Master* (1969; repr., London: MacMillan Caribbean, 2003). Subsequent references appear parenthetically in the text. Here the geopolitics of place matters. UK-based critics have already begun the project of recuperating Gladwell's work. See Sandra Courtman, "Women Writers and the Windrush Generation: A Contextual Reading of Beryl Gilroy's *In Praise of Love* and Children and Andrea Levy's *Small Island*," *EnterText*, "Special Issue on Andrea Levy" 9 (2012): 84–104; Suzanne Scafe "The Caribbean," *Journal of Commonwealth Literature* 39, no. 4 (2004): 29; Suzanne Scafe "The Embracing 'I': Mothers and Daughters in Contemporary Black Women's Auto/Biography," *Women: A Cultural Review* 20, no. 3 (2009): 287–298.

2. See Courtman's interview in the introduction to Gladwell, *Brown Face, Big Master*.

3. Sandra Pouchet Paquet, *Caribbean Autobiography: Cultural Identity and Self-Representation* (Madison: University of Wisconsin Press, 2002), 111–131.

4. Referenced in Gladwell, *Brown Face, Big Master*, 139. See Madeline Kerr, *Personality and Conflict in Jamaica* (London: Collins; and Kingston: Sangster's Book Stores, 1963).

5. Kobena Mercer, "Decolonization and Disappointment: Reading Fanon's Sexual Politics," in *The Fact of Blackness: Frantz Fanon and Visual Representation*, ed. Alan Read (Seattle: Bay Press, 1996), 114–131.

6. Peter J. Wilson, "Reputation and Respectability: A Suggestion for Caribbean Ethnology," *Man* 4, no. 1 (March 1969): 70–84.

7. Carolyn Cooper, *Noises in the Blood: Orality, Gender, and the "Vulgar" Body of Jamaican Popular Culture* (Durham, N.C.: Duke University Press, 1995); Heather A. Horst, "Landscaping Englishness: Respectability and Returnees in Mandeville, Jamaica," *Caribbean Review of Gender Studies* 2 (2008): 1–17; Belinda Edmondson, "Public Spectacles: Caribbean Women and the Politics of Public Performance," *Small Axe* 13 (March 2003): 1–16; Carla Freeman, *High Tech and High Heels in the Global Economy: Women, Work, and Pink-Collar Identities in the Caribbean* (Durham, N.C.: Duke University Press, 2000).

8. Belinda Edmondson's *Caribbean Middlebrow: Leisure Culture and the Middle Class* (Ithaca, N.Y.: Cornell University Press, 2009) is a notable exception. See also Raphael Dalleo, "On Reading Brownness, Seriously: Belinda Edmondson and Caribbean Middle Class Culture," *Anthurium: A Caribbean Studies Journal* 9, no. 1 (2012): Article 8.

9. See Michelle Rowley on the agential working-class black female subject as the dominant Caribbean feminist imaginary. Michelle Rowley, "Whose Time Is It? Gender and Humanism in Contemporary Caribbean Feminist Advocacy," *Small Axe* 31 (March 2010): 1–15.

10. Frantz Fanon, *Black Skin, White Masks* (New York: Grove Press, 1967).

11. Belinda Edmondson, *Making Men: Gender, Literary Authority, and Women's Writing in Caribbean Narrative* (Durham, N.C.: Duke University Press, 1999).

12. See Edmondson, *Caribbean Middlebrow*.

13. For this Anglophone preindependence period, Edmondson goes to the white creole writer Jean Rhys. But situating Joyce Gladwell in this sea of male writers at once unsettles the spatio-temporal gender chronology Edmondson identifies between London-based male *exilic* writers of the 1960s anticolonial/independence period and the *immigrant* ethos evinced in the writings of 1980s US-based women authors. See Edmondson, *Making Men*.

14. The press is now named InterVarsity Press. It was first established in 1947 with a mission to "change the world" through experiences with God (see http://www.ivpress.com). Through the circulation and distribution network of the InterVarsity Christian Fellowship Press, Gladwell's 1969 autobiography sold out its first run of 21,000 copies, and she became a part of a transnational imagined community of Christians—mainly of the British Commonwealth. See Courtman's introduction to the memoir.

15. Beryl Gilroy, *Black Teacher* (London: Cassell, 1976).

16. Joni Miltenburg, "New WICC Building Named after Joyce Gladwell," *ObserverXtra*, April 3, 2009, http://observerxtra.com/2/featured/new-wicc-building-named-after-joyce -gladwell/.

17. Debbie Millman, "Interview with Malcolm Gladwell and Joyce Gladwell," Audio Design Matters Archive, *Voice of America Business*, http://observermedia.designobserver .com/audio/malcolm-gladwell-joyce-gladwell/9187/.

18. Malcolm Gladwell, *Outliers: The Story of Success* (New York: Little, Brown, 2008), 271–273.

19. Miltenburg, "New WICC Building Named after Joyce Gladwell."

20. Faith Linton, *What the Preacher Forgot to Tell Me: Identity and Gospel in Jamaica* (Pickering, Ont.: BayRidge Books, 2008).

21. In her excellent recent study of Fanon's Mayotte Capecia, Tinsley explains how Capecia literally has to clean up her working-class genealogy once she accepts a marriage proposal and moves to Paris to take on the public life as a writer. Herself a twin, Capecia was born to an unwed mother and an already-married father who would not give his twin daughters his surname. Establishing the legitimacy of her birth by attaining her father's surname is the first detail Capecia attends to before migrating. The prospect of entering a marriage with a white Parisian was, for her, "to enter another class construction of sexuality," which in the Caribbean was usually the domain of middle- or upper-class women. Omise'eke Natasha Tinsley, *Thiefing Sugar: Eroticism Between Women in Caribbean Literature* (Durham, N.C.: Duke University Press, 2010), 141.

22. The phrase is George Lamming's from *The Pleasures of Exile* (1960; repr., Ann Arbor: University of Michigan Press, 1992).

23. Kuan-Hsing Chen, "The Formation of a Diasporic Intellectual: An Interview with Stuart Hall," in *Stuart Hall: Critical Dialogues in Cultural Studies*, ed. Kuan-Hsing Chen and David Morley (New York: Routledge, 1996), 484–503.

24. It is also important to note that Gladwell's mother secures the initial funds to get Joyce abroad from their neighborhood Chinese grocer.

25. She travels with a similarly unaccompanied group of students, twenty passengers on the banana boat going second class—first class was reserved for the bananas. Marcus Garvey's son, then en route to study law, was among her travel companions (112).

26. University College London celebrates the fact that it was the first university in England established without a religious foundation.

27. Once again, in this moment black femininity as ontological state is produced through its encounter with whiteness (146–148).

28. Gladwell, *Outliers*, 284.

29. Here I have in mind Carole Boyce Davies's recent *Left of Karl Marx: The Political Life of Communist Claudia Jones* (Durham, N.C.: Duke University Press, 2008). In this book, Boyce Davies is able to recuperate Claudia Jones for a Marxist black radical tradition.

30. See Curdella Forbes, *From Nation to Diaspora: Samuel Selvon, George Lamming and the Cultural Performance of Gender* (Kingston: University of West Indies Press, 2005).

31. For this autobiographical tradition, see Rosie Stone's 2007 memoir, *No Stone Unturned* which chronicles her positive HIV status resulting from her husband's sexual indiscretions. Rosemarie Stone, *No Stone Unturned: The Carl and Rosie Story* (Kingston: Ian Randle, 2007). See also Stacey Ann Chin, *The Other Side of Paradise* (New York: Scribner, 2009).

32. Robin D. G. Kelley, *Freedom Dreams: The Black Radical Imagination* (New York: Beacon Press, 2003).

Elma Napier's Literary Sense of Place

EVELYN O'CALLAGHAN

Haunted by a history of transplantation and loss, Caribbean writing has consistently revisited constructions of land and landscape in an effort to establish what Elizabeth M. DeLoughrey, Renée Gosson, and George Handley call "a sense of place."[1] This history witnesses centuries of transportation to the Caribbean of people from across the globe, the motives hugely problematic and the means horrifically disparate. Most arrivants found themselves in landscapes so alien, and usually hostile, that their initial accounts struggle to even articulate their responses, which range from confusion, fear, alienation and a longing for the land left behind, to grudging admiration for the beauty of the new and considerations of its possibilities. To endure, to survive, and, for some, to prosper necessitated finding a means of connecting to the place where, for better or worse, they were all in a sense castaways. While Caribbean literary histories of the Windrush "genesis" have foregrounded this transportation/ migration as a defining trope, the direction of travel is, however reluctantly, almost always away from the region. I am interested in writing that focuses on land and land use in establishing a sense of place in the Caribbean proper. But is it possible to reconnect imaginatively with a vanished early landscape? The physical contours of the Caribbean have been so radically transformed by colonial conquest, plantation, and state-sponsored "development" from the seventeenth to the present century that establishing a historically informed "sense of place" inevitably involves some digging—that is, excavating records (whether historical, literary, or visual) to discern how that originary site our ancestors saw has been constructed and reconstructed. Wild and dangerously unhealthy terrain, unspoiled Eden, El Dorado, and contemporary tourism posters of island playgrounds: the Caribbean space has been all—and none— of these. My larger project is concerned with mapping changing Caribbean landscapes in literary (and visual) texts, and teasing out the often painful historical factors associated with these changes. Given that they are living in a place where history is always just under the surface, "imbricated . . . in crucial ways with histories of transplantation, slavery and colonialism and imported European traditions of land and landscape perception and representation," as

Helen Tiffin rightly observes, "Caribbean writers have a complex relationship with their land."[2]

For twentieth-century literary landscapes, one usually turns first to texts by those migrant writers who sought to establish a West Indian "sense of place"—Lamming's Barbados, Naipaul's Trinidad, Mittelholzer's Guyana, McKay's Jamaica—from abroad. The link between exile and literary production is well documented; for example, Vera Kutzinski's introduction to *A History of Literature in the Caribbean* concludes that "at the end of the 1960s, the majority of Anglophone Caribbean writers, many of whom that decade had propelled into international prominence, were quite removed from West Indian local existential realities. Most of these first generation emigrant writers were male and middle-class."[3] Such histories make no mention of writers like Elma Napier, a white Scottish woman who, long before Lamming, Naipaul, Mittelholzer, Selvon, and the rest of the Windrush generation traveled to the "Mother Country," had published two novels and several stories intimately bound up in the natural and human worlds of her chosen Dominican home. Nor do they notice that, unlike the later migrant writers, her locally situated and very specific sense of place is clearly informed by care for the land—that is, by an early environmental consciousness.

As noted, land has been at the center of the Caribbean colonial project and the development of society in the region. Accordingly Windrush authors—and those since—detail how the relationship between landscape and power informs all aspects of the lives of (for instance) the peasant characters in the early novels of Selvon and Lamming. And yet, note the editors of *Caribbean Literature and the Environment: Between Nature and Culture*, "ecological concerns seem surprisingly absent" from readings of this literature.[4] Regardless of whether this lack is due to long periods of exile or subsequent critical blindness, Napier's centering of land, as well as its ownership and stewardship, constitutes an early, even pioneering contribution to the development of ecological consciousness in the Caribbean literary tradition. Her Dominican memoir, *Black and White Sands*, movingly records her love of the island's physical terrain and calls for a careful balance between development and progress and the protection of natural resources; her novel *A Flying Fish Whispered* co-opts literature in defense of a natural world threatened by the reimposition of colonial and plantation economies.

Who was Elma Napier (1892–1973), and what was her relationship to the Caribbean? The unconventional daughter of a Scottish aristocrat, she married English businessman Lennox Napier (1891–1940) in Rangoon in 1924. They traveled extensively, but Elma, conscious of her privileged status, was quick to dissociate herself from the stereotype of the colonial memsahib keeping up appearances in exotic places: "Thank God," she writes, "I have never been one to walk through the fields in gloves, a fat white woman whom nobody loves."[5] Introducing *Black and White Sands*, Polly Pattullo relates how the couple were enchanted with Dominica, encountered during a Caribbean cruise in 1931.[6] By 1932 they had wrapped up their affairs in England and moved the family to Calibishie, on the isolated north coast of Dominica, subsequently becoming deeply involved in the life of their community and the island in general. White, British, and privileged they were; yet they could not have been more different from most of Dominica's tiny white expatriate society. "While the other wives baked cakes and gossiped about the servants," Pattullo observes, "Elma wrote articles for the *Manchester Guardian*, talked to men about politics and learned about the landscape and culture of her adopted island."[7] Their commitment to progressive politics is evident. Lennox was popular locally for representing the dire state of Dominica's peasantry to the Colonial Secretary in London in 1932, prior to the Moyne Commission visit of 1939. In 1937 he was elected representative for the extensive North Eastern District, and in this capacity he championed the campaign for boat landing and seashore rights for the villagers of Woodford Hill and Wesley in 1938, eventually guaranteeing the access rights of Dominicans to their beaches. By the time he succumbed to tuberculosis in 1940, Elma was a familiar literary and political presence, and was persuaded to take over as representative for the district, serving for some ten years.[8] The first woman elected to a Caribbean parliament (in 1940), she was also the first to serve in Dominica's Legislative Assembly. Elma pioneered cooperative efforts, encouraged the formation of village boards and self-help programs, and campaigned (along with Lionel Laville, a member of the Legislative Council)[9] for the construction of the Transinsular Road, which finally connected the north to the south of the mountainous island.[10] "There is nothing escapist about her life," wrote English travel writer Alec Waugh; "not only has she written three or four books there, but she is active in local politics."[11] Elma Napier died in 1973 at the age of eighty-one and is buried on her land at Calibishie, a final testimonial to her sense of place.[12]

Critic Elaine Campbell considers Elma Napier one of the early writers and artists whose work transitioned "literature about Dominica away from the detached report of the literature of colonization and away from the romantic picture-painting of nineteenth century commentators. It moves the literature about Dominica towards a literature of concern about Dominica by Dominicans."[13] Napier's evocation of Dominica is indeed an insider's perspective: it is precise, particular, and celebratory at a period when many West Indian–born poets were rendering their landscape with reference to classical or English literary models or as exotic postcard "views." The "project of literary decolonization," Alison Donnell observes, "has been very much involved with developing a language through which to name, affirm and cherish the beauty and sustenance that is found in a Caribbean landscape."[14] Napier's writing participates in this project, but her admiration for the land does not blind her to the hardships and challenges it posed for less-privileged inhabitants. Verbally "painting" scenery, she never falls into the trap of arranging "natives" as picturesque adornments to the prospect. They emerge, rather, as vivid personalities whose lived realities are clearly familiar to the author.

To illustrate, compare Napier's portrayal of the Caribbean with that of another long-term British resident of the region, Esther Chapman of Jamaica.[15] Chapman's travel guide, *Pleasure Island: The Book of Jamaica*, offers a virtual island tour, pausing to note "the tropical beauty of palm tree and cane field" and comment on the scenery around the Rio Grande, which reminds her of "a great tropical waterway, and were it not for the Jamaican accent of the boatman, one could imagine oneself on the mighty jungle-clad rivers of South America."[16] The guidebook format might account for the removed gaze, the gesturing to the seasoned traveler, and the homogenizing clichés about Jamaica's natural beauty. But in her novel *Too Much Summer: A Novel of Jamaica*, there is still no sense of connection, of attachment to place, for Chapman's female protagonist, an Englishwoman who comes to the West Indies and never leaves: "Jamaica was a lovely country . . . but after ten years one had perhaps had enough scenery and sun and entertainment."[17] Chapman also rehearses the tired stereotype of Jamaican "natives" as poor but "happy and cheerful, for their needs were few and easily satisfied. A little work, a little rum, a little love."[18] Neither is there much concern for the preservation of the gorgeous environment that her tourist guide fulsomely promotes; indeed, Chapman advertizes "pastimes" like hunting turtles and shooting crocodiles and wildfowl, seemingly unaware of the irony that her list of game birds includes "the Jamaican Blue Pigeon, which unfortunately is on the point of extinction."[19] Chapman evokes the Jamaica of her time; yet there remains a curious disconnect, a lack of personal response to or feeling for her island "home." Similarly, although Alec Waugh—a repeat visitor to Dominica— expresses sincere admiration for the island in travel sketches written between 1930 and 1958, he too evinces little sympathetic connection to the land or its people. Like Chapman, his narrative tone conforms to a condescending and generalized colonial perspective: "Dominica is the Ireland of the Antilles. It is the loveliest of the islands and it is the most difficult to manage."[20] Approvingly, Waugh notes the self-sufficiency of the peasants who live in harmony with their environment and produce "just exactly what they needed for themselves."[21] Yet these same peasants are reified as the grinning chattering proletariat. I am sometimes infuriated by their casual, lazy improvidence, but it is impossible to be angry with them for long. They are basically so good natured, always ready to dance and sing and laugh; they are born comics. They contribute immensely to the visitor's enjoyment.[22]

The rehabilitation and valorization of the West Indian peasantry that preoccupied West Indian writers in 1950s London counter precisely this kind of distanced essentializing.

Some twenty years earlier, the expatriate Napier actively disassociates her family from what, in the late 1930s, seemed to her an anachronistic colonial mindset:

> We had made our entrance in Dominica at the end of an act, when the orchestra was already playing a new one.... Gloves and stockings, silver salt cellars and tea equipages, the White Man's Burden and the prestige of the Master Race.... This attitude was rigidly maintained until the tide of democracy and commonsense, to say nothing of war conditions, swept it away.[23]

Loyal to empire when war breaks out, Napier is nonetheless clear-eyed about Britain's disregard for the welfare and long-term needs of the peoples of the West Indian colonies. The Napiers clearly recognized the need for social change and self-government: Lennox's name appears on a petition for Dominican self-government in the mid-1930s. Moreover, the Napiers' appreciation of nature is not at the expense of the real, human needs of Waugh's "grinning chattering proletariat," and they championed practical infrastructural development that would make life less arduous for the rural population. Elma's dedication to the campaign to build the Transinsular Road, which enormously improved intra-island transport and trade, finds its way into her 1952 story "The Road" as well as being described in *Black and White Sands*.[24] At the same time, her writing registers wariness about the ecological cost of the road: "Where a few years ago we had walked in the twilight of trees there was now a bare hillside strewn with axed stumps, half hidden already by razor grass and wild eggplant."[25] Napier's care for her island leads Pattullo to term her an "early environmentalist, [who] fought to preserve the island's great forest ranges."[26] The "extraordinarily beautiful island" of Dominica has been celebrated, Campbell points out, precisely "because it had not been successfully exploited by the planters who ravaged other West Indian islands."[27] Napier's writing dramatically reminds us of the need to be aware of this, now more than ever.

Despite her literary, environmental, and political engagement, Napier is not mentioned in mainstream critical studies of the Windrush writers or, for that

matter, their predecessors; her work is usually relegated to a footnote in most
Caribbean literary historiography. Non-Caribbean birth, as well as her whiteness and class, probably accounts for this erasure. Further, attention to writing
by women is relatively new, and several authors are yet to qualify for places in
the literary record. Early canon formation was at best partial; hence Campbell
questions why Sylvia Wynter cites Ada Quayle (1927–?) as *the* first West Indian
woman novelist, ignoring Napier, Jean Rhys, and Phyllis Shand Allfrey, all of
whom published much earlier.[28] Perhaps, as Donnell suggests with regard to
early West Indian women's poetry, such writing was ignored or dismissed as
"embarrassing and undesirable" because it was considered overreliant "on colonial forms and ideologies."[29] Critical marginalization or even exclusion, then,
has to do with assessments of "relevance" as much as quality, and in Caribbean
literary contexts the former category has generally been related to judgments
about authorial race, class, politics, or place of birth, as well as the appropriate-
ness of subject matter. Reaffirming Napier's place in Dominica's literary record,
Campbell's legitimizing impulse is evident in the reminder that Napier's family
"is now in its third generation in Dominica . . . [and her] forty-one years in
Dominica combine literary and political activity."[30] Since Campbell's intervention, notions of what constitutes a Caribbean literary tradition have been revisited so that the work of Napier and other (then anomalous) writers can now be
accommodated. Yet while articles, reviews, and books have been written about
Allfrey and Rhys, Napier's writing will still be new to many readers. Only the
recently republished *A Flying Fish Whispered* and her Dominican memoir are
in print, and it is with these texts that I want to engage.

In *Black and White Sands*, she mentions being delighted (if amused)
when a tourist tells her that "your Flying Fish Whispered is the best book
ever written about the West Indies."[31] The tourist's claim may be somewhat
inflated, but the novel warrants attention not simply because it is informa-
tive, amusing, gripping, lyrical, and evocative but also because it foregrounds
the relationship between land, land use, and power that is central to Caribbean history. This is the central plank, for example, in Sylvia Wynter's seminal
article "Novel and History, Plot and Plantation" (1971), which consolidated a
binary model for the ways land came to be read in Caribbean literature: either
as slave *plot* (small tracts of land, vital resources on which those who were
enslaved grew food and sold/bartered any excess) or master's *plantation* (a
system for efficient exploitation of natural and human resources in the service of profit). The Caribbean was "planted" with people, Wynter argues, not
in order to form societies, but to implement and maintain plantations with
the sole purpose of producing single crops for the market.[32] In her formula,
Caribbean peoples came into being as adjuncts to the product (sugar) that

they produced. So while the plot prioritizes *use value* in which human needs determine what is produced, the plantation operates according to *exchange value*, where the product—determined by market demand—is more important than the needs of people. For Wynter, the commodification of land in the plantation economy alienated those who were forced to work it, while traditional West African notions of land as sacred reinforced the value placed on slave plots/gardens. Wynter's article called on Caribbean critics to declare their alignment with either the plot (and all it represented: Brathwaite's Afro-Creole "little" tradition) or the plantation (signifying colonial and imperial power, the Euro-creole "great" tradition). Thirty years earlier, Napier's *A Flying Fish Whispered* (1938) depicts a white creole protagonist forced to declare her ethical commitment to one or the other, and choosing to assert the values and rights associated with the plot over those of the plantation.

In what follows, I read Napier's 1930s novel in conjunction with some of the stories and journalism she published during the 1950s, as well as her 1960s memoir *Black and White Sands* (published only in 2009). This literary output covers the period from prewar stirrings of the labor movement and the rise of nationalism in the Caribbean through to the serious consideration of political independence, and reflects Napier's sensitivity to changes in local opinion and a growing concern with extending political and environmental rights to the peasant class whose cause was later, and with more flourish, championed by the Windrush writers.[33] Aspects of her writing, then, can be read from an eco-critical perspective with particularly gendered concerns, concerns quite different from the generic and political preoccupations of her midcentury male counterparts. *A Flying Fish Whispered* centers on a love affair between an Englishwoman, Teresa Craddock, long resident in the Caribbean island of St. Celia, and the married white creole Derek Morrell, recently arrived from nearby Parham Island. St. Celia is configured as a place where there is an *interrelationship*, a mutual connection, between people and their natural environment. Conversely, Derek's imported Parham Island ethos constructs land and labor as commodities to be bought and sold, and his management of the plantation he has acquired clashes with communal-minded local conceptions of land rights and ownership. He and his frugal Scottish wife are Methodists who intend to "succeed financially as planters" whatever the cost: he moves tenants off his land, razes their "gardens" (plots) to make way for sugarcane planting, and threatens to withdraw access to the beach. But, asks Teresa, "How would the people get their fish?" Derek's wife speaks for him: "That, Miss Craddock, would be their business, not ours."[34]

Refusing villagers the fallen coconuts to which—like the beach and the river—they traditionally had access, the Morells demonstrate the planter's

commercial ethos with regard to land as exchange value. Their jealous guard-
ing of property rights is something Teresa terms "the lust of possession."[35]
Since only one of the 1,500 acres of Derek's estate is planted in coconuts, there
is more than enough land for his intended plantation; but like the prover-
bial dog in the manger, he insists that "I might need these [coconuts] some
day. Anyway, it's the principle of the thing. The nuts are mine."[36] By contrast,
Teresa shares the concept of land for mutual use value articulated by a local
priest: "is it not so that when one buys or inherits a property one acquires
at the same time certain responsibilities, the duty of administering the land
for the greatest good of the greatest number?"[37] Derek will have none of this.
Bitter at the loss of his family's estate in Parham Island (modeled on Anti-
gua), a dry, flat sugar island whose peasantry is kept in dire poverty by estate
owners descended from slaveholders, he affirms his allegiance to the plantocracy: "I was heir to a house three hundred years old, one of those heavy
stone mansions that still had slaves' quarters, and a mill with an immense
stone chimney."[38] His inflexible "lust of possession" leads to open conflict with
the community when one of his cattle goes missing, presumably stolen. To
Teresa's dismay, Derek resolves to punish the entire village: it is of no account
that they will starve without their livelihood. His plantation mindset prioritizes profit over human needs and the exploitation of resources (both land
and people) to this end.

The novel makes Napier's sympathies abundantly clear, and these are reinforced in *Black and White Sands* when she sardonically reports an American
estate owner whining about how hard "it is . . . to get a jelly-nut for my own
use because the people still pilfer. They don't reckon it is stealing to take a nut
or a fig from the old estate. It is as though it were still our business to feed
them."[39] The paternalism on the part of "us" toward "the people" links these
new landowners with the old slaveholding planters and their commodification of nature and labor. Both fiction and memoir echo actual events that
illustrate the Napiers' activism on behalf of their constituents. In 1938 Captain
Stebbings, whose estates occupied almost eight miles of foreshore, had forbidden local fishermen from landing their boats on his beach, the only safe
landing spot on that stretch of coastline. His excuse was suspicion that one or
more of them had stolen coconuts and a cow from his property, supposedly
for export to Guadeloupe. He also forbade washing in the river on his land,
and right-of-way to or from the beach without his permission. Two fishermen
who did not remove their boats were prosecuted and fined three pounds each,
an exorbitant sum at the time, which, having no income as a result of the ban,
they were unable to pay. "Ominous murmurings reach us from the Northern
District," reports the *Dominica Tribune* of January 8, 1938. "The villagers of

Wesley are asking why the Government has done nothing to restore them the right, which they believe is theirs by user [rights] from time immemorial, to beach their fishing boats on the foreshore at Cariboa Bay." Outraged, "the villagers of Woodford Hill and Wesley approached Mr. L. P. Napier, the elected member of the Legislative Council for the district, and asked him to prepare a petition to the government for the restoration of what they honestly believed to be their rights."[40]

The case led the governor to institute an investigation, and, as a result, Stebbings was told to allow the villagers some access to the beach and the river mouth for laundry purposes. He refused to compromise with regard to Cariboa Bay, banning the Wesley fishermen. "Mr. Napier pointed out that times were changing, that it was now recognized that landlords had obligations as well as rights," and that it was grossly unfair to penalize these fishermen (who had paid boat licenses) and the community for an alleged theft. The *Tribune* warns the government that the infringing of "not only their legal rights but also of their rights as human beings" could result in "a very ugly mood" in the area. What the newspaper highlights and Napier's fiction acknowledges is a growing Caribbean awareness of the rights of all citizens to natural resources. It also suggests that Napier may usefully be read alongside her Caribbean contemporaries' configuration of land use and power relations, particularly Claude McKay's celebration of the hills and peasantry of Jamaica in his poetry, his novel *Banana Bottom* (1933), and his posthumous autobiography, *My Green Hills of Jamaica* (1979). Significantly, McKay was the son of a farmer and studied agriculture; his writing promotes diversified small-scale agriculture in Jamaica as opposed to corporate monocrop (banana) cultivation.[41] Like Napier, he wrote against the social and economic plight of the peasantry and for sustainable agriculture, and he implicitly endorsed, as she did, the concept that natural resources are held collectively by the community.

The spiteful self-righteous parsimony of the historical Stebbings, echoed in the stance of Derek Morrell, clearly outraged Napier, as the motif of the stolen coconuts reappears in her story in *Bim* "No Voyage for a Little Barque" and later in her memoir; and, of course, it marks the end of the romance in *A Flying Fish Whispered*.[42] Teresa is repulsed by Derek's disregard for local places and people and breaks with him. Knowing her sympathies lie with the powerless villagers, he offers to stop persecuting them if she will sleep with him, echoing the stereotypical colonial conflation of Caribbean woman's body with land forced to yield up its treasures. Teresa resolutely refuses, and the novel ends with her acknowledgment of the harm caused to innocent people by "her desire for a white man who had turned out to be a person not of her own creed or understanding."[43] In actuality, the Cariboa Bay affair was resolved, and landowners in Dominica were obliged to recognize a tenet of environmental justice: that *all* citizens have a right to access the earth, the rivers, and the sea. In her fiction as in her life, Napier advocates a holistic sense of ownership and responsibility vis-à-vis the land. Her writing insists that the needs of the poor majority outweigh the rights of capitalists and plantation owners. Organized politics and her role therein are discussed toward the end of *Black and White Sands,* but the fictions already demonstrate a political commitment to her local and national community (Teresa and her brother are constantly called on to fetch doctors or medical supplies, provide transport, loan money, and give legal and other advice).

A *Flying Fish Whispered* not only records the exquisite beauties of Dominican nature, but it also expresses an enlightened ecological awareness. Teresa loathes careless deforestation for agricultural development, whether on a large scale (Derek's dream of a sugar plantation) or small, as in the peasants' slash-and-burn land clearance method and the resultant soil erosion.[44] The text is driven by horror at what the island faces, in human and natural terms, from the planter mentality of Morell: "Drink to our success here," Derek said, "to the ultimate downfall of the forest."[45] Like her author, Teresa is keenly aware of the cost of progress and development: "if he found what he wanted, rich alluvial soil . . . then the axe would follow, and the cutlass, and a burnt desolation. Chatagniers, gommiers, bois riviéres, would lie . . . in mud."[46] Naively, she trusts the island to withstand human destruction: "the red cliffs would remain, and the sea. The most determined planter would never tamper with these."[47] In Napier's first novel, *Duet in Discord* (1936), also set in a fictionalized Dominica, the protagonist rejoices at the failure of a Canadian lumbering company in the island: "Once again the forest rejected the white man."[48] And in *Black and White Sands,* Napier dryly mocks the inability of the Rank Organization film crew and its "continuity girl" to make nature fit their shooting schedule: they "could not control the beat of the waves nor the cloud formation in the sky."[49] The implacability of Dominica's natural world is a construct shared by Jean Rhys's *Wide Sargasso Sea* and Phyllis Shand Allfrey's *The Orchid House.* These two novels, along with Napier's, clearly illustrate Èdouard Glissant's claim that the Caribbean "landscape in the [literary] work stops being merely decorative or supportive and emerges as a full character."[50]

More explicitly, Napier's memoir prophetically links development, particularly tourism marketing, with the pollution of the very landscape being promoted. Will the bottles and cans discarded by the film crew "lie forever and forever in the sand," she wonders, "until the day when the New World was rediscovered by some new Christopher Columbus, perhaps from another planet, after the next Dark Ages."[51] A *Flying Fish Whispered* underscores the implications of "Parham Island ways" with regard to environmental as well as social and economic justice. Visiting Parham, Teresa describes the disfigurement of its "white-sanded beaches" toward which "drifted the refuse of the Atlantic."[52] Napier's work ominously prefigures the degradation of the Caribbean environment to which we are now, reluctantly, waking up. Back in St. Celia, Teresa traces the careless disregard for ecological issues back to the indifference of the island's British government representative, who, after all, "would never see the island again, nor care, after his departure, if it were networked with concrete highways, or left in pristine innocence."[53] Like Napier, Teresa sides with the local population, black and white, against environmental (and other types of) mismanagement by colonial expatriates concerned only with keeping "'the Empire for the English.'"[54] Today, the sands of the Cattlewash coast in Barbados are compromised by tar and other debris washed ashore: bottles and cans litter the beaches, and every weekday morning sees gridlock on the network of concrete highways. My anecdotal evidence only underlines the prescience of Napier's warning that environmental destruction correlates with unregulated development, partially promoted by accounts like Waugh's and films of the kind mocked by Napier. Her very personal use of the trope of a poisoned Eden, a beloved landscape threatened with disease, has clear relevance for readers today.

To conclude, Napier's work attends to two representations of the relationship between power and Caribbean land/nature, anticipating Wynter's paradigm of plot and plantation. It also precedes Wilson Harris, Antonio Benítez-Rojo, Derek Walcott, and others in considering the ecological issues that necessarily accrue to these opposed relationships. Ironically, Wynter would have dismissed Napier's insight; relegated to the peripheral category of elite expatriate observer, Napier's warning went unnoticed by those concerned with the literary work of nation building. Certainly Napier's affiliation with her beloved Dominica overlaps with her connection to empire; the same is true for writers like Claude McKay and C. L. R. James, who, as Donnell notes, embraced European literature *as well as* the need for West Indian political transformation.[55] Given the complex constitution of "Caribbeanness," its literary history, as Kutzinski observes, will necessarily be a "partially, and unequally shared, messy" one: critics would do well to heed Harris's caution against the orthodox policing of literary boundaries, striving instead for the active imagining of "new less-bounded identities."[56] In this spirit, an examination of Napier's life and literary output can serve to open up concepts of Caribbean nation and belonging. Exiled from the land of her birth, she spent half her life involved in furthering the political and environmental rights of the black peasant class about which Lamming, from his London exile, wrote so passionately. However ill it may fit with the conventional narratives of West Indian literature, Napier's writing partakes of one of its fundamental concerns, underscoring the significance of a sense of place as encoding an awareness of the value of Caribbean landscape and an obligation to maintaining the integrity of its lived environment.

Notes

1. Elizabeth M. DeLoughrey, Renée Gosson, and George Handley, eds., *Caribbean Literature and the Environment: Between Nature and Culture* (Charlottesville: University of Virginia Press, 2005), 14.

2. Helen Tiffin, "'Man Fitting the Landscape': Nature, Culture and Colonialism," in DeLoughrey, Gosson, and Handley, *Caribbean Literature and the Environment*, 200.

3. Vera M. Kutzinski, "Introduction," in *A History of Literature in the Caribbean*, ed. James Arnold (Amsterdam: John Benjamins, 2001), 2:11.

4. DeLoughrey, Gosson, and Handley, *Caribbean Literature*, 26. However, they concede, it is arguable that many early writers were more concerned with agendas such as "reclaiming a historical Caribbean subject than engaging with the natural environment. Wilson Harris has sustained the most vocal critique of the ways in which the adoption of a realist history for the Caribbean novel has prevented an engagement with the 'numinosity' of the landscape" (9). Napier, however, *does* engage with environmental concerns within a realist fictional framework.

5. Elma Napier, *Winter Is in July* (London: Jonathan Cape, 1949), 230.

6. Polly Pattullo, "Before Dominica: A Portrait of Elma Napier," in Elma Napier, *Black and White Sands: A Bohemian Life in the Colonial Caribbean*, ed. Polly Pattullo (London: Papillote Press, 2009), iv.

7. Ibid., v–vi.

8. Elma Napier had written two memoirs before she came to Dominica, *Youth Is a Blunder* (London: Jonathan Cape, 1948) and *Winter Is in July*, as well as a volume of travel sketches, *Nothing so Blue* (London: Cayme Press, 1927). She finished the third part of her autobiography, *Calibishie Chronicle*, in Dominica in 1962, now published as *Black and White Sands*, ed. Polly Pattullo (2009). Her two novels set in the island, *Duet in Discord* (London: Arthur Baker, 1936) and *A Flying Fish Whispered* (London: Arthur Baker, 1938), were both published under the pseudonym Elizabeth Garner (possibly because of their frank sexual content). She contributed to the local press and the regional literary journals *Bim* and the *West Indian Review* in the 1950s and 1960s, and was encouraged by a friend of her husband's family to contribute pieces about her travels to the *Manchester Guardian* and *Blackwood's Magazine*.

9. In private correspondence, Lennox Honychurch provides some background to Lionel Laville, a farmer and small landowner descended from the original "petite blanc" (poor white) settlers who had retreated from Guadeloupe and settled in Dominica in the early eighteenth century. The family had mixed with Kalinago/Carib indigenous people and "free

people of color," and in the first half of the twentieth century were considered to be among the higher level of "colored" peasant proprietors. Lionel Laville operated a small pottery-making enterprise mainly producing a type of clay goblet, popularly called "carafe" in Creole, for holding drinking water. When universal suffrage was introduced in 1951, Elma Napier became a nominated member in the new legislature, and Laville took over her constituency. Laville won the North Eastern District seat again in the general elections of 1954 and 1957, when he was made minister of communications and works under the newly introduced system of ministerial government. He quit politics in 1961.

10. To illustrate how much this achievement improved transport and trade in the island, Elma's son Michael recalls that previously there "were no roads to the south of the island so journeys to [the capital] Roseau involved driving [across the island] to Portsmouth and then a three hour boat journey along the leeward coast, stopping at villages on the way." Michael Napier, "History of Pointe Baptiste," http://www.pointebaptiste.com/history.html.

11. Alec Waugh, *The Sugar Islands* (New York: Farrar, Straus, 1949), 100–101.

12. For this biographical sketch, I have drawn on Pattullo's introduction to *Black and White Sands*; Virginia Blain et al., eds., *The Feminist Companion to Literature in English* (London: B. T. Batsford, 1990), 786; and Lennox Honychurch, *A to Z of Dominica Heritage*, http://www.lennoxhonychurch.com/heritage.cfm?Id=121.

13. Elaine Campbell, "Literature and Transnational Politics in Dominica," *Journal of Postcolonial Writing* 24, no. 2 (1984): 356.

14. Alison Donnell, *Twentieth-Century Caribbean Literature: Critical Moments in Anglophone Literary History* (London: Routledge, 2006), 58.

15. Chapman was a journalist for the *Jamaica Daily Express*, founded and edited the *West Indian Review* in 1934, and wrote a play and two novels set in the island (as well as two tourist guides) between 1927 and 1953.

16. Esther Chapman, *Pleasure Island: The Book of Jamaica* (London: Constable, 1928), 140–141.

17. Esther Chapman, *Too Much Summer: A Novel of Jamaica* (London: Chantry, 1953), 1.

18. Ibid., 167.

19. Chapman, *Pleasure Island*, 200.

20. Alec Waugh, *Love and the Caribbean: Tales, Characters and Scenes of the West Indies* (New York: Farrar, Straus and Cudahy, 1958), 30.

21. Ibid., 296.

22. Ibid., 308–309.

23. Napier, *Black and White Sands*, 92.

24. Elma Napier, "The Road," *Bim* 4, no. 16 (June 1952): 264–265; Napier, *Black and White Sands*, 228.

25. Napier, *Black and White Sands*, 230.

26. Pattullo, "Before Dominica," vi.

27. Campbell, "Literature and Transnational," 355.

28. Elaine Campbell, "An Expatriate at Home: Dominica's Elma Napier," *Kunapipi* 4, no. 1 (1982): 82–93. So scanty is research on Ada Quayle that at the time of writing, her official date of death could not be confirmed.

29. Alison Donnell, "Difficult Subjects: Women's Writing in the Caribbean pre-1970" (paper presented at the Sixth International Conference of Caribbean Women Writers and Scholars, Grande Anse, Grenada, May 18–22, 1998).

30. Campbell, "Literature and Transnational," 357.

31. Napier, *Black and White Sands*, 168.

32. Sylvia Wynter, "Novel and History, Plot and Plantation," *Savacou* 5 (1971): 95.

33. The Windrush writer most associated with a deep, sensory investment in land is no doubt Wilson Harris. I suggest that Napier anticipates Harris's protoecological message in her focus on landscape, locality, and ethics.

34. Elma Napier, *A Flying Fish Whispered* (1934; repr., Leeds: Peepal Tree Press, 2011), 80.

35. Ibid., 57.

36. Ibid., 65.

37. Ibid., 174.

38. Ibid., 72.

39. Napier, *Black and White Sands*, 138.

40. "Cariboa Bay: An Appeal for Action," *Dominica Tribune*, January 8, 1938. I am grateful to Napier's grandson Lennox Honychurch (Dominica's foremost historian/ writer/anthropologist/environmentalist) for the newspaper clipping to which I refer.

41. I thank Leah Rosenberg for pointing out that in poems such as "King Banana," McKay challenges corporate agriculture and asserts the superiority of peasant over plantation farming.

42. Elma Napier, "No Voyage for a Little Barque," *Bim* 4, no. 14 (June 1951): 85–87; Napier, *Black and White Sands*, 24–25; Napier, *Flying Fish*, 190.

43. Napier, *Flying Fish*, 232.

44. Ibid., 167.

45. Ibid., 79.

46. Ibid., 69.

47. Ibid., 74.

48. Napier, *Duet in Discord*, 250.

49. Napier, *Black and White Sands*, 243.

50. Édouard Glissant, *Caribbean Discourse: Selected Essays* (Charlottesville: University of Virginia Press, 1992), 105–106, quoted in DeLoughrey, Gosson, and Handley, *Caribbean Literature*, 4.

51. Napier, *Black and White Sands*, 244–245.

52. Napier, *Flying Fish*, 132.

53. Ibid., 223–224.

54. Ibid., 158.

55. Donnell, *Twentieth-Century Caribbean*, 55.

56. Kutzinski, "Introduction," 16–17.

Part Three

The Politics of Literary Production and Reception

The BBC's *Caribbean Voices* and Its "Critics' Circle": Radio Criticism and the Development of Anglophone Caribbean Literature

GLYNE A. GRIFFITH

In April 1940 Jamaican poet and cultural activist Una Marson, who was living in London, organized a radio program feature for the BBC Overseas Service. Broadcast to the Anglophone Caribbean, the program titled "Calling the West Indies" offered London-based servicemen from the English-speaking Caribbean the opportunity to read messages of sentiment and the occasional poem over the air as one aspect of maintaining contact with relatives back home. After a brief while, as a result of Marson's initiative, the program began to include more literary and cultural items relevant to the Caribbean. Thus the stage was set for what would become *Caribbean Voices*, a dedicated literary radio program. When, as a result of illness, Marson returned to Jamaica in 1946, the BBC temporarily employed English writer Mary Treadgold to run the program until Henry Swanzy, an Irishman, was hired as the program's permanent editor and producer in July 1946.[1] For the next eight years, Henry Swanzy shaped and guided *Caribbean Voices* in significant and lasting ways until he was transferred to Accra in November 1954 to serve as head of programs in the Ghana Broadcasting Service.

As a result of his effort and vision, *Caribbean Voices* became one of the most important early influences on the development of literature in the Anglophone Caribbean as it helped to consolidate the nascent literature into a coherent body of work and to provide early writers, scattered as they were across the archipelago of British colonial territories, with a sense that they were connected by means of the BBC to each other in a shared creative and critical endeavor. At the same time, the program inadvertently encouraged a nationalist gaze in much of the early work as a consequence of Swanzy's demand that submissions reflect what he called "local color." A significant number of prose fiction submissions sent to London and broadcast during the early period of Swanzy's eight-year editorship met his call for local color by representing the vernacular speech of diverse peasant and working-class characters in the fictional renderings of specific island territories. Numerous poetry submissions also highlighted specific territories and localized cultures in various ways, not least of which were poems that sustained an unabashed nationalist tone. During one program in March 1948, for example, *Caribbean Voices* broadcast the poems "Jamaica" by Micky Hendricks, "This Is Jamaica" by Carl Rattray, "Trinidad—I Am of Thee" by Barnabas Ramon-Fortuné, "My Sweet Barbados Home" by Olga Hoad, "Portrait of British Guiana" by Frank Dalzell, and "Trinidad" by Sam Selvon.

This circumstance was somewhat ironic since British policy in the region, as the various Caribbean territories were being prepared for a not too distant decolonization, emphasized political federation and regionalism rather than individual territorial nationalisms. Anne Spry Rush suggests that Swanzy was not unaware of the potential link between his submissions guidelines and the developing nationalist tendencies apparent in the work broadcast:

> At Swanzy's insistence, Caribbean settings, themes, and characters were preferred over work set outside the region.... Nationalist voices were not uncommon on the program, and in later years, Swanzy himself suggested that his openness to West Indian nationalism might have contributed to the BBC's decision to transfer him to another department.[2]

Caribbean Voices also had the effect of encouraging prose fiction that relied primarily on social realism, as opposed to other modes of representation, as a consequence of the limitations of the program medium and the relatively short broadcast time. That *Caribbean Voices* and Henry Swanzy's editorial work contributed to the shape of literature emerging from the Anglophone Caribbean in the decades of the 1940s and 1950s has already been acknowledged in broad terms by several critics.[3] This essay examines the particular influence of the critical preferences the program highlighted and the effect of the broadcast medium on the developing writing, and does so by engaging a succinct combination of close reading and archive-based contextualized literary history. Given the essay's subject matter and method, complementary interventions regarding the emergence of African and Caribbean literatures in midcentury London, in particular Gail Low's *Publishing the Postcolonial: Anglophone West African and Caribbean Writing in the U.K. 1948–1968*, have some contextual relevance.[4] Like Low, I use archival research into the British institutions that disseminated Caribbean literature in the 1950s to illuminate the processes that selected and shaped it. As with Low's study of English literary presses, my research on the BBC's contribution to literary development in the Anglophone Caribbean reveals both the cosmopolitanism of early Caribbean writers in exile in London and the complexity of the relationship between metropole and colony in the production of postwar writing. That Swanzy promoted "local color" and an emphasis on territorial cultural particularities despite the fact that this was in conflict with British government policy toward the region makes clear that the BBC did not simply impose metropolitan economic interests, political policy, ideology, or taste in an unmediated manner on Britain's colonized authors.[5]

Swanzy helped to shape the developing literature not only because he had the final word regarding which submissions sent from the Caribbean would be broadcast but also because early in his editorship he organized regular segments devoted to criticism of the emergent literature. Early in 1947 he assembled a small group of mostly Caribbean writers based in London and formed the "Critics' Circle." This group met periodically in the broadcast studio and offered critical opinions on previously aired submissions. After *Caribbean Voices* was lengthened from twenty to thirty minutes in February 1948, Swanzy began devoting entire programs to literary criticism, and the Critics' Circle became a regular feature of the broadcasts. As editor, Swanzy had become conscious of the radio program's potential for assisting the development of literature in the English-speaking Caribbean by focusing on criticism. Since the program was produced in London and broadcast only to the Anglophone Caribbean under the auspices of the BBC Overseas Service, he was keenly aware of the colonial politics vested in his position, but he was also significantly motivated by his own personal desire to help fledgling writers who did not have ready access to substantive criticism or to significant publishing outlets.

Responding, in writing, to a letter from a Trinidadian listener, Rowell Debysingh, who had found fault with some of the Critics' Circle comments during a broadcast, Swanzy provided a sense of what he thought the Critics' Circle as a feature of *Caribbean Voices* was poised to achieve:

> I think you are a little unfair to Mr. Roy Fuller [an early member of the Critics' Circle] who is perfectly well aware of most of the points we made. We realize, for instance, that any criticism from London might well be doing what we complained of in the past, that is, the imposition of alien standards to a regional culture which ought to develop of itself. On the other hand, we are certainly under the impression that comment by literary men, as opposed to schoolmasters, is likely to help build up a better tradition than the "heritage" of English literature, which has not, so far as I am aware, produced any valuable West Indian writing in the past.[6]

And so the Critics' Circle, comprising John Figueroa of Jamaica, Gordon Bell of Barbados, Ulric Cross of Trinidad, and English writers Roy Fuller and Arthur Calder-Marshall, became an integral part of the overall concept of *Caribbean Voices*, as Swanzy sought to provide professional criticism as a means of assisting the development of an Anglophone Caribbean literary tradition. Occasionally, other Caribbean and English literary personalities would make guest appearances, but the regular participants were the individuals named above. The usual approach was to offer close readings of previously broadcast poems and short stories so that, as a result of the general discussion that ensued in the studio, listeners in the region could derive a sense of which previously aired submissions had succeeded and which had not met the program's critical standards.

Swanzy preferred to focus on criticism grounded in close reading and discussion of form rather than entertain theoretical or other abstract discussions. He expressed his interest in formal rather than theoretical or ideological criticism in particularly strong terms when Fernando Henriques of Jamaica was a guest critic for Critics' Circle No. 5, broadcast on October 12, 1947. Henriques had been silent for a long while as John Figueroa and Gordon Bell continued to make their critical remarks about the selected submissions. When Swanzy eventually invited Henriques to weigh in, Henriques remarked:

> The reason [I have been silent] is that I don't quite agree on this method of criticism. West Indian poetry is suffering from very much more than the use of rhymes of words. Its fundamental fault is that it is derivative. For example, these four poems [being considered] have nothing new about them. Wouldn't it be more profitable for us to discuss in general what nature poetry should be?[7]

Swanzy then responded, "In some special program later perhaps, but now we are really at the carpenter's bench."[8] Swanzy's admonition led the other participants back to the close reading of previously broadcast poems, but even so, on this occasion the discussion soon headed back to broader contextual and philosophical concerns as the critics were invited to comment on two poems that had been submitted by Trinidadian schoolmaster and aspiring poet Harold Telemaque. The two poems, "They Have Not Seen Adina's Dancing Beauty" and "Tobago in January," elicited different responses from Figueroa and Henriques. Figueroa thought that the two poems failed to convey to the reader, or the listener, the subject matter suggested by their titles. On the contrary, Henriques argued that the poems did succeed in conveying the poet's point of view to the reader and listener. The different interpretations led the discussants back to broader literary concerns in spite of Swanzy's earlier admonition that they focus on the "carpenter's bench" approach, or structural concerns, which he preferred. In exploring their different responses to Telemaque's two poems, Figueroa wondered whether it was possible for the reader of a poem to understand that poem completely if he or she had not had the same kind of experience as the poet. Henriques thought that the reader ideally needed to have a similar kind or level of experience if the poem were to be fully appreciated. Figueroa then suggested to Henriques that if one followed the latter's line of argument, one could suggest that it might not be possible to read John Donne or T. S. Eliot, for example, without sharing their philosophy. Henriques responded:

> Well, in one sense we can't, at least with Donne. With Eliot, it is possible to understand, at least for someone who lived in Europe after 1918, for whom *The Waste Land* is a reality expressing a world they knew. But I am inclined to doubt whether it is the same thing in Jamaica or Barbados, whether you can really appreciate Eliot—you have to have lived through something similar.[9]

Consequent on Henriques's comment, and before Swanzy could interject and move the critical discussion back to narrower matters of poetic structure, Bell interjected:

> So far as the Caribbean is concerned, I think these are good poems and this point shows our dual problem: first, it is very difficult [from the perspective of a Caribbean individual] to experience the background of even the best metropolitan writers: and secondly, what is sometimes overlooked, is that they cannot always experience our background and build on to what is so frequently an apparently shallow reaction to tropical nature.[10]

Here Gordon Bell called attention to the typically stark material and cultural differences between metropolitan middle-class life at the various centers of empire and the quotidian existence of the majority of colonized subjects such as those in the British Caribbean. At the same time, he was also drawing attention to the limited view of many metropolitan writers of the day in terms of their engagement with Anglophone Caribbean life and culture. However, as in the exchange between Swanzy and the other members of the Critics' Circle, Swanzy did not promote a space during these early broadcasts on criticism for the examination of important matters of cultural and existential difference between developing writers in the Anglophone Caribbean and established writers in Britain. The criticism he promoted, as we have seen, remained more narrowly focused on the structural matter of craft.

In one sense this is understandable because Swanzy comprehended his role primarily as a nurturer of underexposed talent. He wanted to get greater exposure for good writing from the British Caribbean, and he wanted to help develop good writers so that the best among them could gain access to publishing houses in Britain and thus establish themselves professionally. Given such a focus and the reality that each *Caribbean Voices* broadcast was relatively brief, Swanzy thought that there could be little space for entertaining broad philosophical concerns. Instead, he tried to ensure that the limited time was spent engaging in a carefully focused structural critique of the nascent literature. Indeed, when one examines the program scripts, it is clear that the various critical comments that were actually broadcast were robustly edited in terms of available airtime to favor the "carpenter's bench" type of analysis that Swanzy actively promoted. For example, the section of Figueroa's statement above regarding Donne and Eliot, as well as Henriques's statement about *The Waste Land* and Europe after 1918, was edited out of the broadcast. The program scripts reveal lines drawn through sections of text with the occasional word or short phrase inserted for the sake of continuity and coherence in what was actually broadcast. Thus, regarding Henriques's stated concern, the listening audience would have heard only: "I am inclined to doubt whether in Jamaica or Barbados you can appreciate Eliot, say,—you have to have lived through something similar." With the deletion of the contrast offered in the original scripted text, the radio audience was deprived of the sense of cultural comparison, with the attendant resonances in terms of the differing responses between Europeans and Caribbean peoples regarding a significant global event such as the First World War, that Henriques's initial intervention implied. Different ideological responses to the same global event would likely produce different artistic renderings, not only of that event but also of critical reactions to it. An Anglophone Caribbean modernist poet, for example, might not have understood himself or herself to be writing out of the same sense of modernity that, let us say, informed T. S. Eliot and, by extension, *The Waste Land*. It is conceivable that the Caribbean modernist poet might have written out of an ideological context that was much less informed by absurdity, despair, and hopelessness in the aftermath of that major European conflict, but this circumstance would not have made him or her any less a poet working within the historical and artistic continuum of modernism. This is a consideration and recognition that might have resonated with the listening audience in the Anglophone Caribbean if the full discussion, at that juncture of the broadcast, had been aired. It is also a consideration, coincidentally, that facilitates a ready acknowledgment of the accuracy of Gail Low's observation, albeit without the presumption of irony that she suggests is characteristic of the situation described:

The presence of a literary circle of exiled writers in London created, ironically, a sense of a metropolitan identity that helped establish common ground between exiled Caribbean writers and the London literary establishment. The content of the Anglophone Caribbean writers was distinctive, aesthetically innovative and—significantly—also anti-colonial, yet their connections with a London literary elite, their commitment to literary excellence, and their modernist outlook made them seem different but, crucially, not *too* different, and helped pave the way for their championing by the men of letters in London.[11]

Since the ideological nature of colonialism, as well as its quotidian practices, meant that both colonizer and colonized, metropole and periphery, were embroiled in the same epistemic conjuncture, it need not be construed as ironic that these Caribbean writers were simultaneously exiles from their various British colonies and cosmopolitan residents in the metropole. They were, at the same time, aspiring Caribbean writers from their respective colonial outposts and also articulate interlocutors within the discourse of modernity at the center of empire. Nevertheless, neither the limited broadcast time allotted to *Caribbean Voices* nor Henry Swanzy's emphasis on poetic craft allowed for a comprehensive airing of these kinds of philosophical and ideological concerns on the program, at least not during the early period of the twenty-minute broadcasts, the period of *Caribbean Voices* when this particular Critics' Circle broadcast was aired.

Given its prominence on the program, the Critics' Circle undoubtedly had a significant impact on aspiring writers in the Anglophone Caribbean. When we examine the influences informing choices made by the program's critics, we discover that it was not only literary style and taste but also the requirements of broadcast technology that had an impact on some of their pronouncements. The efficient use of available airtime influenced the critics' expectations and demands. In an exchange among Bell, Henriques, Figueroa, and Swanzy, for example, Figueroa admonished Henriques to re-read a submitted poem in its entirety in order that he might consider revising his judgment of a line. Figueroa said: "I think you ought to read it, man. Read it to the end. You will see what I mean."[12] Bell then interjected that the difficulty was that one could not spend time reading the poems several times on air, and he argued that it should have been possible to play the recordings of the readings several times during a Critics' Circle broadcast. Swanzy then intervened and stated: "Ideally, yes, but that is why I think radio poems must be easy and declamatory to be entirely successful."[13] Here we observe that the intersection of literary choice and broadcasting limitation produced a critical statement from Swanzy that encouraged a particular notion of syntactical and structural efficiency. There is also evidence that aspiring writers in the region responded to the Critics' Circle discussions, as can be seen, for example, regarding Harold Telemaque's poem "Adina." This poem was broadcast on July 27, 1947, along with eight other Telemaque poems and was, later that year, the subject of discussion during the Critics' Circle broadcast referenced above. The poem was then published two years after its broadcast and critique on *Caribbean Voices* in *Poetry of the Negro, 1746–1970*, the anthology edited by Langston Hughes and Arna Bontemps.[14] In the published version of "Adina," one key word was revised in apparent response to the Critics' Circle analysis. Lines three through six of the first stanza of "Adina" as broadcast on *Caribbean Voices* read as follows: "They have not seen Adina's velvet figure / Swimming uncovered in our rivers' bubbles / They have not seen the bamboo's slow manoeuvre, / The light reflecting round her shapely ankles." These are the exact lines read by Fernando Henriques during the Critics' Circle broadcast, and he and Figueroa then discussed word choice, imagery, and syntactical precision. They considered whether Telemaque's word selection at this point in the poem was precise enough to let the hearer, or reader, of the poem imagine what the poetic persona had observed. Figueroa argued that, at points, Telemaque's word selection was not precise enough, but Henriques countered that it was, saying, "Well, it really depends entirely on your judgment of his choice of words, but personally I think 'bamboo's slow manoeuvre' is remarkably graphic and exact."[15] The relevant lines of "Adina" as they then appeared in the 1949 Hughes and Bontemps anthology were rendered as: "They have not seen Adina's velvet figure / Swimming uncovered in our rivers' bubbles / They have not seen the bamboo's slow manoeuvre / The light refracting round her shapely ankles."[16] The subtle but significant change from "reflecting" in the *Caribbean Voices* version to "refracting" in the Hughes and Bontemps publication addresses the matter of precise word choice and enhanced imagery, the very subject of the Critics' Circle discussion between Figueroa and Henriques regarding Telemaque's poem. Drawing attention to the "refracted" rather than "reflected" light around Adina's shapely ankles as she swims in the river is not only a more precise word choice in terms of representing the physical properties of light transmission, but the idea of the bending light, as is made explicit in Telemaque's use of "refracting" in line six, facilitates a representation of movement in that line that parallels the movement of the bending bamboo, a visual complement to the "bamboo's slow manoeuvre" in the preceding line. This gives the first stanza of the published poem an additional literary coherence. In addition, the repetition of the phrase, "They have not seen . . ." in alternating lines satisfies Swanzy's statement, referenced above, that successful radio poems be "declamatory."

Telemaque's poetry was broadcast with increasing regularity on *Caribbean Voices*, and he was often held up by members of the Critics' Circle, and particularly by Swanzy, as an example that other aspiring poets in the Anglophone Caribbean might emulate. In short, Swanzy's praise of Telemaque's talents at this juncture was also an emphasis on the sort of writing he hoped to see from the region. Indeed, just three months after the Critics' Circle No. 5 broadcast, when Henriques and Figueroa had discussed the relative merits of Telemaque's handling of imagery, Swanzy praised his literary ability and dedication to craft during a broadcast on January 11, 1948:

> He has one supremely important attitude which I have not been able altogether to sense in most other writers and that is that he seems dedicated. For him poetry is not something you fall back on when you can't be with your girl, or you see the moon and remember the old folks at home. It is an art; it is a discipline, itself your mistress and mother. And because of this attitude, Telemaque is able sometimes to achieve the essential purpose of the poet which is to give a universal value to private images.[17]

Swanzy's admonishment that successful *Caribbean Voices* submissions should at some level reveal local color is captured here in his statement that the writer's purpose is to give "universal value to private images." During this broadcast in 1948, he also provided a survey of the previous year's submissions and lamented the fact that some writers in the Anglophone Caribbean were not participating in *Caribbean Voices*. He then attempted to better articulate what he meant by local color:

> There are a lot more writers discreetly keeping silent. Perhaps it is because they object to that Oxford voice. . . . I suspect that there is another reason, and that is the belief that one is only interested in what one might call topographical poetry. That, of course, is quite wrong. We only ask for this local writing because literature, all literature, is nothing if not concrete and particular (as opposed to science which is abstract and general) and it is also a fact that most people talk best about themselves and their own work.[18]

These ideas would have been difficult for aspiring writers to ignore if they hoped to gain some recognition by means of *Caribbean Voices*, and while Swanzy's critical positions were not proscriptive, his emphases and the expressed concerns of the Critics' Circle had an impact on the shape of writing emanating from the Anglophone Caribbean. This was not only true for poetry but also for prose fiction.

Regarding the bulk of prose fiction submissions broadcast in 1948, Swanzy observed that they were in the tradition of social realism. He observed that "all these prose writers are realists: they report a scene, sometimes doing little more than that. Probably that is because a radio story has to be on the short side, and pictorial."[19] Swanzy's comment that some of the realist submissions did little more than report a scene hints at his desire for writing that did more, but he nevertheless surmises that this circumstance was likely the result of writing for radio broadcast. Aspiring writers in the listening audience would have been keenly aware of the time constraints of the radio broadcasts and Swanzy's often-stated demand for writing that exhibited local color. The combination of limited broadcast time, the need to localize the writing in terms of a Caribbean cultural milieu, and the additional preference for writing that relied primarily on pictorial sensibilities militated against literary approaches that moved too far afield of these parameters. In terms of prose fiction approaches, magical realism, surrealism, and perhaps even science fiction writing, for example, would not easily have met the guidelines articulated by Swanzy and the Critics' Circle. It is not surprising, therefore, that the trend in prose fiction submissions was predominantly toward social realism. In addition, members of the Critics' Circle, such as Arthur Calder-Marshall, admonished prose fiction writers to begin in medias res and employ short, declarative sentences. This is not to suggest that such critical advice might not be well-founded in some particular aesthetic sense, but rather that the demands of the medium, as we have seen, played a significant role in determining what the members of the Critics' Circle represented as good craft to the listening audience dispersed throughout the English-speaking Caribbean. We can only speculate about the degree to which the members of the Critics' Circle were self-conscious about what portion of their critical decisions derived from aesthetic sensibilities and what part resulted from the demands and limitations of the particular medium of transmission. Whatever their degree of awareness, we can observe some of the ways in which these critical voices influenced the shape of the developing literature.

As indicated above, English writer Arthur Calder-Marshall served as a member of the Critics' Circle, a sort of critic-at-large on *Caribbean Voices*. More often than not, he critiqued prose submissions, and, on one such occasion during a March 1948 broadcast, he offered critical commentary on two short stories read in that broadcast. The stories were Sam Selvon's "The Sea," read by Gordon Woolford, and H. V. Ormsby-Marshall's "The Earthquake," read by Pauline Henriques. Unlike previous instances where the criticism of a work was heard in a later, separate broadcast, Calder-Marshall's commentary followed immediately after Woolford and Henriques had read the stories. This new broadcast format represented Swanzy's success at remedying the problem identified earlier by Gordon Bell, where readings and criticism were done in separate broadcasts. Doubtless, it was the ten-minute increase in *Caribbean Voices* broadcast time, beginning in February 1948, that had made this enhanced programming possible.

In examining Calder-Marshall's critique of the two short stories, we can observe the standards the program had established for aspiring prose fiction writers. Selvon's story was read first and presented listeners with the tale of six seamen desperately trying to survive in an open lifeboat adrift at sea after the schooner on which they worked, the *Ocean Pearl*, developed a leak and sank just two-days' journey off the coast of Barbados. When the story begins, the unfortunate men have been adrift for almost a week, and, in addition to the threat of exposure and dire thirst, the narrative reveals that they are also threatened by one among them, a Trinidadian seaman named Menklep, who had murdered the schooner's captain, Fedson, as the crew abandoned the doomed schooner for the lifeboat. Menklep had viciously dispatched the old captain in full view of all the men already in the lifeboat in order to secure a place for himself there. He knows that any one of the survivors in the lifeboat can give evidence against him in a court of law if they all manage to survive the ordeal at sea, and so he determines that if they do not each succumb to the ravages of the elements, he will readily kill again to save himself from the court's judgment. The story concludes with the eventual death of each seaman, including the mate, Michael, who manages to outlast the others only to be murdered by Menklep. As sole survivor, Menklep sights the Trinidad coast and steers the lifeboat toward land. He comes ashore on the rugged north coast of the island and attempts to climb a steep cliff face to escape the battering waves, but slips near the top and falls to his death on the rocks below.

In Ormsby-Marshall's story, a medical doctor from the English-speaking Caribbean who has studied in England returns to his island homeland and devotes himself to assisting his fellow citizens, not only in terms of their physical health but also by trying to eradicate those folk beliefs that, as he construes it, militate against their social progress. He regularly travels treacherous country roads in his old Austin car to attend to his patients, and, on this occasion, he visits the farmhouse of Mr. Jackson and his wife. Mr. Jackson is ill and has taken to bed. Both Mr. Jackson and his wife are convinced that his ill health, which has rendered him unable to leave his bed without assistance, is the result of obeah. The Jacksons believe that others in the community envy their financial success as owners of several acres of arable land and that someone has employed obeah to make Mr. Jackson gravely ill. As the doctor is in the bedroom attending to his patient and seeking to disabuse him of the notion that his illness is the result of necromancy, the old farmhouse begins to shake violently. Recognizing that there is an earthquake occurring and they are both in danger, the doctor insists that Mr. Jackson exit the house immediately and without any assistance. Fearful that he might lose his life should the house collapse around him, Mr. Jackson jumps out of bed unaided and follows the doctor outside to safety. Once outside, the doctor tries to convince his patient that his unassisted exit to safety is proof that his only true ailment is his abiding belief in obeah. Mr. Jackson, however, is now convinced that divine intervention in the guise of the earth tremor has produced his miraculous recovery. He is adamant that the earthquake literally shook him free of the obeah spell.

In both stories, several characters speak creole, and the textual rendering of speech patterns in each case is sufficiently well crafted to suggest to the listener, or reader, Trinidadian colloquial speech in the Selvon story and Jamaican colloquial speech in the Ormsby-Marshall story. Thus the combination of colloquial speech patterns and the descriptive settings specific to each story serves, at one level, to satisfy Swanzy's demand for local color. In addition, Ormsby-Marshall's use of obeah as an element in her story further enhances the sense of a Caribbean cultural locale. Commenting on the stories, Calder-Marshall suggested that "there could scarcely be a greater contrast than between the second story and the first. The first was written simply and plunged straight into the story. The second doesn't really start until it's almost half way through. And the prose it's written in is specially written, we're told, for broadcasting."[20] He then read a long sentence from the Ormsby-Marshall story to illustrate his point:

> In spite of the skill he had to employ in handling the wheel of the ancient model, the doctor still found the opportunity for exchanging a cheery greeting with all who passed his way, from the Resident Magistrate of the parish whose new-modeled Austin made his own look still more outdated, to the market women who rode astride the heavily loaded hampers of their donkeys, and the draymen who conveyed cartloads of coconuts or hewn timber for sale in the nearest town.[21]

Calder-Marshall sarcastically concluded his critique of the Ormsby-Marshall story by use of emphatic repetition: "And this is 'specially written for broadcasting!'"[22]

What is evident in such commentary, even if we judge the Ormsby-Marshall story to be less well crafted than the Selvon tale, is that the demands of the broadcast medium helped to bolster admonitions from members of the Critics' Circle that short stories begin in medias res and that the successful story should employ declarative statements and brief, realist depictions rather than lengthy abstractions. As such, Selvon's story fits these guidelines much better than the Ormsby-Marshall submission. Despite its shortcomings, we can still see the attempt in the Ormsby-Marshall story to satisfy the demand for local color. Indeed, the section of the story that Calder-Marshall references above as an example of uneconomical language use might simultaneously be read as the writer's attempt, by means of description, to satisfy Swanzy's expectation regarding local color. In other words, the story's description of the doctor cheerily greeting "the market women who rode astride the heavily loaded hampers of their donkeys, and the draymen who conveyed cartloads of coconuts or hewn timber for sale in the nearest town" is obviously part of Ormsby-Marshall's attempt to provide local color by means of extended descriptive passages. Thus, even where submissions were employed to illustrate literary shortcomings, as in this case, we can still observe the attempt on the part of these writers to craft submissions according to the guidelines established by Swanzy, Calder-Marshall, and the other influential members of the Critics' Circle.

Although Calder-Marshall described "The Earthquake" as a poorly crafted effort and suggested that it was more of an anecdote than a short story, he nevertheless concluded that it offered a "more important subject than that which Selvon has chosen."[23] Perhaps this was the reason he chose this particular failed story to contrast with Selvon's "The Sea." But if Ormsby-Marshall's story, despite its perceived limitations, still offered a more significant subject matter than the Selvon story, it might be profitable to briefly assess each story's framing of content to glean something of Calder-Marshall's reasoning.

Selvon's story, as indicated above, deals with the plight of six surviving seamen adrift for five or more days without food or potable water. The story reveals that while one of the men, Michael, seems somewhat more formally educated than the others, there is little class difference among the castaways in the lifeboat. Furthermore, respective seamen's rank matters little to these survivors as each man tenuously clings to life for as long as possible. The initial focus of Selvon's story is the narrative tension produced when we learn that there is a murderer among them who is determined to ensure that if he survives the ordeal at sea, no one else will. After we discover that Menklep does indeed outlast the others and that he then murders the only other survivor, Michael, as they gain sight of the Trinidad coast, the focus shifts to the story's moral tone. We wait to discover whether Menklep will somehow be punished for his crimes or whether he will escape judgment. His fall from the cliff face to his death on the rocks below provides a conclusion that satisfies the typical reader's sense of moral justice. If we conclude that the thematic concern of Selvon's tale is each person's social and moral responsibility to his or her fellow human, particularly in a context where the gaze of society is absent, then surely this is an important subject, a subject that Selvon addresses within the cultural milieu of the Anglophone Caribbean by employing Caribbean working-class characters.

The focus of Ormsby-Marshall's story is the social commitment of a local medical doctor working in a rural district in the British Caribbean. The particular island is never named, but the creole speech of Ormsby-Marshall's rural characters, as indicated above, suggests a community somewhere in rural Jamaica. As previously stated, the physician is not only interested in the physical well-being of his patients but also in their cultural and social uplift. He is resolved to help "the people of the undeveloped areas to shake off some of their silly innate beliefs . . . myths which were holding them back from true progress."[24] Thus, unlike the Selvon story, "The Earthquake" features a middle-class Anglophone Caribbean protagonist who has benefited from his education in England and has returned to the Caribbean to improve the material and cultural lot of the rural, uneducated poor. The story's subject matter, quite clearly represented by the doctor's thoughts regarding the country folk, is cultural uplift and moral responsibility in a context where the working class and the poor are construed as generally backward, nonprogressive peoples. From the perspective of this story's protagonist, it is the responsibility of the educated middle classes in the British Caribbean to take up the burden of their enlightened class position and lead the lower classes out of superstitious folk belief and into the sweetness and light of progress and modernity. This is the ideological framework undergirding Calder-Marshall's conclusion that the Ormsby-Marshall story, despite its structural problems as he perceives them, addresses a more important subject than the Selvon story.

If we briefly consider one important aspect of the overall logic of early BBC radio broadcasts to the Anglophone Caribbean, we can better understand the foundation of Calder-Marshall's reasoning. As Anne Spry Rush indicates regarding official BBC policy of the day in the British Caribbean:

> Anybody, no matter what their ethnic or geographical background, could be welcomed into the fold as long as they valued the middle-class perspective and, in particular, the BBC's policy of cultural uplift. It is not then surprising that those persons who worked with or for the BBC's Colonial Service, regardless of whether they were native Britons or West Indians, almost without exception identified themselves as middle-class.[25]

BBC policy of the day revealed the ideological linkages between the formation of Anglophone Caribbean middle-class cultural sensibilities and notions of British middle-class respectability. *Caribbean Voices* was not devoid of such ideological perspectives, and, indeed, the Calder-Marshall example is indicative of yet another influential force acting on the burgeoning literature in the Anglophone Caribbean during the 1940s and 1950s. The salient point here is that *Caribbean Voices*, and particularly its Critics' Circle, had a significant influence on the development of literature in the region because aspiring writers were regularly exposed not only to critical positions and stylistic preferences focused on literary form and supported by a particular view of poetics but also to deeply seated ideological and epistemological tendencies, as the foregoing examples illustrate. The technologically new and developing social medium of radio broadcast in the 1940s and 1950s exerted a significant influence on literary development in the Anglophone Caribbean. However, this should not be construed in a one-dimensional manner as merely the colonial center imposing its influence on the periphery. Henry Swanzy's work with the BBC and *Caribbean Voices*, given his own complex personality, suggests a far more dynamic cultural relationship than such a reading of Anglophone Caribbean literary history might offer. When we add to this dynamic the creative tensions revealed by the intersection of two simultaneously developing technologies, the still developing social medium of BBC radio broadcast and the developing social medium of literature in the Anglophone Caribbean, we recognize that what this period of intersecting technological and cultural development also represented was an enhancement of the discursive continuum within the project of modernity in the English-speaking Atlantic world.

Notes

1. For a detailed account of Una Marson's life and her contribution to the radio program that evolved into *Caribbean Voices*, see Delia Jarrett-Macauley, *The Life of Una Marson: 1905–65* (Kingston: Ian Randall, 1998).

2. Anne Spry Rush, *Bonds of Empire: West Indians and Britishness from Victoria to Decolonization* (New York: Oxford University Press, 2011), 198.

3. See Philip Nanton, "What Does Mr. Swanzy Want: Shaping or Reflecting? An Assessment of Henry Swanzy's Contribution to the Development of Caribbean Literature," *Caribbean Quarterly* 46, no. 1 (March 2000): 61–72; and Glyne A. Griffith, "Deconstructing Nationalisms: Henry Swanzy, *Caribbean Voices* and the Development of West Indian Literature," *Small Axe: A Caribbean Journal of Criticism* 5, no. 2 (September 2001): 1–20.

4. Gail Low, *Publishing the Postcolonial: Anglophone West African and Caribbean Writing in the UK, 1948–1968* (New York: Routledge, 2011); and see also Franco Moretti "Conjectures on World Literature," *New Left Review* 1 (January–February 2000): 54–68.

5. See, for example, Low, *Publishing the Postcolonial*, 99–105.

6. Henry Swanzy to Rowell Debysingh, October 18, 1948, Swanzy Archive, University of Birmingham, UK.

7. *Caribbean Voices*: "Critics' Circle" No. 5, October 12, 1947, BBC Written Archives, Caversham.

8. Ibid.

9. Ibid.

10. Ibid.

11. Low, *Publishing the Postcolonial*, 106.

12. *Caribbean Voices*: "Critics' Circle" No. 5.

13. Ibid.

14. Langston Hughes and Arna Bontemps, eds., *The Poetry of the Negro, 1746–1970* (1949; repr., New York: Doubleday, 1970), 349–350.

15. *Caribbean Voices*: "Critics' Circle" No. 5.

16. Hughes and Bontemps, *Poetry of the* Negro, 349–350.

17. *Caribbean Voices*: "Talk by Henry Swanzy," January 11, 1948, BBC Written Archives, Caversham.

18. Ibid.

19. Ibid.

20. Ibid.

21. *Caribbean Voices*: "Critical Comment," March 14, 1948, BBC Written Archives, Caversham.

22. Ibid.

23. Ibid

24. Ibid.

25. Rush, *Bonds of Empire*, 189.

John Hearne's Plantation Fantasy

KATE HOULDEN

Between 1955 and 1961, John Hearne published five novels—*Voices under the Window, Stranger at the Gate, The Faces of Love, The Autumn Equinox*, and *Land of the Living*. Although well received in the United Kingdom, these texts were criticized within the Caribbean on the grounds of Hearne's alleged failure to reflect the lives of those on the bottom rung of West Indian society: they were perceived to be an anachronistic and depoliticized swansong for the white plantocratic class. There is some truth to this claim, as these novels undeniably romanticize aspects of plantation life, framing that culture as a resource for the beleaguered light-skinned middle classes of postwar Jamaica. In this, Hearne writes against novels like Herbert de Lisser's *The White Witch of Rose Hall* (1929) and Ada Quayle's *The Mistress* (1957), with their sensationalized narratives of white degeneracy. In so doing, his novels not only enact the growing pains of a light-skinned middle-class elite in the face of an expanding proletarian national consciousness, but they also attempt to construct a "New World" model of national belonging that includes a wider range of subjects than was often the case in writing from the period.

Yet this mobilization of what the author sees as the plantation ethos is undermined in a number of ways. Hearne's novels offer a reinvigorated version of plantation culture by taking the unusual step of inviting those previously excluded—men and women of color—into his gentrified fictional world. However, at the same time, the horrors of slavery are pushed to one side of his narratives. In the hands of his modern-day Afro-Creole planters, the violence of their ancestors is erased, and the novels ultimately betray an inability to come to terms with the past. Complicating matters further, Hearne himself was, at best, only distantly related to that elite group whom he nominates as the bulwark (both past and future) of his nation, this despite attempting to align his own familial heritage with the plantocracy. Finally, Hearne demonstrates a troubling lack of awareness as to the evasions and nostalgia of his novels, which, I suggest, limits the reader's ability to engage with his plantation vision.

The most famous denunciation of Hearne's writing is that by George Lamming in *The Pleasures of Exile*, a work ordered around the claim that "it is the West Indian novel that has restored the West Indian peasant to his true and original status of personality."[1] Unsurprisingly, Lamming finds Hearne's engagement with the plantocracy a cause for concern, wondering whether this group can even constitute "a proper subject for fiction."[2] In keeping with his overall theme, Lamming concludes that Hearne's novels are "not an example of that instinct and root impulse which return the better West Indian writers back to the soil."[3] There is no doubt that this emphasis on the laboring individual served an important function in the postwar years, legitimating the literary exploration of the lives of those historically disenfranchised. However, it is when looking at Sylvia Wynter's analysis, "We Must Learn to Sit Down Together and Talk About a Little Culture," that an alternative strand of literary-critical engagement can be discerned.

In her article, Wynter begins similarly by acknowledging Hearne's "failure to grasp" the peasant's "sacramental union" with the landscape.[4] She demonstrates greater sympathy for the author, however, when she views this as an "understandable failure," one rooted in the "marked and deep" colonial divisions of the Caribbean.[5] More positively, Wynter recognizes that those in the Great Houses also had a relationship with the land, albeit one built on the labor of slaves. Provocatively, therefore, Wynter frames Hearne's impulse to celebrate Brandt's Pen, the much-revered estate house appearing across the novels, as being "the same as Lamming's to re[-]create Papa, and his house."[6] Here, Wynter recognizes the validity of elite claims to national belonging, providing an early acknowledgment of the diversity of voices constituting Caribbean selfhood. Her assessment of Hearne complicates what Leah Reade Rosenberg has described as the "surprisingly resilient" emphasis on the "peasant novel," a focus that has continued to affect negatively the status of Hearne's work within the canon.[7]

Lamming's response to Hearne's novels is also illustrative of the dramatic shift in fortunes experienced by Jamaica's lighter-skinned inhabitants (Hearne among them) during the post–World War II years, when a social order long built on white privilege was increasingly undermined. As fellow author Andrew Salkey made clear, "the Jamaica that he [Hearne] knew and wrote about just evaporated in front of his eyes."[8] In viewing this as the major tragedy of Hearne's creative writing, Salkey is supported in this contention by Hearne himself. Reflecting on the gaps in his publishing record, Hearne explained:

> I had painted five good canvasses in a certain style, but my society was changing too quickly around me. And my understanding not about my society itself but my imaginative use of my society, my imaginative setup, as it were, that had been formed by a particular local set of situations.[9]

Perhaps as compensation for this sense of marginalization, both Hearne's novels and, arguably, his reminiscence of his own family heritage display nostalgia for the certainties of early plantation life. In a 1984 interview, Hearne laid out the peculiar and, to contemporary ears, strangely feudal privileges of his background when describing how

> there was a curious sense of ownership of the entire country, there was a curious sense of that [sic] every acre belonged certainly not to my family, but we knew somebody to whom, every other acre belonged. . . . I have come to realize the extraordinary sense of confidence it gave to one.[10]

He also portrayed a familial relationship between master and servant, claiming that

> although there were very rigid class divisions, there was certainly for my sort of family an easiness of relationship between those who served and those who were served. It really was a family relationship . . . one was aware of an extraordinary sort of continuity of relationship that had persisted in many cases for two or three generations between those who, as I said, were served and the servants.[11]

In the context of a lessening in white political power and privilege, Hearne's emphasis on ownership and continuity marks this recollection as being out of step with the political imperatives of his time.

Parallels can be traced between this evocation of the author's familial past and his portrayal of the plantocracy in his factual histories of Jamaica, such as "Landscape with Faces." In this, Hearne is careful to acknowledge the negatives of plantocratic society, claiming that

> to this day, a few Jamaicans whose features are predominantly European will look at each other over their drinks and wryly acknowledge the central place on History's stage from which their island was pushed by the greed and sheer lack of imagination of their eighteenth century ancestors.[12]

Equally damning of the culture they engendered, Hearne also argues that "a community that is nine-tenths slave is corrupted beyond redemption," with the free being "only technically different from the bond: otherwise they are possessed, without realising it, by slavish perceptions, slavish attitudes, slavish morality."[13] Elsewhere, however, he qualifies these criticisms, pointing to the "closely-knit" nature of the plantation world and cautioning: "It must be remembered that in the simpler society of eighteenth and early nineteenth century Jamaica the master and slave mingled, in their daily lives, with a great deal of casual intimacy."[14] So, too, the political independence of the planters receives Hearne's cautious approval, as he describes them as being "self-confident in a way that the colored Jamaicans who succeeded them did not begin to emulate until our own times."[15] The positive values that Hearne ascribes to this era appear to have infused his portrayal of his own, much later childhood, rendering it curiously nostalgic.

This nostalgia also carries through to the novels, which, I suggest, provide Hearne with the opportunity to reimagine plantation culture without its worst excesses. A gap therefore opens up between the Jamaican past as seen by Hearne the historian and those more problematic idealizations of plantation life that filter through his childhood recollection and find fruition in his fiction. In this, postemancipation whites still manifest the values of domesticity and confidence Hearne attributes to plantation culture, but the coarseness and barbarity of earlier times have been screened out. Only Hearne's first novel, *Voices under the Window* (1955), appears concentrated on the future prospects of the island. This text, however, sees the vision of its middle-class protagonist, the politician-hero Mark Lattimer, stall. Hearne proves unwilling to engage in the nostalgic re-creation of the later books, and is unaccommodated within the tumultuous present of the new Jamaica. His attempt to engage with the political future of his country is foiled, and ultimately there is no narrative outlet for Mark but death. Following this initial portrayal of failed political engagement, Hearne's four succeeding works abandon any serious attempt to place their protagonists within the contemporary political realm, although wider, regional politics do continue to frame their action. Rather, the books narrow in focus, as the continuity, confidence, and longevity of plantation life are marshaled as resources for Jamaica's Afro-Creole middle classes, ostensibly for the contemporary moment, but unmarked by any explicit reference to that moment's concrete reality.

Traces of the domestic intimacy and supreme confidence Hearne highlights can be observed across the books. In *Strangers at the Gate* (1956), the character Roy visits Brandt's Pen and notes the "incestuous, happy, kindly closeness where every personal contact is never let go, and where everyone fits into his place like a cork into a bottle."[16] Equally, *The Autumn Equinox* (1959) sees a young Cuban American visitor, Jim Diver, who, after meeting a group of aged Cayunan grandees, concludes that "whatever challenge had come to these men in their lifetimes had come too late to be important; if they ever worried about that challenge, it was for the sake of stimulation. Assurance and righteousness had stained them to the bone."[17] It is the freighted site of Brandt's Pen, however, that best illustrates Hearne's desire to reimagine a new, ethical society based on older values. Appearing across the books, this estate house—and its patriarch, Carl Brandt—epitomizes those civilized values that Hearne ascribes to plantocratic culture, with Carl himself being discussed in terms of his "nobility of soul."[18] Even those antagonistic to the ethos represented by the Brandts turn to them for assistance. In *Strangers at the Gate*, for example, Carl Brandt harbors a deposed Communist leader at the behest of a childhood friend, placing personal loyalty over and above political considerations.

In *The Faces of Love* (1957), meanwhile, Hearne introduces Carl's cousin, Andrew Fabricus, a man descended from the "real old plantocracy" whose family has, thanks to his father's poor business dealings, lost their land and much of their wealth.[19] Looking out over Brandt's Pen, Andrew informs the reader:

> All sorts of people had told me that places like this were bad. And I had read one or two books which said the same thing. But, for me it was one of the places where the life of my country had been cast and carefully nourished. Whatever people had done since then, nobody had been able to make anything so efficient, so beautiful, and so enduring.[20]

Here plantation culture is offered as a productive template with which contemporary Jamaicans might reinvigorate national life. The repetition of "so" emphasizes the distance between "then" and the failings of "now," while the definitive "nobody" makes clear the extent to which Andrew views his society as having degenerated, a process he appears to attribute to a failure of care on the part of the island's civic and political leadership. With *The Autumn Equinox* making clear that the Brandts have lived on Cayuna since the seventeenth century, there is no mistaking the fact that Andrew is eulogizing what was once a slave plantation.[21] However unpalatable, there is some truth to his assertion that this was one of the primary locales in which Caribbean life was forged. Andrew's words therefore serve as a rebuttal to Lamming's question as to whether the plantocracy were a fit subject for fiction. They also implicitly make a claim for the inclusion of white elites within the postindependence future of the region, gesturing toward a broader framework of national belonging.

At the same time, however, the evident difficulties of such a statement cannot be ignored. An undeniable failing of Hearne's novels lies in the fact that they disregard the complicity of their elite families in the horrors of the past. When Hearne does allude to slavery, for example, it is framed as an unfortunate state of affairs from a distant time and is pushed to one side of the narrative. Andrew Fabricus is desperately saving to buy his own estate house and lands and, with no apparent sense of irony, inducts his mixed-race fiancée, Margaret, into his plantation vision with stories of how "in the slave days all the big revolts used to start around the Head. Our house was burnt down three times," a statement eliciting her laughter and the improbable response, "I love you."[22] In similarly blank tones, Andrew later rides around Brandt's Pen and informs the reader, "we got to Soldier Blood Gap. It was called this because a party of runaway slaves . . . had once ambushed a double company of the Forty Second Regiment here and killed every man."[23] Great house or slave rebellion, soldier or runaway, all are elided into a curiously neutral historical backdrop; one would hardly guess that Andrew's or Carl's recent ancestors had any hand in such events. In actuality, however, many fair-skinned Jamaicans were not so comfortably distant from the slave-owning society Hearne carefully condemned in his factual accounts. As the historian Patrick Bryan makes clear, white hegemony in the late nineteenth century, for example, was still "assured by relative wealth, by the political and constitutional order, and by that special authority which had been associated with skin color in a multi-ethnic community dominated by one segment. . . . The plantation ethos had not died."[24] Such words are equally applicable to the twentieth-century context of these novels, despite Hearne's attempt to distance the Brandt and Fabricus families from the horrors of the plantation past.

Hearne is, however, scrupulous in condemning more immediately racist sentiments, clearly realizing the need both to acknowledge the endemic prejudice of the plantocracy and, more important, to exclude their descendants from it. Although figures such as Andrew's father—who believes "you can't trust black people"[25]—reveal the racist tendencies of their group, Andrew and his peers are quick to dismiss such bigotry as "something horrid from the way we were brought up to think."[26] Going further, Hearne also attempts to reinvigorate plantation culture by showing his modern-day planters inviting those previously excluded from plantation life—men and women of color— into their gentrified world. This project is epitomized in the figure of Jojo in *The Faces of Love*. Invited to Brandt's Pen by Andrew, this black builder and ex-convict quickly endears himself to the group, proving a fine shot and showing himself to be appreciative of the family history. Ultimately distinguishing himself by the daring rescue of Oliver when they are caught unaware by a hurricane, Jojo gains the approval of none other than Carl Brandt. At the same time as he displays these noble qualities, however, Jojo is also a flashy, "assertive, confident, explosively moving man" frequently likened to his scheming lover, Rachel.[27] Although capable of entering into the plantocratic ideals of the novels, this pair also embodies those emerging entrepreneurial classes threatening the existing elite, such that the critic Wilfred Cartey has characterized them as "the new people of power" in Cayuna.²⁸ Coupled with their racial heritage, it is no wonder that Jojo and Rachel unsettle the very fantasy Hearne attempts to draw them into, as demonstrated when Jojo describes the sanctuary of Brandt's Pen as "dead," much to Andrew's chagrin.²⁹

Hearne refuses to allow this rejection of plantocratic values within the frame of his novel. Accordingly, the troublesome pair is killed off, with Jojo murdering Rachel after discovering her infidelities, before being sentenced to death himself. Having proven too unstable an influence within Hearne's plantation fantasy, their removal only reinforces the sanctity of its values, with the book closing on Andrew vowing to "try harder" with his father.³⁰ The significance of this pledge is indicated by Andrew's earlier rejection of this figure, for whom we were told: "all he needed to fill out the picture was a grinning little black boy in striped Osnaburg pants offering him a long cool drink."³¹ Jojo and Rachel are eventually put back in their place, and in this instance at least, the rigid world of the plantation reasserts its primacy in Hearne's novelistic vision.

Despite Hearne's failure to integrate Jojo and Rachel into his plantation world, they nevertheless represent an earnest attempt to reinvigorate the plantocratic heritage in which he was so invested. Their presence, I suggest, also connects with a further and seemingly contradictory strand in the author's thinking: his attraction to a "New World" model of belonging based on ideas of regional unity, creolization, and creativity. For example, Hearne has claimed that "I am an American writer. And for me the American experience begins in Alaska and ends in Argentina."³² Expanding on this, he explains how, following a conversation with celebrated left-wing Mexican author Carlos Fuentes, he concluded:

> We shared a perception that we belonged to what was almost totally a New World of expression. . . . We had to establish a new kingdom of the imagination here between Alaska and Argentina that the older civilizations, or rather the other continents, Europe, Africa and Asia, whose nomads we were, could take for granted. It gives us a peculiar strength . . . because we are in a sense all nomads, all castaways, all Robinson Crusoes, that any piece of any culture is valid for our consumption if it can establish a seemly and original habitation on a desert isle. . . . That is what we strive for, and you can see it in the best work from North America.³³

Going on to draw William Faulkner into the same frame of reference as Gabriel García Márquez and Carlos Fuentes, Hearne positions himself within an alternate literary axis running across the Americas, one with a degree of creolization at its heart.

This is made even more explicit in his 1976 introduction to the CARI-FESTA Conference proceedings, where he states:

> I know and revere my distant cousin the European, the African, the Asian. But the brother at my table, even if he does not speak a language I can understand, is Césaire, the black, Retamar, the Hispanic white, Walcott and Guillén, the mulattoes, Naipaul, the East Indian, Dobru, the beautiful mix from Suriname, and William Faulkner, the Anglo-Saxon searcher after justice from Mississippi.[34]

These sentiments gesture toward an expansive Caribbean vision not often associated with Hearne, despite the fact that in his youth he was engaged with left-wing politics and interested in events in Cuba and Haiti. It is this vision that fuels Hearne's desire to invite those previously excluded into his plantation world, as demonstrated by the fact that even so illustrious a figure as Carl Brandt admits, "it was rather a good thing, all this mix-up of races."[35] Such references to racial mixing recur throughout the books and are illustrated by the scientist Stefan in *The Land of the Living* (1961), who describes how, in Cayuna, "the essentially coarse colonial mind has been sharpened and made flexible by . . . the rich *pot-au-feu* of race that simmers in their genes."[36] This biological analogy is extended into numerous further examples, as when Stefan describes a fisherman's wife as "one of those strange, disturbing mixtures—not black, not brown, not any conventional formula of stirred colours—that you only see in Cayuna. You felt that here was an experiment of biology that had already justified its risk because of the new, troubling beauty and vigour it had."[37] Although the gendered implications of this description offer some cause for concern, what I want to emphasize here is the newness and sense of hybridity animating Hearne's description. His nostalgia for the plantation can be viewed as having been tempered by the greater fluidity of the regional vision outlined above. Within the novels, however, this kind of mixing can only succeed as long as those domestic, self-confident qualities Hearne attributes to plantation life are maintained.

This regional vision is helpful in understanding the tension between Hearne's novelistic celebration of the plantation and his recognition of its barbarities as displayed in his historical writings, for in these, the author also acknowledges the slave's capacity to produce culture: "The present miracle of the Jamaican people is that we managed to preserve (or assemble intuitively) the decencies of human intercourse which are now established."[38] Slave populations, despite their "psychic injuries . . . stubbornly fashioned a way of life tough enough, flexible enough, wide enough in scope to survive decently the tremendous shock of freedom."[39] The plantation, as Hearne sees it, not only allowed the self-confidence and domestic qualities of the planter class to flourish, it was also the foundational locale where enslaved people helped create the very culture of the Caribbean. At points in his discussion, however, Hearne avoids the implications of culture and biological heritage and too easily draws equivalence between master and slave. "Nomads," "castaways," and "Robinson Crusoes," for example, are not comparable identities; the former two were colonized, whereas the latter was a colonizer.[40] Similarly, there are points where Hearne unconsciously appears to align himself with the master, rather than the slave. In asserting that "perhaps all of us in the New World are informed by this common humility: that we all belong to the new found land *we seized and exploited* [emphasis added] with such desperate temerity," Hearne adopts the persona of Carl Brandt's European ancestors rather than embracing all aspects of the "mixed" heritage he purports to celebrate.[41] It is slippages such as these in the historical accounts that reveal Hearne's own investment in the plantocratic society of his fiction. Equally, when turning to the novels, characters such as Andrew and Carl are presented positively, with the reader being encouraged to see these men as the ideal types to lead the new Jamaica. The novels' narrative voice, meanwhile, often appears to share in the views articulated by such characters. The opening pages of *Strangers at the Gate*, for example, with their lavish description of the "smooth teak" floor, "soft pink light," "old, handsome room," "grinning" dogs, and "warm and close" stable of Brandt's Pen, hardly read as neutral description.[42] Rather, they appear to support Andrew Fabricus's claim as to the beautiful and enduring nature of plantation life.

In this light, Wynter's alternative critical engagement with Hearne's fictional project again proves useful. Although more sympathetic to the author than Lamming, she astutely observes, "Carl Brandt and his like needed an idealized version of themselves to evade the reality of injustice that would otherwise press in too closely on them."[43] This emphasis on evasion accords with Hearne's seeming lack of awareness as to the tensions of his plantation vision. It also bears comparison with Svetlana Boym's definition of restorative nostalgia. Boym characterizes this form of nostalgic longing as "a transhistorical reconstruction of the lost home ... [that] does not think of itself as nostalgia, but rather as truth and tradition."[44] While Hearne's novels can clearly be read in nostalgic terms, both the author and his characters refute this charge. Carl Brandt's uncle, Hector Slade, for example, asserts that "we have almost no nostalgia."[45] Similarly, Hearne himself, in a published excerpt of his journal, proclaims, "perhaps the most solid achievement of the Jamaican people up to now is the way they have divested themselves of nostalgia."[46] Presenting plantation culture as truth and tradition, Hearne's refusal to acknowledge the nostalgia of his vision allows him to evade those injustices he recognizes in his historical writings. Equally, his attempt to include those whose ancestors suffered on the plantations can be viewed in terms of Roberta Rubenstein's discussion of nostalgia as something that allows us to "fix" the past, to "*correct*—as in *revise* or *repair*."[47] Yet Rubenstein's formulation again hinges on a certain level of *awareness* on the part of the author, with this forming the crux of my critique of Hearne's fictional world—for he appears remarkably *unaware*, at an emotional level at least, of the contradictions and problems of his nostalgic celebration. Despite the measured condemnation of his histories, in his novels, Hearne's authorial voice is harder to disentangle from that of his protagonists: it seems *too* emotionally invested in the restitution of the heritage he himself wished to share. While intellectually he may be all too cognizant of the fact that he is "engaging in a potentially compromised and ideologically questionable enterprise"—as John J. Su characterizes the hazards of nostalgia—the subtextual messages of Hearne's novels do not reveal such doubts.[48] His fictional eulogizing of the plantation estate acknowledges little, if any, fault with this past. As a result, his nostalgic vision proves untenable. A valiant attempt, it is nevertheless ethically problematic.

However, Hearne's work merits attention on the grounds that it stands alone within the postwar West Indian canon in making an overt attempt to deploy plantation culture as a resource in the present day. This is so even if some correspondence can be drawn with Peter Hulme's characterization of Jean Rhys's *Wide Sargasso Sea* (1966)—of which Hearne was wholly approving—as a "creole family romance."[49] Hulme describes Rhys's novel as "fundamentally sympathetic to the planter class ruined by Emancipation," terms echoing Hearne's eulogization of plantation culture.[50] Echoes of Hearne's negation of the horrors of slavery can also be found in Rhys's *Wide Sargasso Sea*, which "occlude[s] the actual relationship between ... [her] family history and the larger history of the English colony in Dominica," most pertinently her family's violence against enslaved and later emancipated Afro-Caribbeans.[51] Moreover, Hulme's recognition of the complex interplay between Rhys's own family history and its fictional re-creation reflects the uneasy negotiation between fact and fiction in Hearne's novels.

These works also bear some commonality with that vein of twentieth-century British writing concerned with the decline of the English country estate (in the wake of authors such as Evelyn Waugh or Angela Thirkell). Like Waugh in the English context, Hearne makes the country estate an "ideal metaphor for the enduring nation," in which, as Su puts it, "individual members might change but whose essential structure remains relatively consistent."[52] In much of this work, as Su describes, the estate serves as "a site that promises to maintain 'civilization' itself," words echoing Andrew's insistence in *The Faces of Love* that the house at Brandt's Pen, with its "solid elegance," represents civilized values.[53] Su's framing of such texts as "a reaction to the social, economic, and cultural tensions" that "accompanied the loss of the Empire" proves equally applicable to Hearne's disenfranchised elite for, if anything, their plantation estates were even more closely intertwined with the fortunes of British imperialism.[54]

Hearne's fiction is immensely revealing of the challenges facing light-skinned populations during the age of West Indian nationalism, proving an important vehicle for articulating the voices of this often disregarded group. He therefore stands within the tradition of what Kim Robinson-Walcott has identified as those white writers from the region whose "burden . . . involves struggling with a sense of marginalization as a dwindling minority in an environment of increasing Afro-or Indo-centricity."[55] Bringing vividly to life the unease of these communities as they learned to live as equals with precisely those they were "brought up to despise and fear," Hearne's novels, despite their flaws, stand as a humanizing corrective to many literary portrayals of the plantocracy.[56] Ultimately, however, their author's nostalgia for the plantation reveals the stubborn discordance at the heart of his novels' imagined regional community. As such, they predict many of the political problems that emerged for Caribbean nations in the postindependence era. While Hearne has been dismissed—and to some extent rightfully, given all the contradictions in his fictionalized political vision—he nevertheless provides a more complete picture of the nascent nation-state and its troubles, prefiguring the political fault lines of the future and highlighting the elisions and negotiations of canon formation itself.

Notes

My thanks to Kim Robinson-Walcott for her helpful discussions about John Hearne and to J. Dillon Brown and Leah Reade Rosenberg for their thought-provoking editorial input.

1. George Lamming, *The Pleasures of Exile* (1960; repr., Ann Arbor: University of Michigan Press, 1992), 39.

2. Ibid., 45.

3. Ibid., 46.

4. Sylvia Wynter, "We Must Learn to Sit Down Together and Talk About a Little Culture: Reflections on West Indian Writing and Criticism, Part 2," *Jamaica Journal* 3 (March 1969): 35.

5. Ibid.

6. Ibid.

7. Leah Reade Rosenberg, *Nationalism and the Formation of Caribbean Literature* (New York: Palgrave Macmillan, 2007), 4.

8. Frank Birbalsingh, "Andrew Salkey: Bright as Blisters," in *Frontiers of Caribbean Literature in English* (London: Macmillan Education 1996), 33.

9. Wolfgang Binder, "'Subtleties of Enslavement': An Interview with the Jamaican Writer John Hearne," *Komparatistische Hefte* 9/10 (1984): 101–113, 108.

10. Ibid., 101–102.

11. Ibid., 101.

12. John Hearne, "Landscape with Faces," *Caribbean Quarterly* 54, nos. 1/2 (March–June 2008), http://catalogue.ulrls.lon.ac.uk/search~S22?/tcaribbean+quarterly/tcaribbean+ quarterly/1%2C2%2C2%2CB/c8561077233&FF=tcaribbean+quarterly&1%2C1%2C%2C1 %2C0.

13. Ibid.

14. John Hearne, "European Heritage and Asian Influence in Jamaica," in *Public Affairs in Jamaica No. 1: Our Heritage*, ed. John Hearne and Rex Nettleford (Kingston: Department of Extra Mural Studies, University of the West Indies, 1963), 21–22.

15. Ibid., 18.

16. John Hearne, *Strangers at the Gate* (London: Faber and Faber, 1956), 141.

17. John Hearne, *Autumn Equinox* (London: Faber and Faber, 1959), 140.

18. Ibid., 41.

19. John Hearne, *The Faces of Love* (London: Faber and Faber, 1957), 64.

20. Ibid., 147.

21. Hearne, *Autumn Equinox*, 14–15.

22. Hearne, *Faces of Love*, 150.

23. Ibid., 169.

24. Patrick Bryan, *The Jamaican People, 1880–1902: Race, Class, and Social Control* (Jamaica: University of the West Indies Press, 2000), 8–9.

25. Hearne, *Faces of Love*, 205.

26. John Hearne, *Land of the Living* (London: Faber and Faber, 1961), 26.

27. Hearne, *Faces of Love*, 81.

28. Wilfred Cartey, "The Novels of John Hearne," *Journal of Commonwealth Literature* 7 (July 1969): 49.

29. Hearne, *Faces of Love*, 166.

30. Ibid., 267.

31. Ibid., 64.

32. Binder, "Subtleties of Enslavement," 105.

33. Ibid.

34. John Hearne, "Introduction," in *Carifesta Forum, An Anthology of 20 Caribbean Voices, 1976* (Kingston: Institute of Jamaica and Jamaica Journal, 1976), ix.

35. Hearne, *Strangers at the Gate*, 61.

36. Hearne, *Land of the Living*, 59.

37. Ibid., 41.

38. Hearne, "Landscape with Faces."

39. Ibid.

40. Binder, "Subtleties of Enslavement," 105.

41. Hearne, "Landscape with Faces."

42. Hearne, *Strangers at the Gate*, 9–10.

43. Wynter, "We Must Learn to Sit Down Together," 35.

44. Svetlana Boym, *The Future of Nostalgia* (New York: Basic Books, 2001), xviii.

45. Hearne, *Strangers at the Gate*, 107.

46. Hearne, *Strangers at the Gate*, 107; John Hearne, "From a Journal," *Tamarack Review* 14 (Winter 1960): 139.

47. Roberta Rubenstein, *Home Matters: Longing and Belonging, Nostalgia and Mourning in Women's Fiction* (New York: Palgrave, 2001), 6.

48. John J. Su, *Ethics and Nostalgia in the Contemporary Novel* (Cambridge: Cambridge University Press, 2005), 11.

49. Peter Hulme, "The Locked Heart: The Creole Family Romance of *Wide Sargasso Sea*," in *Colonial Discourse/Postcolonial Theory*, ed. Francis Barker, Peter Hulme, and Margaret Iversen (Manchester: Manchester University Press, 1994), 75. See also John Hearne, "The *Wide Sargasso Sea*: A West Indian Reflection," *Cornhill Magazine* (Summer 1974): 323–333.

50. Hulme, "Locked Heart," 72.

51. Cited in ibid., 76.

52. Su, *Ethics and Nostalgia*, 123.

53. Ibid., 124; Hearne, *Faces of Love*, 142.

54. Su, *Ethics and Nostalgia*, 121, 123.

55. Kim Robinson-Walcott, "Taking, or Spurning, the Imperial Road: White West Indian Writers and Their Black Protagonists," *Sargasso* 1 (2005–2006): 149.

56. Hearne, *Land of the Living*, 171.

John Hearne: Beyond the Plantation

KIM ROBINSON-WALCOTT

Every privilege that we've got, because of an accident of history, has imposed these real obligations, this necessity that we must fulfill of making this place more than just a plantation.
—John Hearne, interview with Roberto Márquez

It is not at all by chance that so much of the action of West Indian novels takes
place outside, in the open air. This is a long way away from the muted whisper in
the living-room cell or the intellectual stammering which reverberates through
the late night coffee caves.

The West Indian who comes near to being an exception to the peasant feel is
John Hearne. His key obsession is with an agricultural middle class in Jamaica. I
don't want to suggest that this group of people are not a proper subject for fiction;
but I've often wondered whether Hearne's theme, with the loaded concern he
shows for a mythological, colonial squirearchy, is not responsible for the fact that
his work is, at present, less energetic than the West Indian novels at their best.[1]

In 1960 George Lamming published the above comments on John Hearne,
words that have lingered in the consciousness of literature scholars and, I
would argue, affected considerations of Hearne's inclusion in the West Indian
literary canon ever since. Hearne had in the period 1955–1959 published
four novels: *Voices under the Window*, and three of his four Cayuna novels:
Stranger at the Gate, *The Faces of Love*, and *Autumn Equinox*. The fourth and
final Cayuna novel, *Land of the Living*, would follow in 1961.[2] Lamming's criticism of Hearne's work evidently focused primarily not on *Voices* but on the
three Cayuna novels that had been published, all set in the fictional island of
Cayuna and all having as a common reference point the physical and social
world of wealthy near-white landowner Carl Brandt.

Nineteen-sixty: It was the beginning of a tumultuous decade in which
the first countries of the British West Indies would gain their independence;
the US civil rights movement and Black Power would explode and affect
the Caribbean; Marcus Garvey's body would be returned to Jamaica,[3] and
his status changed from embarrassment to national hero; the significance of
the antiestablishment Rastafari movement would finally be acknowledged

academically and officially;[4] the "Rodney riots" would erupt.[5] It was not a decade in which the sensibilities of the colonial squirearchy would easily have found favor with the intelligentsia.

Nevertheless, Hearne's ranking among the foremost West Indian writers to have emerged in that explosion of literary creativity in the 1950s remained at least until the mid-1960s. Reviews of *Voices* and his Cayuna novels in United Kingdom newspapers in the late 1950s had proclaimed him "among the very best of West Indian writers,"[6] and "the most accomplished of the new school of Caribbean writers."[7] Caribbean reviewers echoed these accolades: Edward (Kamau) Brathwaite, in a 1960 review, acclaimed him for having a "compact, atomic-like economy of observation and feeling, rare among West Indian writers";[8] and in a 1966 anthology of Caribbean literature he was referred to as the "most outstanding of living Jamaican novelists."[9] However, by the time Kenneth Ramchand published his landmark study of the West Indian novel in 1970, he found it necessary to defend Hearne: "Lamming accuses Hearne of being obsessed with 'an agricultural middle class in Jamaica.' . . . Such a charge does little justice to Hearne's probing of the painful gap between personal allegiances and political conflict."[10]

One reason Ramchand may have felt a need to defend Hearne was that Hearne had been heavily criticized by Sylvia Wynter in her seminal 1969 essay, "We Must Learn to Sit Down Together and Talk about a Little Culture: Reflections on West Indian Writing and Criticism." She noted dryly that in novel after novel, "all the potential threats to the basic arrangement of Cayuna society are eliminated" while "the Brandts live on, serenely . . . and come hell or high water these human values must be preserved by the few who can afford them."[11] Wynter goes on to state:

> One can only hope that Hearne's next novel . . . will break new ground . . . for it is only there . . . that Hearne will cross his Rubicon; will learn, through a new emotional identification, how to see the white Mahler through the black Henneky's [*sic*] eyes; how to define the "insider" Lattimer through the outsider's eye of a Tiger Johnson. This new kind of eye, the outsider's eye, will mean that Hearne, having paid his dues, will have learnt how to really sing the blues for a Henneky [*sic*]; he would then have no need of a borrowed suffering.[12]

Wynter's irritation with Hearne is clear in that essay, and his public response to it—merely a correction, albeit a scathing one, of her misidentification of a piece of classical music—would not have helped.[13] Although Wynter may have been as hasty in her condemnation as she was in her fact-checking, her critique of Hearne is not without value; on the contrary, it is an extensive and provocative analysis of Hearne's first five novels.[14] Certainly some of Hearne's protagonists display instances of nostalgia for the plantocracy that are disturbing, but Wynter appears to have missed significant nuances in Hearne's work. The Brandts do not in fact live on serenely, but in a fragile and diminishingly safe space. These are not happy-ever-after stories where the cherished plantocrat lifestyle is saved, but rather tragic depictions of good intentions gone awry, of idealism crushed by human failings.

Hearne may have had need of a "borrowed suffering." Yet his depiction of the middle class was in itself immensely valuable. Those characteristics of the Cayuna novels critiqued so heavily by Lamming and Wynter—their concern with the sensibilities of the colonial squirearchy, their light-skinned middle-class identity—are the very features that make them significant. Hearne was perhaps the only author of his generation to move beyond stereotype to illuminate the motivations, actions, and beliefs of this historically vilified segment of the Jamaican population.[15] That very mulatto or middle class has in fact played a critical, if vexed, role in shaping Jamaican politics, society, and literature. A "borrowed suffering" was surely what propelled the most prominent of those national leaders who led the decolonization and postindependence movements. The chief architects of Jamaica's independence, Norman Manley and Alexander Bustamante,[16] were near-white/brown middle class.[17] Again, the main figures in the country's early postindependence development—principally Norman's son Michael Manley and Edward Seaga—were near-white middle class.[18] The woman widely accepted as the "mother" of modern Jamaican art and culture, Edna Manley, was white middle class.[19] Hearne was in tune with the politicized minority within the middle class: those who had responded to the sound of "voices under the window" (the urban poor, referred to in Hearne's first novel) or "voices at the workplace" (a term later used by Michael Manley).[20]

Middle-class figures, then, would be the ones shaping the Jamaican political, social, and cultural identity in the early postindependence period and were widely celebrated as such by the Jamaican intelligentsia. In Wynter's poetic tribute to Norman Manley, published after his death, she writes, "Through hills dressed in drought and bronze / You played your piper's song, / Came to our tawdry Samarkand / Crying wares for our pain . . . / Your melody was rare."[21] I suggest that Hearne's melody, too, was rare. Hearne, in fact, did break new ground—though not in the way that Wynter may have liked. Far from being out of touch, then, Hearne was a spokesman for the political and cultural vision of the mainstream educated middle class of the 1950s and early 1960s. In fact, Hearne's works mirrored the developing, then retreating, radicalism of the Jamaican middle class in the 1950s, and explored the complications of political engagement by that class, so that a reconsideration of his work elucidates the development of the political landscape in pre- and postindependence Jamaica.[22]

Voices under the Window: A Borrowed Suffering

The protagonist in John Hearne's debut novel, *Voices under the Window*, is the lawyer-politician Mark Lattimer, a near-white Jamaican of the upper classes. Mark is caught in a riot when it erupts in Kingston, and is injured; the novel covers the few hours between his injury and his eventual death, during which Lattimer reflects on his life. *Voices* paints a picture of a Jamaican preindependence society in turmoil, with its black majority seething with resentment, threatening to explode. Hearne's opening lines set the scene:

> A crowd of unemployed men had waited for the Minister of Labour outside the House of Representatives since early morning. In a way they had been waiting for a number of years: waiting and looking for jobs they were promised at election time; waiting for food, for clothes, for a little money to feed the children their women had once a year . . . they were very tired of waiting, and by this time, after all these years, they had become quite angry. (9)

Lattimer becomes a victim of this resentment; when the riot erupts he is downtown, in the heart of the inner city, accompanied by his East Indian friend, Ted, and his black mistress, Brysie. Much more so than his companions, he is in the wrong place at the wrong time because he is the wrong color. The resentment of the crowd toward the white minority that has long oppressed them is translated into a single machete chop unexpectedly leveled at Mark when he swoops up a child who is in danger of being trampled by the crowd: "Put him down, you white bitch" (180). So Mark, then, is a victim—his act of heroism misinterpreted sinisterly because someone of his color would not be expected to be concerned about the welfare of any poor black person. Ironically, Hearne demonstrates in the course of the novel that Mark may care more for the black underclass than politicians like the black minister of labor, who had once been a truck sideman but now has begun "to show the curve of good eating on his buttocks and in his big thighs" (10): "Oh to hell wid dem all, dem will never do nuttin' fe' we," the crowd declares (10). Mark is also indirectly a victim of the indifference and opportunism of those politicians who, because of their color and class backgrounds, would have been assumed by the black electorate to be more caring than he—those who are *not* experiencing a borrowed suffering.

Yet Hearne makes sure to point out that in a larger, more important sense, Mark is no victim. He has enjoyed the benefits of his skin color in a society that privileges whiteness. Brought up among the landed gentry, he has displayed an awareness of this privilege since childhood, as demonstrated when he assures a servant who is trying to warn him about the inadvisability of shooting birds out of season that the police "wouldn't trouble" him; "they don't trouble white people" (35). This moment is also a turning point in his childhood. The servants at his affluent uncle's home make sure to point out to him, "Missah Mark, *you* not white, you know" (36), and Mark is given a rude awakening not only to the fact that he is not really white but also to the resentment of the black majority to those of his color who illegitimately claim whiteness. Although for much of his time abroad in the RAF he has persuaded himself that his color is of no consequence—that, rather, what matters are bravery, honor, commitment to an ideal—this changes abruptly one night when the racist comments about "niggers" made to Mark by some white sailors who mistake him for white reveal to him the burden of blackness, and impel him to proclaim his black side, and thereafter to make a political commitment in support of that side that will last for the rest of his life.

Lattimer is injured because of his color and class, the result of a misinterpretation of his good intentions due to a miscommunication based on the race and class divide, and later will be rescued because of that color and class (though the rescue comes too late). Lattimer is uncomfortable with his favored treatment; he feels his integrity has been compromised.

Bleeding to death in an alien downtown ghetto space as he waits to be rescued and transported to safe territory uptown, he feels that he deserves to die because he is unworthy of redemption—primarily because "the people out there aren't a part of me. . . . They knew it, the people out there, the people I've tried to love. They smelt out the failure and the fear; that's why they chopped me" (113–114). Appropriately, he has been chopped by a machete, symbol of manual labor on the sugarcane plantation, and symbol, therefore, of colonialist oppression/resistance.

The people out there, under the window, are represented by a block of sound, "a clamouring, deep roar of sound. It was lonely and a little mad; frightened, and full of hate raised to the place where it was ready to destroy. . . . Out of the sound they heard the nerve-cracked voice of the speaker on the drum falling on the people like a whip. It was all as sad a thing as any of them had ever heard" (27). It is this chorus—the "sullen and abandoned sounds of the people" (141)—that he recognizes to be "the sound [he's] always heard . . .

the music [he has] moved to for so long" (28). The sound contains echoes of slavery—the drum, the voice cracking like a whip falling on the people.

The sound is also an index of his unbelonging—"The black people bellowing at me to get off their necks, and the whites too, screaming nervously, not so often, more refined, whenever I came nearer than a certain limit" (28).[23] Hearne's descriptions of animalistically "bellowing" blacks versus "more refined" whites might seem to support the concerns of critics in their exposure of middle-class prejudicial views, but they also highlight Lattimer's dilemma of alienation from both groups: he does not identify socially or psychologically with the "bellowing" blacks with whom he identifies politically, the people he has "tried to love," and he is not accepted socially by the "more refined" whites with whom he might be more inclined psychologically to identify despite his political disapproval of them.

On another level, Hearne may be implying that blacks have been reduced to animal status through slavery. The sobbing of Lattimer's mistress, Brysie, as she grieves over his death is disparagingly dismissed by the white police superintendent: "It's only a black woman . . . could cry like that" (163). Of course, as Hearne has implied, it is only the black population that *would* cry like that—only the black population that has suffered so long and so hard. Unlike the superintendent, Lattimer can sympathize with her social class, but someone of his color and background has not shared the experience of suffering and may be better able to sympathize than empathize. As Lattimer's fate illustrates, the gulf caused by this lack of shared experience can be deadly: "Driving through the grey morning, with the slime and gutter smell mingling with the rank odour from the houses where people slept fourteen in a room, he had realized that perhaps it was a mistake for one of his colour to be here to-day. This morning, more than he could ever remember, he had felt the weight of the years' oppression and suffering" (12).

In her critique of Hearne, Wynter had compiled a wish list for *Voices*:

If he had shown us that the political commitment of his hero was as much an upper-middle-class privilege, as much a product of the social and political arrangement of his society as was his colour of skin, quality of hair, of education, of feeling, of conscience; if he had shown us that in taking over the running of the system Latimer [*sic*] was merely coming into an inheritance, and that in . . . seeking the destiny of the poor he was in fact fulfilling nothing but his own private destiny, easing nothing but the private property of his conscience, then his death . . . would not have been by accident; but the result of a terrible logic. For then the unknown murderer would have been seen also as . . . a man who kills aimlessly in an aimless existence which is the lot of his inheritance. But Hearne draws back from such a conclusion.[24]

It would have been difficult for progressive, radicalized Wynter, in that heady, early postindependence period of burgeoning national socio-politico-cultural consciousness, to assess a Lattimer figure without impatience. But Lattimer's borrowed suffering as a member of the educated elite is exceptional. As Shivaun Hearne has noted, protagonists like Lattimer should be judged as much for what they are as for what they would otherwise have been had they not risen above the complacent self-interest of the mainstream upper classes.[25]

The figure of Lattimer is a familiar one to those acquainted with Jamaican history; Hearne's inspiration was presumably the 1938 riots that saw the emergence of trade unions and the rise to political prominence of the lawyer Norman Manley and the trade unionist Alexander Bustamante. Hearne was a young man at the time of the riots, but the near-white/brown middle-class Roger Mais, with whom he later formed a close friendship and whom he admired greatly, was a leading activist. Nineteen thirty-eight, then, was significant in Jamaican race/class history in that it was a moment of radicalization of members of the near-white/brown middle class.[26] The 1938 riots would lead to the granting of universal adult suffrage in 1944, which resulted in the election of a House of Representatives led first by Bustamante and then, in 1955, by Manley. Hearne shared with the majority of the country's middle-class intelligentsia a preference for the genteel, refined Manley over the brash, less-educated Bustamante.

Manley was a deep-thinking intellectual; but perhaps, like Hearne's Lattimer, he was unable to identify fully with or feel the pulse of the masses, as demonstrated first by his inability to lead his party to electoral victory until 1955, then his disappointing losses with the referendum of 1961 and the general election of 1962. His ill-fated decision to call an unprecedented referendum on the issue of West Indies federation, however much due to his "commitment to principle" whatever the consequences—qualities Lattimer would have applauded—was also probably the result of his mistaken conviction that "the electorate would accept his advice and assurances that Jamaica's interests had been protected."[27] Though devastating, the defeat may not have been really surprising. Just as Lattimer, when delivering his political speeches, "wasn't sure they understood it all" (148), Manley's granddaughter Rachel Manley recollected that "the campaign leading up to the referendum became . . . futile. . . . Perhaps this was the most remote and isolated he ever felt from his own people. . . . His arguments somehow left him stranded . . . as he fought against a tide of incomprehension."[28] On hearing about the referendum defeat,

Manley allegedly said, "I am finished. . . . I don't want to go on. There is nothing to go on for . . . the people have spoken, they've rejected it, they've rejected me."[29] We recall Lattimer's sense of rejection by both blacks and whites as he lies dying. Lattimer's disillusionment and eventual death in *Voices*, then, could be read as symbolically reflecting as well as predicting Manley's own political disillusionment and disappointments.

The Cayuna Novels: Beyond the Plantation

The role of the near-white/brown middle class in Jamaican decolonization politics is reflected in Hearne's Cayuna novels—though in a more muted way than in *Voices*. *Stranger at the Gate* juxtaposes the conservative near-white landowner Carl Brandt with his closest friend, the Communist lawyer Roy McKenzie, and the deposed Franco-Caribbean Communist president Henri Etienne. Brandt agrees to help McKenzie shelter Etienne despite his disapproval of Etienne's revolutionary politics; he does this out of loyalty to McKenzie. Over the course of the novel, however, Brandt comes to admire and respect Etienne, recognizing that "whatever conduct of life he, Carl, could never approve or accept or condone, it had been come by passionately and bravely" (251). When McKenzie sacrifices his life at the end of the novel in order to ensure Etienne's safe escape, Hearne depicts him as a true hero—brave, committed, passionate in his beliefs, selfless—qualities that Brandt recognizes he himself lacks. *The Faces of Love* is less overtly concerned with political idealism, dealing instead with the private politics of race, class, and gender among a group of white, brown, and black upper- and middle-class protagonists. It is sufficient to note here that again in this novel, Hearne uncovers honor in unexpected places—or places surprising to his white or near-white privileged protagonists, thereby upturning long-held assumptions about race and class.[30]

However, the third Cayuna novel, *Autumn Equinox*, returns to questions of idealism and radicalism. Told alternately by the aging ex-revolutionary white Cayunan merchant Nicholas Stacey, his adopted "niece" Eleanor, and her lover, the American Jim Diver, who has been sent by Stacey's old comrade Luis Corioso to Cayuna on an undercover mission in support of a revolutionary movement in Diver's mother's neighboring Hispanic-Caribbean homeland, the novel explores the contrasting ideological positions of the two men. Jim is young and burning with unfulfilled desire to help his mother's oppressed countrymen and women and ultimately prove his manhood. Nicholas, in contrast, is timeworn:

I am only sorry now that, at his age, Luis Corioso should still be wasting his energy and experience on this sort of revolution. Surely he must have learnt by now how ephemeral is the life of what passes for justice which such revolutions achieve. A change of governors is all that happens; no change of government. A brief, intoxicating week-end in which those who have fought for truth and liberal catch-words use up their honesty, and then the take-over bid by the realists.... I should have thought that by now Luis would have realized the sickness of governors is not in the abuse of power, but in the desire to govern. Power merely serves to make the disease obvious. (100–101)

For Jim, ideology is more important than love; for Nicholas, love is all that matters in the end. Hearne does not overwhelmingly promote either side, though Nicholas's wisdom does seem to transcend cynicism and, gently, to outweigh Jim's insecurities and feverish idealism. But here there are no clear-cut heroes or villains: Nicholas, a brave fighter in his revolutionary days, is racked by guilt over his callous treatment of Eleanor's mother; Eleanor, beautiful, impulsive, passionate, treats her black servant, Sonny, like a dog; Sonny may indeed act like a dog—lazy, unreliable, dishonest—but is seething inwardly, and justifiably as Hearne demonstrates, about societal inequalities and the class divide; Peter Conroy, Jim's irritating, nihilist/anarchist American partner in his undercover operation, displays surprising moments of insight. All the same, perhaps the person whose portrayal is most straightforwardly sympathetic is the local madman, the Franco-Caribbean exile Pierre Auguste, demented from abandonment; yet his childlike clinging to distant ideals of liberty comes across as sadly admirable.

In both *Stranger* and *Autumn Equinox*, the revolutions taking place are in the distance, within the region but outside the still-safe (but fragile) world of Cayuna—reflecting the geopolitical realities of the 1950s where Haiti and the Hispanic Caribbean heaved with social unrest and revolutionary fervor while the Anglophone Caribbean remained stable. The fourth and final Cayuna novel, *Land of the Living*, locates the social instability within Cayuna. Here Hearne again features a white, foreign protagonist, this time the Jewish survivor of World War II Stefan Mahler, now employed as a zoologist at the local university, who through his involvement with the brown-skinned working-class Bernice becomes acquainted with her father, Marcus Heneky, head of the Rastafari-like black church, Sons of Sheba. Heneky, whose philosophies bear a strong resemblance to those of the Jamaican pan-Africanist Marcus Garvey, is, as Garvey was, dismissed by the upper classes as a madman and a troublemaker; but Mahler, himself with a personal history of disenfranchisement and oppression, can relate to Heneky's extremist philosophies of racial segregation and black empowerment. In his view, Heneky is trying to erase "the lie that the black man was faceless," trying "to give the black man the sort of vision of himself that would make him free. And make the whites and browns free, because they were shackled to the lie too. But it wasn't just a matter of giving the black man a vote, . . . or an equal income. . . . There is something else needed. . . . A territory the heart can occupy" (109–110). As Heneky explains to Mahler, "The white man race take mine away from his truth. For the heart of the black man never make the journey with his body" (158). Even the English police superintendent acknowledges that "stories and history that are part of a big pattern don't belong to [black Cayunans]," that they "don't have any legends or history that's [their] own to build on. . . . It's why you get somebody like Heneky" (260).

Yet Heneky is fighting a losing battle. Although Mahler "identifies" with Heneky, it is with "his violent, faithful, wrongheaded witness to the inspiration of an impossible dream" (240). Herein lies the tragedy in this novel. Heneky is doomed to failure, because he threatens the stability of the colonialist society. Years later Hearne would write of Garvey:

> There was a genius and vision of a scope and originality that make him quite unique. His organizing powers were exceptional. . . . But, politically speaking, . . . he was before his time. . . . The executive, the planters, the big merchants—and the Press that spoke for them—feared his unceasing claim for black mass entry into the systems of power and wealth controlled solely by whites. Their careful denigration of his character and motives, with its half-lies, truths and sneers, makes for unpleasant reading even now. . . . The response of the middle-class radicals and emerging nationalists was more ambivalent. They could not, in conscience, deny him their measure of admiration for his brilliant and original assertions of black pride, black self-reliance, black equality. . . . However, [they] could never subscribe to . . . his concept of a "new" Africa. . . . Their ideas on political advancement were, in essence, the products of their readings in the great liberal, socialist and Marxist-Leninist texts of Europe.[31]

So the planter-turned-progressive-politician Andrew Fabricus recognizes that Heneky is "bred by the sort of injustice we've had here for three hundred years" (108), but regards him nevertheless as "a poor old lunatic" full of "back to Africa nonsense" (110).

Heneky's "passionate and accomplished voice [lays] siege to accepted meanings" (203); he upturns the social and political order by dismissing both parties in the established political hierarchy and telling his followers not to vote; he declares that "the white man's vote is a snare and a delusion" (205).

Heneky, it seems, is right to dismiss the two existing political candidates. As the white Cayunan journalist Oliver notes,

> Andrew uses Littleford [the black candidate] as a sort of moral excuse for giving a lot of old prejudices an unconscious airing. You see a chap like Littleford, black, probably illegitimate, aggressive as hell. Everything poor old Andrew was brought up to despise and fear. Then Andrew gets decency like religion: social conscience, colour blindness.... And there is a Littleford on the other side representing everything Andrew has abandoned, all the greed, privilege, corruption and the like. He's almost worse than Andrew's lot used to be. So Andrew pays for everything he doesn't know he hasn't forgotten, deep down, by attacking, justifiably, the sort of man he never thought of except as a servant until he was nearly grown up.... It'll be a good thing when all my generation in Cayuna is dead. All of us. Black, white or brown. We tracked too much of the old dirt in with us. Most of us without knowing it. Worse, pretending that we didn't. This island won't be able to clean house properly until we're all gone. (172)

Hearne offers no hope in this bleak picture of the political landscape. The colonial masters became "carriers of an agreed myth" (251) despite their "terrible treatment" of blacks in the past (259). The myth was so successfully imparted that now blacks like the policeman Cowell or Heneky's brown bartender daughter, Bernice, have bought into it, and discard Heneky's extremism and "African foolishness" (163), wanting instead "progress and order and what a man has to work for and build up" (258). When Mahler accuses Bernice of being a "hopeless bourgeois" (163), her response is "axiomatic": "Is only a fair[-skinned] man and a bought woman can afford to not be respectable in this island" (164). Unlike *Stranger*, where Roy's ideological commitment was presented as brave, true, and ideal, and unlike *Autumn Equinox*, where Jim's ideological commitment was weighed against Nicholas's pragmatism with no clear-cut winner, Hearne's position in *Land* seems to be captured in Mahler's words: "I . . . rested for a few minutes in abstract and unfeasible dreams of freedom" (206). Mahler can afford to rest only for a few minutes in these dreams. And Mahler's last line in the novel is telling: it is hard to explain life, and hard, also, to keep the faith, regenerate—"It's hard to find a beginning sometimes" (280).

Mahler, as outsider and as "exiled Jew,"[32] can see clearly the shortcomings of the colonialist preindependence Cayunan society, and particularly those of the white/near-white elite. Although Hearne's elite Cayunan protagonists display moments of insight, these moments are usually short-lived. In *Land*, Oliver's insightful summary of the political scene does not translate into any significant remedial efforts on his part. Carl's uncle, Hector Slade, in *Stranger* is a reasonable man but will not tolerate disruption of the status quo. Meanwhile, Hector's daughter, Janice, is narrow-minded and racist; so too is Andrew Fabricus's father; indeed, so too, to some extent, is Eleanor in *Autumn Equinox*, who refers to the black Sonny as an "idiot" (12) and "ape" (15). In *Land*, an upper-class woman mentions "the nicest gathering [she has] attended in years. . . . There wasn't a dark face except for the servants" (238).

Hearne, nevertheless, did appear to struggle with a conflict between a romanticized view of the plantocracy and being himself a member of an increasingly radicalized educated middle class.[33] One is tempted to read it as Hearne's own voice when, in *Stranger*, Carl Brandt repeatedly derives comfort from the fact that his lifestyle has been the same for two centuries ("It was an old, handsome room and the heads of the Brandt family had slept in it for two hundred years" [9]; "Two centuries of polish had brought the table to a texture where the cloths looked as if they were floating on black water" [15]); or in *Faces*, when Andrew Fabricus, visiting Brandt's Pen, states:

> To come here was to pass from a world where people did things more or less well, but untidily, and to enter a place that had moved for a long time with a secure, confident rhythm, like the beating of a powerful heart. All sorts of people had told me that places like this were bad. . . . But for me it was one of the places where the life of my country had been cast and carefully nourished. Whatever people had done since then, nobody had been able to make anything so efficient, so beautiful, and so enduring. (147)

Hearne counters this nostalgic sentiment, nevertheless, with Rygin's assertion that Brandt's Pen, however fine, is "dead": "This place is stuck where it was a hundred years ago. If you made it part of a big thing then it would start doing something again. . . . You have to plan big nowadays. You have to add to things and do something new all the time" (*Faces*, 166). For Hearne, both sides of the story are worth presenting. Even the Communist McKenzie in *Stranger* finds comfort in the stability of the Brandts: "[This] is the thing that could really corrupt me. Not the wealth of it . . . [but] the closeness of it that could change me. This incestuous, happy, kindly closeness where . . . everyone fits into his place like a cork into a bottle" (151).

Throughout the Cayuna novels, then, there is a repeated message that life is complicated; issues are not simply black or white but various shades of gray (or brown). In the first Cayuna novel Hearne does promote the value of radical ideological commitment to the extent of the sacrifice of lives for the greater good, as shown in the epigraph "For none of us liveth to himself, / and no man dieth to himself." As his imaginary Cayuna world evolves in subsequent novels, however, Hearne's view of this complexity develops, and he points us unambiguously to this view with his epigraph to *Autumn Equinox*: "Yes, but all the living / Make the mistake of drawing too sharp distinctions." Finally, as the epigraph to *Land* states, "The earth is green where our fathers died—but no greener than where our fathers did not die." Not that Hearne embraces the nihilism of a Peter Conroy; there are issues that are absolutely right, and these are all life-affirming: social justice, honor, bravery, friendship, loyalty, passionate commitment, and love. However, the message is clear: any blinkered, violent radicalism is a misguided waste of lives, and doomed to failure.

After Cayuna

In the mid-1960s Hearne, now living in Jamaica permanently after years of moving between Kingston and London,[34] started work on *The Sure Salvation*. As the decade progressed, work on the novel proceeded slowly. This may or may not have been partially due to the negative criticism condemning his novels as inadequately radical or progressive.[35] Another, probably more critical contributory factor was his increasing political activity in the early 1970s. Hearne, by now a close friend of Michael Manley, was, like much of Jamaica's educated middle class, an enthusiastic supporter of the People's National Party (PNP) when it campaigned in the 1972 general election with its promises of social reform. However, Hearne, again like most in his class, began gradually to demonstrate a disaffection with the radicalism of Manley and his party—a disaffection that turned to outright disillusionment in the mid-1970s when it appeared that a series of violent events in Kingston had been instigated by the PNP. Hearne's exposure of this alleged complicity in his newspaper column caused a permanent rift in his relationship with the PNP and an abrupt end to his personal friendship with Manley.[36]

Given Hearne's high esteem of the values of friendship and loyalty as expressed in his Cayuna novels, this perceived treachery would have been debilitating. Hearne was heartbroken. The eventual publication of *The Sure Salvation* in 1981 did not help significantly; the novel received quiet critical acclaim, but did not succeed in restoring Hearne to the canon of Jamaican literature. Although a radical departure from Hearne's previous works, *Sure Salvation* did not satisfy the criteria of his early critics. Set on a slave ship becalmed in the Atlantic in the early nineteenth century, it was debilitatingly bleak in its outlook: black slaves and white sailors were equally irredeemable; there were no heroes. As Barbara Lalla has noted, *Sure Salvation* demonstrated "points of view other than those that are politically correct."[37]

Sure Salvation, then, expressed a disillusionment with humankind that may have been influenced by Hearne's personal disillusionment. Yet that nadir of disaffection was the logical endpoint of a gradual downward trajectory from idealism that was evident in the evolution of his fiction, from *Voices* through the Cayuna novels. When *Sure Salvation* was released, the Jamaican mainstream middle class had begun to demonstrate a political cynicism, a disaffection with radicalism that had begun in the early 1950s,[38] that plunged again in the mid-1970s when Manley's policies took an extremist turn,[39] and that would have its last breath in the horrific aftermath of the Grenada revolution in 1983.[40] It would take another couple decades, however, before the extent of political cynicism among that group would descend to the level expressed in *Sure Salvation*.[41] Where Hearne's early work explored the politicization and then subsequent deradicalization of the Jamaican middle class, his final work may indeed have predicted the eventual depoliticization of that class.

In 1971 Hearne wrote:

> For nearly ten years I have been trying to discover something to be confident about. This long drought ... has not been caused, I think by a failure of nerve as to what I can do, but by the nature of the engagement between me and the history of our territory.
>
> I had to come back [to Jamaica]. There was that moment when the territory, and the logic of the situation, claimed me and I had to return.
>
> And ever since I have hung on to a hope of relevance that has diminished with every year.[42]

Contrary to Hearne's despondent claim, and contrary to the strident critical voices of the 1960s, Hearne's body of work was relevant from the time it was written, and may be even more relevant today. Hearne's writing reflected the motivations of the class that was, and is still, instrumental in the process and realization of independence. More critically, it described the limitations of that class, and the tensions and complications of Jamaican national realization that actually occurred. Hearne's work, then, offers a new way of thinking about the political dilemmas and search for solutions that Jamaica experienced over his lifetime and continues to experience today. Hearne himself observed, in relation to a biographer of Edna Manley: "He suggests, rather than describes in detail, the mood of those intense, bewildered years before 1938: years which we must understand if we hope to make sense out of what has happened in Jamaica since."[43] If we substitute 1962 for 1938, Hearne's words apply to his first five novels; and, if we substitute a later date, they may extend to his work as a whole.

Notes

This essay is dedicated to the memory of my friend Leeta Hearne. I am grateful to Shivaun Hearne for her sharing of information and insights, which have greatly enhanced my appreciation of her father's life and work.

1. George Lamming, *The Pleasures of Exile* (1960; repr., Ann Arbor: University of Michigan Press, 1992), 45–46.

2. John Hearne, *Voices under the Window* (1955; repr., London: Faber and Faber, 1973); John Hearne, *Stranger at the Gate* (London: Faber and Faber, 1956); John Hearne, *The Faces of Love* (London: Faber and Faber, 1957); John Hearne, *Autumn Equinox* (1959; repr., New York: Vanguard Press, 1961); John Hearne, *Land of the Living* (1961; repr., New York: Harper and Row, 1962). Subsequent references appear parenthetically in the text.

3. Garvey's body was brought from the United States in 1964, in an initiative spearheaded by then minister of development and welfare Edward Seaga.

4. A 1960 study of the Rastafari movement conducted by University of the West Indies (UWI) lecturers led to government-sponsored missions to Ethiopia in 1961 and 1962, which in turn resulted in the official visit of His Imperial Majesty Emperor Haile Selassie I, regarded as the messiah by Rastafari, in 1966. See Roy Augier and Veronica Salter, eds., *Rastafari: The Reports* (Kingston: Caribbean Quarterly, University of the West Indies, 2010).

5. Guyanese UWI lecturer Walter Rodney had been engaging in activities regarded as incendiary by the Jamaican government; as a result, a decision was taken to refuse him entry to the country in October 1968. In response, UWI students led Kingston-wide riots. See, for example, Rupert Lewis, "Jamaican Black Power and Walter Rodney in 1968," *Jamaica Journal* 32, nos. 1–2 (August 2009): 42–49.

6. B. Evan Owen, review of *Stranger at the Gate*, *Oxford Mail*, May 10, 1956.

7. John Davenport, review of *The Faces of Love*, *London Sunday Observer*, April 28, 1957, 13.

8. Edward (Kamau) Brathwaite, review of *Autumn Equinox*, *Bim* 8, no. 31 (July–December 1960): 216.

9. G. R. Coulthard, *Caribbean Literature: An Anthology* (London: University of London Press, 1966), 38.

10. Kenneth Ramchand, *The West Indian Novel and Its Background* (London: Faber and Faber, 1970), 6.

11. Sylvia Wynter, "We Must Learn to Sit Down Together and Talk about a Little Culture: Reflections on West Indian Writing and Criticism," Part 2, *Jamaica Journal* 3, no. 1 (March 1969): 37.

12. Ibid., 39.

13. Hearne's response was published as a letter to the editor in *Jamaica Journal* 3, no. 2 (June 1969): 2. Wynter would probably not have been impressed by Hearne's seemingly neo-colonial affectations: his British accent, his handlebar mustache, and the busha-style Panama hat that he had probably taken to wearing by then. The importance that he attached to a knowledge of classical European culture would presumably have irked her further, as

indicated by her response to his letter on that same page, where she refers to "the fetishism of the super-culture worshippers." The exchange, signifying the conflict in Jamaica between the European culture of the dominant elite and the African culture of the masses, would be explored a decade later by Rex Nettleford in *Caribbean Cultural Identity: The Case of Jamaica* (Kingston: Institute of Jamaica, 1978).

14. It is not only classical music that Wynter gets wrong but the spelling of protagonists' names, and, more important, plot details. For example, as noted by Shivaun Hearne, Wynter, in her critique of *Land of the Living*, "describes Andrew Fabricus's wife, the educated, brown, middle-class Margaret, 'painting Leda raping the swan [*sic*], creating a classical oasis of Art in a society whose suburbs, by their acceptance of privilege, do violence to the slums . . . day after sour day.' By this, Wynter contends that art is the impenetrable preserve of bourgeois Cayuna. Ironically, the work she refers to is a tapestry of the swan raping a black Leda, created by the black Sybil Hyde, a former factory worker, who has, in her own way, done violence to the 'serene' world of middle-class Cayuna through her art and by marrying a white man, Oliver Hyde." Shivaun Hearne, *John Hearne's Life and Fiction: A Critical Biographical Study* (Kingston: Caribbean Quarterly, University of the West Indies, 2013), 56.

15. The mulatto or middle class has been marginalized in much Jamaican/Caribbean fiction and writing as a whole, from Bryan Edwards's early nineteenth-century observations to the contemporary works of Anthony C. Winkler. I discuss this point in greater detail in my book *Out of Order! Anthony Winkler and White West Indian Writing* (Kingston: University of the West Indies Press, 2006).

16. Norman Washington Manley (1893–1969), a leading lawyer in the 1920s, was, along with his trade unionist cousin Alexander Bustamante (1844–1977), an advocate of universal adult suffrage, which was granted to the colony in 1944. Manley was the first leader of the People's National Party (PNP), founded in 1938. Bustamante, originally a member of the PNP, founded the Jamaica Labour Party (JLP) in 1943. Both men led their respective parties until 1967. Bustamante was the colony's first chief minister when the position was created in 1953. Manley served as chief minister from 1955 to 1959, and as premier from 1959 to 1962. As a result of his defeat in a 1961 referendum on the island's participation in the West Indies Federation, Manley called a general election in 1962, which his party lost, as a result of which Bustamante became the country's first prime minister when Jamaica was granted independence in August 1962.

17. Manley's father, son of an English merchant and a slave, was an agricultural businessman; Manley's mother was the daughter of an Irish penkeeper and his mixed-race wife. Bustamante (neé Clarke) was the son of an Irish planter and his mixed-race wife. Manley and Bustamante shared the same grandmother.

18. Michael Manley (1924–1997) became prime minister of Jamaica in 1972 after his party, the PNP, won the general elections, and remained in power until the party's defeat at the polls in 1980. He was again prime minister from 1989 to 1992, when he retired from active politics. Edward Seaga (1930–), son of a Lebanese merchant father and Scottish-Indian-African mother, was leader of the opposition JLP from 1974 until 1980, prime minister from 1980 to 1989, and leader of the opposition until his retirement in 2005.

19. See, for example, Petrine Archer-Straw and Kim Robinson, *Jamaican Art: Then and Now* (Kingston: LMH, 2011). Edna was the wife (and first cousin, through their mothers) of Norman and mother of Michael. Both Norman and Edna were Bustamante's second cousins.

20. Michael Manley, *A Voice at the Workplace: Reflections on Colonialism and the Jamaican Worker* (London: Andre Deutsch, 1975).

21. Sylvia Wynter, "A Tribute to Manley: Moritat for a Lost Leader," *Jamaica Journal* (December 1969): 2.

22. The PNP, led by Norman Manley, in its early years leaned toward Fabian socialism. However, in the early 1950s the party moved toward a more moderate path, as indicated by the expulsion in April 1952 of four radical members of the party known as the "4 H's"—Richard Hart, the brothers Frank and Ken Hill, and Arthur Henry—because of their supposed Communist beliefs. Ten years later newly installed prime minister Alexander Bustamante immediately established his country's foreign policy: "We are with the West." See Holger Henke, "Jamaica's International Relations: Between the West . . . and the Rest," *Jamaica Journal* 34, nos. 1–2 (August 2012): 32–37.

23. The colored man's unbelonging status as portrayed by Hearne is a theme familiar to those conversant with the works of contemporary near-white Jamaican writers such as Michelle Cliff, Honor Ford Smith, and, more recently, Diana McCaulay. See Robinson-Walcott, *Out of Order*.

24. Wynter, "We Must Learn to Sit Down Together," 37.

25. Hearne, *John Hearne's Life and Fiction*, 53.

26. I am grateful to Fragano Ledgister for highlighting, in an informal conversation in June 2012, three moments of Jamaican middle-class radicalization: 1938 (the labor riots), 1968 (the Rodney riots), and 1999 (the gas riots). All three moments saw the emergence of prominent near-white/brown middle-class activists: notably, Bustamante, Manley, and Richard Hart in 1938; Honor Ford-Smith, cofounder of the working women's Sistren Collective, in 1968; and Carolyn Gomes and Susan Lumsden, founders of the human rights group Jamaicans for Justice, in 1999.

27. Theodore Sealy, *Sealy's Caribbean Leaders: A Personal Perspective on Major Political Caribbean Leaders Pre and Post Independence* (Kingston: Kingston Publishers, 1991), 168; Richard Hart, "Federation: An Ill-fated Design," *Jamaica Journal* 25, no. 1 (October 1993): 16.

28. Rachel Manley, *Drumblair: Memories of a Jamaican Childhood* (Kingston: Ian Randle, 1996), 246–247.

29. Ibid., 264.

30. The novel's first-person narrator is the cynical Andrew Fabricus, son of a bigoted former plantocrat, employee, and ex-lover of the mercurial, ruthlessly ambitious mulatto newspaper editor Rachel Ascom, and close friend of Rachel's black lover, the builder/entrepreneur Jojo Rygin. Andrew himself, as the novel casually reveals, is somewhat dishonorable, especially in his treatment of women; those who are, perversely, revealed to have most integrity are the straightforward, hardworking, ambitious, loyal, brave, and curiously naive Jojo and, surprisingly, Rachel herself who, like Roy in *Stranger*, sacrifices her life for a greater cause—this time the life of Michael Lovelace, an English colleague thought to be but the latest in her string of sexual conquests but revealed to be someone she truly loves.

31. John Hearne, introduction to *The Search for Solutions: Selections from the Speeches and Writings of Michael Manley*, ed. John Hearne (Oshawa, Ont.: Maple House Publishing, 1976), 1314.

32. Wynter, "We Must Learn to Sit Down Together," 37.

33. Although Hearne's paternal ancestors were wealthy landowners, his own family was professional, urban middle class: his father was a civil servant, and his mother a secretary. Hearne, *John Hearne's Life and Fiction*, 4.

34. According to his daughter Shivaun, Hearne moved from Jamaica to England in 1952, back to Jamaica in 1956, back to London in 1958, and back to Jamaica in late 1961, when he accepted Norman Manley's invitation to work with the newly formed Jamaica Information Service (JIS). When Manley lost the election a few months later, however, Hearne, through loyalty to Manley, resigned from the JIS. He subsequently accepted a post at the UWI, where he would remain until his death. *Voices, Stranger, Faces*, and *Land* were written in England, while *Autumn Equinox* was started in Jamaica and completed in England. See Hearne, *John Hearne's Life and Fiction*, 40–60.

35. Shivaun Hearne suggests that this probably had little impact on Hearne since he paid scant attention to local critics (email communication, June 28, 2012).

36. Manley responded to Hearne's critical *Gleaner* column with a march to the *Gleaner* offices, during which Hearne's life was threatened. Hearne felt betrayed by his friend (as, indeed, did Manley) and, his wife and daughter have suggested in personal communications, never fully recovered. See Hearne, *John Hearne's Life and Fiction*, 70–74.

37. Barbara Lalla, *Defining Jamaican Fiction: Marronage and the Discourse of Survival* (Tuscaloosa: University of Alabama Press, 1996), 152.

38. Sealy, *Sealy's Caribbean Leaders*; Hart, "Federation."

39. The PNP came to power for the first time since independence after winning the 1972 general elections, strongly supported by the middle class. By the time the party was reelected in 1976, however, it had become much more left-wing in orientation, declaring a policy of democratic socialism and embracing close ties with Cuba, and alienating many from the business and middle classes as a result. The loss of middle-class support contributed significantly to the PNP's defeat in the 1980 general elections.

40. The execution of Maurice Bishop in 1983 shocked the socialist and Communist factions in the region, which had given the Grenada revolution their full support, and effectively killed the left-wing movement in Jamaica and the Anglophone Caribbean.

41. This growing disengagement among the middle class and indeed the population as a whole is perhaps best illustrated by comparing voter turnout figures in general elections in recent decades: in 1980, the turnout was 86.91 percent; in 1989, 78.38 percent; in 2007, 60.40 percent; and in 2011, 53.17 percent. See "Voter Turnout for Jamaica," International Institute for Democracy and Electoral Assistance, http://www.idea.int/vt/countryview .cfm?CountryCode=JM.

42. Hearne, "An Emigre's Journal," May 5, 1971, typescript, 238, as quoted in Hearne, *John Hearne's Life and Fiction*, 65.

43. Hearne, *Search for Solutions*, 19. Hearne was referring to Wayne Brown's biography, *Edna Manley: The Private Years, 1900–1938* (London: Andre Deutsch, 1975).

Part Four

Alternate Geographies

Kingston Calling: Mais's Paris, 1954

FAITH SMITH

"I have a feeling that you are happier, more extended, than you have been for a number of years. It's worth it for that alone. You ought to hang on to France or at least the continent. England becomes less and less a good soil for the artist. Snobbery grows too many weeds here." So wrote John Hearne from London in a March 13, 1954, letter to Roger Mais.[1] After moving to London from Kingston in 1952, Mais moved to Paris in early 1954, and to the south of France from around June to October, at which time he returned to London briefly before traveling to Jamaica at the end of that year. Hearne's suggestion invites us to explore not only what it would mean to locate a Windrush-era novelist in relation to France instead of England but also how a focus on Mais's commitment to painting during that time might alter our view of a period that we tend to think of in terms of *literary* pursuits. My focus on the journalist, painter, short story writer, poet, playwright, and novelist in an anthology devoted to destabilizing the canonical certainties of the period would seem to be counterintuitive. Both the fiery anti-colonial journalism that got him jailed for sedition in 1944 and the portraits of rural and urban Jamaica in novels such as *Brotherman* and *Black Lightning* were hailed as icons of preindependence nationalism. As early as Norman Manley's introduction to the 1966 edition of his novels, Mais was positioned as "one of those we are encouraged to remember through anthologies and critical studies."[2] How could one of the period's major figures possibly take us "beyond Windrush"?

It is Mais, after all, who in George Lamming's famous 1960 indictment serves as the poignant and damning proof that the Caribbean's "dense and grinning atmosphere" in the 1950s forces its writers to leave or kills them.[3] Since Mais left *and* returned, dying shortly afterward, he tragically justified Lamming's accusation. "You had the feeling of a man who was in a hurry, as though he felt that he was near the end of something," Lamming has said more recently.[4] Certainly a sort of feverish intensity marks Mais's life and work, particularly in those final three years of his life. Having abandoned the United States as a viable market for his short fiction some time earlier, Mais accepted the advice of Hearne and other writers to join them in London.[5] To raise money for his impending departure, he exhibited his paintings at the

Junior Institute on East Street in Kingston, and then boarded the *Reina del Pacifico* for England in August 1952. He already had a contract with Jonathan Cape to publish *The Hills Were Joyful Together*, and he also had with him the completed manuscript of *Brotherman*, written, according to Hearne, in an intense and rainy two-week period in late 1951.[6] In London, he oversaw the publication of *Hills*, unsuccessfully tried to place his fiction with the BBC and in popular magazines, and, crucially, painted. Deciding that Paris would be a more hospitable city for painting and for exhibiting his work, he moved there in January 1954. There he proofread the now canonical national novel *Brotherman*, worked on a new novel, and produced dozens of canvases. By the time he returned to Jamaica by way of London in the last week of 1954, he was still trying to work feverishly. The Institute of Jamaica held an exhibition of his French paintings in April 1955, but Mais missed the opening because of illness and succumbed to cancer in June.

"What I have never quite worked out with him," Lamming muses, "was the *exceptionalism* of him, coming out of that background. At what point did he make that kind of break away from the world [he came from] and make the very genuine identification with that other world?"[7] Lamming refers, for example, to Mais's interaction with Rastafarian communities in the decidedly nonrespectable world of August Town, St. Andrew.[8] Certainly Mais's personal and professional renunciations of social and colonial allegiances, and the social worlds traced out in his fiction and nonfiction, constituted a divergence from and critique of the respectable and relatively privileged world of Liguanea, St. Andrew, where his family resided.[9] A *break within* the colony is alluded to here, as Mais crosses worlds within Jamaica, necessitated by "that lonely desert of mass indifference, and educated mass treachery" of which Lamming speaks in *The Pleasures of Exile*, and which justifies the *break away* from these societies altogether, toward the exile of London.[10]

But if Lamming's representation of the writer vis-à-vis Caribbean colonial society is true, then it is not the only truth, I want to suggest here. In Mais's letters to his mother and sister in particular, we may discern his Jamaican family and colleagues' investment in him as a prestigious and hard-working writer who was producing the representative fiction of his generation—though, for his family, he was also a beloved, disappointing, indebted, and not-yet-famous son and brother. For his own part, Mais is seen to be conflicted about being recognized as a distinguished writer rather than a down-to-earth manual laborer, or about competing for patronage and being seen to be doing so. We see him reassuring others that he is working hard and that he is not being distracted by sensual pleasures. Even if such reassurances are precisely the terrible cost of living in the conservative, philistine Caribbean that Lamming describes, the emotional ties that are reflected in Mais's letters are not disabling, or are not *only* disabling. In what follows I want to trace the extent to which Mais's time in France, as revealed in his correspondence, indicates a *continuity with* rather than a "break away from" the respectable middle-class subject who was the son, brother, uncle, and friend pulled emotionally—and not always unwillingly—toward the Caribbean.

Letters moving back and forth between Jamaica and France or Jamaica and Canada, where his sister resided, keep multiple locations in view simultaneously but also multiple circuits of travel, rather than the unidirectional trajectory that Caribbean writers' migration to Europe sometimes suggests. We can think about potential travelers of that era in relation to a Caribbean they have already left, have not yet left, or will never leave, or to which, like Mais, they are shortly to return. Sylvia Wynter helps us to keep multiple locations in mind when she traces a dialectical relationship between those who leave the Caribbean to write fiction during this period and those who enter the region to assess this fiction. She comments on the fact that Louis James, an English scholar teaching at the University of the West Indies, edited *The Islands In Between*, an early and influential collection of critical essays on Anglophone Caribbean literature that appeared in 1968. Wynter excoriates his "objective" discussion of the inevitability of exile for Caribbean writers in London and of their intellectual debt to England. As she sees it, James chooses to ignore the fact that colonial economic and political arrangements thus profited England as they made the Caribbean less profitable: "The writer wanting market and audience had to go to England; as the West Indian emigrant wanting a living wage had to go to England. As the West Indian University wanting skilled personnel had to turn to England. The presence of Louis James in the Caribbean and the absence of the writer in London are part of the same historical process."[11]

Speaking of his own travels, Lamming also helps us to keep multiple locations in a dialectical relationship with each other when he recalls that he and others expected Vic Reid to join them in London: "'What happened? I mean we were expecting you.' And then he told me the story. . . .' My last daughter was finishing off at school and I just didn't know how I would make it with two or three children. And I panicked.'"[12] This perfectly reasonable decision to stay produces anxiety on behalf of someone who is perceived of as being prevented by parental responsibilities from taking his rightful place as a writer with a vocation. We might think here about their traveling female partners who allayed anxiety because they typed the manuscripts and earned the wages that allowed Caribbean men in Europe to transform themselves from "aspiring" to "published" writers, even as Windrush fictions such as

Samuel Selvon's *The Lonely Londoners* represented Caribbean women as cur-
tailing the freedom of the single male migrant. We might think also about
single traveling women who might well have been perceived of as abandon-
ing domestic duties in the Caribbean, or whose perceived erotic autonomy
caused anxiety in their new location.[13] To chart multiple trajectories is to situate the period's figures in a matrix of journeys, opportunities, and desires that
may or may not be connected to each other, and that may exceed or bypass
altogether the route between the Caribbean and England. We could locate
Windrush-era figures solely in the Caribbean in a period of British-bound
migration; in multiple "Europes," as when Gautam Premnath discusses Selvon's fictional Londoners in relation to the Paris-based journalism of Sen-
egalese writer Sembene Ousmane; or traveling *to* rather than away from the
Caribbean, as James does in Wynter's discussion.[14] This is the period, after all,
in which South African writer Peter Abrahams took Norman Manley up on
his invitation to visit Jamaica and possibly write a book about it; Abrahams
went to Jamaica from Europe in 1955 and has never left.[15]

Mais's time in France allows us to keep in view the continuing claims and
sustenance of the family as he writes letters and receives letters, money, and
packages of food from them. Thinking about him there also allows us to
position an Anglophone Caribbean writer in relation to an imperial center
that is not "his," and that arguably may not be as fraught as we would expect
London to be for a British colonial subject. In addition, in considering Mais
in France, his declaration to his family, "I know I have a big talent for painting—although this fact is not recognized in Jamaica" (RM to M, February 3,
1954), points us to his desire to think of himself primarily as a painter, at least
for a few months, and we can consider how this desire brings him a kind of
freedom, even as it generates anxiety.

My Painting Is as Important to Me as My Writing

On February 25, 1954, Mais had a triumphant vernissage, the opening of an
exhibition of his paintings at the Galerie Zublema at 1, rue Paul-Cézanne. In
attendance were Richard Wright, André Breton, and other members of the
literary and artistic community. A photographer from *Ebony* magazine took
a lot of pictures, Mais told his family. A review published in *Le Monde* on
March 5, 1954, assessed his show and other exhibits of landscapes around the
city: Mais, "Jamaïquain . . . reste sympathique tant qu'il ne s'aventure pas hors
de l'exotisme," which could be rendered as, his work is pleasant enough as
long as it does not venture beyond, or as long as it remains within, an exotic

framework. The exhibition was up until March 17. That *Ebony* appears not to have devoted any space to the event or that the exhibition did not lead to a significant demand for his work is less a reflection on Mais than an indication of the tremendous odds. He had only just arrived in Paris in early January. He had already moved from one hotel to another to cut his living expenses, with his paintings in storage at the train station. That he managed to show his work so quickly and attract the attention of such prominent persons was the result of a delicate dance of begging for loans from his family, and, in Paris, pursuing leads, angling for gallery space, and seeking patronage. In his letters we may discern excitement about actual and potential opportunities, concern about appearing overeager, and desperation.

Richard Wright, the American novelist, was a prominent member of the Parisian literary and philosophical scene. The short fiction of Wright and Mais had appeared in the first issue of a radical Chicago-based journal a decade earlier.[16] In 1953 Wright wrote the introduction to the US edition of Lamming's *In the Castle of My Skin*, noting that Lamming's story was both "his own" and "the story of millions of simple folk . . . sprawled over the world's surface. I too, have been crying these stern tidings, and, when I catch the echo of yet another voice declaiming in alien accents a description of this same reality I react with pride and excitement."[17] It seems reasonable to assume that Mais thought that Wright could be similarly useful to him, though Lamming's relationship to the Parisian literary scene was by no means mediated by Wright: later in 1954, in fact, segments of *Castle* would be serialized in Jean-Paul Sartre's journal *Les Temps Modernes*.[18] Mais told his mother about going to lunch at the home of Richard and Ellen Wright, noting that Richard was valuable to have as a friend since his name opened doors (RM to M, February 7, 1954). Richard talked to him that evening about his recent trip to West Africa. As in other letters from France, Mais described his pleasurable interactions with children, in this case with the Wrights' young daughters. Mais told his family that their apartment walls were covered with paintings and that he hoped Richard would purchase one of his, though he would not ask him to do so.

But if it was Richard Wright who was the celebrity, Mais's visit to their home was equally significant because of Ellen Wright. It was she who negotiated the family's comfort in Europe: the children's schooling, maintenance of an apartment through which many visitors filed, and, perhaps predictably, typing her husband's manuscripts. "Sometimes I think the typewriter was invented to turn quite nice women into weary slaves," Dorothy Padmore, wife of George Padmore, commiserated with her in a letter in June 1953.[19] But Ellen Wright was also a literary agent, representing Simone de Beauvoir's books in the United States and "placing French manuscripts with American houses."[20] Mais's friend Max Schwermer, an American writer who had facilitated his contact with a US publishing agent years earlier and had continued to give him advice about his career, had put him in touch with Ellen Wright. Schwermer asks in a February 17, 1954, letter to Mais: "Did she [Ellen Wright] say anything about my book?" Not just the husband, but the wife might advance his writing career as well, not to mention his friend's. Painting and writing, then, were not necessarily cleanly separable spheres.

Mais's letter to his mother stresses that Richard Wright was charming and friendly, and that while Ellen Wright was as well, he preferred Richard, who was more "large-hearted and warm." The lunch of tender veal was one of the two best meals he had enjoyed since leaving Jamaica; the other had been with a beautiful and talented artist in London of whom he was fond, but only as a friend. I find these epistolary emphases fascinating: the folding of Jamaica into a meditation on pleasurable consumption in Europe; the connection between a white female dinner companion in Paris, and another in London, also possibly white; the clarification (apologetic? defensive? taunting?) of a friendship as platonic and thus not sexual. When it is further considered that Richard had been annoyed by the rapport between Lamming and Ellen when they met the year before, it seems reasonable to wonder if Mais thought that there were sexual undertones swirling around the apartment and if this made an occasion already burdened by considerations of patronage additionally fraught. These complex considerations likely framed his narration of the evening to his mother.[21] We might see the son's comments as reassuring or as defiant, in relation to maternal concerns about a sexually circumspect life suggested by his statements in other letters: he was not "running wild," he assured her just after his arrival in Paris (RM to M, January 13, 1954), and he did not think of Paris as "sinful" or "a cesspool of sin with me being drawn down into the vortex" (RM to M, February 3, 1954).

Ellen Wright seems to have introduced Mais to Madeleine Rousseau, who had just published a book on the history of art and was "interested in Negro Art especially" (RM to JT, January 21, 1954). Rousseau seems to have put him in touch with first one gallery that expressed interest in exhibiting his work and then, when that fell through, with Galerie Zublema. Through Zublema he would meet other dealers who would introduce him to yet others, some of whom took some of his paintings to sell in their galleries. He told his sister of taking paintings to Rousseau's place once when she had five guests who talked about his work as if he were not there: "I am glad that I didn't understand them" (RM to JT, January 29, 1954), perhaps suggesting a discomfort about being scrutinized as an exotic specimen alongside his paintings, by experts in "Negro art."

No matter how influential or helpful his actual or potential sponsors in Paris were, however, it was the financial support of Mais's family in Jamaica and Canada that enabled him to subsist, albeit frugally, and to give the gallery the required funding to mount his exhibition. He told his sister insistently that this was his big chance and that he was trying to find a gallery but that it would cost money. "I must have help. . . . Say, 70 [pounds] at the very least" (RM to JT, January 21, 1954). He did not know where she would get it, but when she did, she was to cable it to Barclays in London. A February 29 letter thanks her for sending the money. Mais's letters to his family are weighted by a sense of debt to them, as well as by the hunger, cold, and labor that justified his need and their support. He thanks "the old man" for raising the loan and tells his mother that he will pay him back with book royalties if the paintings do not bring in revenue. Though he is in Paris, he is "still serious" about his writing and his relationship with Jonathan Cape: "One must go forward, you can't stand still. I must grasp every opportunity, and make the best of every opportunity as it presents itself" (RM to M, February 3, 1954). There seems to be a concession here that any worries they have that his painting is undermining his writing are reasonable, but that his painting will, in effect, be underwritten by income from his writing. A few months later he was urging his mother not to worry about *Brotherman* since he had prepared the proofs and publication was scheduled for June (RM to M, April 5, 1954). He had looked thoroughly into publishing his short stories in England and the United States, but there was absolutely no market for them. He had also, he said, placed three of his watercolors in galleries.

These letters show both Mais and his family to be demanding and anxious. On the one hand: do you appreciate that I am working hard under difficult circumstances? On the other: what do we get in return for our investment in you, particularly when you up the ante by compromising your writing, and in a "foreign" country, to boot? It could not have helped matters when he told his mother that with the warmer weather he was painting watercolor sketches outdoors for tourists, and that a friend had lived off the sales of such sketches for years, or later, that he was moving to the southeast of France. From around mid-June he left Paris to live in a farmhouse near Provence made available to him by an Australian friend, Roy Delgarno. John Hearne and Isaac "Zack" Matalon, a Jamaican actor, his housemates in London, joined him there, until both left him to go to Paris around early October. Mais reported to his family that they were living cheaply in a beautiful old village where the children liked them and that he was doing lovely paintings in the countryside and planning to begin working on a new book. He insisted that he was *"painting"* not *"farming"* (RM to M, July 23, 1954).

This insistence could mean that he sensed that his family thought that farming undermined his prestige as a writer, or that it signified a reduced commitment to his writing. Perhaps his family was at the receiving end of taunts about their son and brother's seriousness about his work. Daphne Morris notes that years earlier, in 1946–1947, Mais had left Kingston to go to the country to farm, frustrated with his writing career.[22] In late 1949 he again took a break from his writing to go to the country and stay with friends. His mother told him that he had rested enough and that he should come back and send his stories to the BBC, since he was not getting any younger. Perhaps these memories now overshadowed mother and son, as he sought to reassure or chide her, and she sought to ensure that he measured up to what she considered to be his primary identity as a writer. From France, he informed her that on her advice he had sent O. T. Fairclough (the editor of the *Jamaica Times*) copies of *Brotherman*; he instructed her to tell Fairclough that the novel was at the top of publisher Jonathan Cape's July list of success-ful novels (RM to M, August 25, 1954). A September 20 letter explained that his letter writing had lapsed because he was "deep" in the novel he was writ-ing. He also encouraged her not to worry about nasty comments that people were making about *Brotherman*, since "the best and biggest people are on my side—the people with the largest perceptions." He hoped that she was on his side too. And, as with all his letters, he apologized that he could not repay his loan just yet.

Here, then, we see that his writing did not diminish his sense that he had to appease his family, but at least it stood for an "authentic" vocation. His resolve to devote time to painting never seems to have supplanted his writing either as a constant concern and activity as he tried to keep up with the demands of his publisher, or as a perceived or actual concern of Jamaican family and colleagues that he felt he had to address. Since painting rather than *farming* also emerges here as an additional concern to painting rather than writing, it is interesting to think about an allusion to manual labor the previous year in a summer 1953 issue of the *Times British Colonies Review*, which featured Mais and Lamming as two major writers working in London who had just had books published in London.[23] According to the article, Lamming said that he worked in factories doing heavy manual labor after arriving in London and found it fascinating at first, then dull: "I could not do it again, not so long as I live." (His biographical description in *Les Temps Modernes* a year later noted that "after working in various factories," he reviewed books for the BBC.)

Mais, it was reported, "would prefer heavy manual labour to anything else," if he were to earn a living other than by painting and writing. The fashioning of the successful migrant writer's labor as intellectual *or* manual, or intellectual *and* manual, is interesting. Did manual labor enhance or undermine the prestige of a "serious" writer? Were both writers self-conscious about the extent to which their careers diverged from the majority of their migrating compatriots, whose labor in English cities was anonymous, unheralded, and even vilified? Were they anxious to connect themselves to such labor? Does Lamming's resolve, born out of actual familiarity with factory work, make Mais's stated preference seem naive or disingenuous, or could we interpret Mais's inclination as being shaped by a pleasurable relationship to working in the soil?

The news that he was going to leave Paris for the country must have been a surprise, since despite the hunger, cold, and struggle to sell his work that are so evident in his letters, it was obvious that Paris was very liberating for him. Ironically, shortly after first arriving in London in 1952 Mais had written to tell his mother that it was "really wonderful" in London: "You feel you are in the heart of things. I don't remember being in command of so much bouncing energy for a long time."[24] His letters from France make clear his hunger and desperation with his circumstances there, as well as his frustration with his family. They also show the pain of separation from them, the tenderness of sentiments for packages given and received, the family member eager to share his pleasurable experiences and respond to news from home. He expresses sorrow about his father's eyesight, happiness that a nephew is engaged, thanks for a moist Christmas pudding even though it was expensive to pay the duties to collect the package, pleasure at gathering wild blackberries in the country, and the anticipation of his family's fruit trees bearing fruit when he returned. His letters are full not just of allusions to life back home but also of attempts to make his experiences in France palpable to his readers with explicit comparisons to Jamaica. Thus Paris's boulevards are longer than Spanish Town Road, and four to six times wider than King Street, or the south of France is not unlike St. Elizabeth, and the town of Montclimer, where he appears to have had another exhibition, is like Brown's Town or St. Ann's Bay. People went out of their way to help strangers, he noted of Paris. The children "sometimes come right up to you and say 'Bonjour' and shake your hands! Some have grubby hands but you can't resist them" (RM to M, May 22, 1954). He recounts an incident at a street intersection when he is approached by a little girl who grasps his hand, crosses the street with him "with the utmost confidence," and finally lets go of his hand when she gets to her gate, where Mais tells her "Au revoir" and she gives him a "small, mischievous smile" (RM to M, February 3, 1954).

It is almost too obvious to contrast this anecdote with Fanon's *Black Skin, White Masks*, in which a similar encounter with a small child in a Parisian public space is the scene of the black person's unmaking: "'Look, a Negro! Maman, a Negro!' . . . . My body was returned to me spread-eagled, disjointed, redone, draped in mourning on this white winter's day."[25] Simultaneously hounded out of and trapped inside of his skin, the splayed black subject's deformation is pivotal to the child's formation as a white subject. Mais does not say that the child is white, but presumably he would have indicated if it were otherwise. Mais's features, lighter-skinned than Fanon's (or those of the composite narrative personae of *Black Skin, White Masks*), could arguably have marked him as North African, and thus subject to the traumatic gaze theorized in *Black Skin, White Masks*, or the child may have assumed that he was white, or been untroubled by his looks either way. A critical element of Fanon's account is missing in Mais's anecdote: the child's mother and the onlookers on the street or on the train—that is, the adults who, in effect, preside over the white child's inauguration into racialized seeing. From the evidence of his letters home, at least, Mais is much more rattled by his family's perceptions of him. In a February 3 letter, he begs his mother not to talk about never meeting him on earth again; did either of them believe that they would never meet again, or was she trying to make him feel guilty? In a letter announcing that he had just signed a contract with Cape for another novel, he chided her for thinking that he did not believe in God and his goodness, or that her advice was stupid; he might not always *follow* her advice, "But who ever does?" (RM to M, October 29, 1954).

A November 5 letter is gentle, apologetic, and also poignantly retrospective. He said he was typing it because he knew it would be easier to read. He had always admired his parents' handwriting, he said, and hers in particular put him to shame, since it was the writing of a gentle old lady at peace with life. But now her spelling was shaky: "You who were such a stickler. . . . Now I feel less at a disadvantage." While he said that he hoped that this was making her laugh, is it also possible to hear a spiteful son whose grammar was always being corrected? Poignantly, he said that he imagined her reading to his father because of his poor eyesight, and that it made him wish that he had been successful sooner. He said he thought of her reading aloud the "lurid passages—especially those about love" from *Brotherman* to his father. He would have to "do something about that" when he next wrote, he said—perhaps implying that he felt guilty about what he had written? Daphne Morris refers to an August 1952 letter in which he had begged his mother to read the advanced copy of *The Hills Were Joyful Together* without judgment: "I wish I could see your face after you have read it. I can just see you trying to tell me that these things are not pleasing to God."[26]

These letters, placed beside his novels, suggest that it was the gaze and desires of the other in the streets and homes of Jamaica, rather than in Paris or London, that remained the most unnerving and compelling for Mais. Since otherness and the gaze were being explicitly theorized in Paris at this historical period, we have a potentially fascinating lens through which to think about Mais. His *proximity* to these existential discussions as they are being worked out in Paris usefully dislodges any inclination toward an English-only perspective of his time in Europe, even as, on my reading of his letters at least, he is not necessarily invested in such discussions. This is the historical moment when Ralph Ellison's *Invisible Man* explored African Americans' relationship to US democracy and citizenship in terms of recognition, or rather a willed blindness, wherein blackness was at once invisible and critical to the capacity of whiteness to be discernible, solid, powerful, and benevolent. In Paris, writers associated with Negritude theorized the material and ideological violence of white supremacy by fashioning an alternative universalism. Could there be a *black* subjectivity in a nonracist future? Could blackness be *universal*, just as an unmarked universal was white by default?[27]

In response, Sartre, invoking the proletariat's objective consciousness of capitalist oppression, compared this to black people's subjective consciousness of racism; Negritude was a sort of dialectical interlude, a necessary but necessarily transient and negative step in the achievement of an affirmative, nonracial, and "universal" humanism.[28] Both Simone de Beauvoir and Fanon posited that a *particular* rather than a universal body experienced freedom— or, more poignantly, the experience of racist or patriarchal oppression—and did so not only at the level of historical consciousness and subjectivity but also of the *body* itself.[29] For Fanon, Sartre's response to the Negritude poets both confirmed his own reservations about the romanticism of some Negritude writers and blithely reduced to an abstraction the particularity of black subjectivity. Shaped by colonialism and racism, the white gaze reveals to the black interlocutor a blackness that is negative, shameful, and disabling. In his own contributions to the period's theorization of the gaze, Lamming addressed the Congress of Negro Writers and Artists held in Paris in September 1956 on the fact of "the Negro" "encounter[ing] himself in a state of surprise and embarrassment" because of "the regard of the Other."[30] Recently he has further discussed the challenge of figuring out how to "colonize that awareness," of wresting sovereignty at the scene of the gaze, in the process of reconstituting the self.[31] Lamming and Orlando Patterson have named French existentialism as key to their intellectual formation in the 1950s and 1960s, and we may thus see their evocations of rural and urban Barbados and urban Jamaica as having this partial provenance.[32]

The review of Mais's Paris exhibition in terms of exoticism is an indication of the extent to which "the regard of the Other" rendered creative work by black artists recognizable and desirable or predictable and profitable as "Negro Art." Mais's *fiction* was also viewed as exotic. For instance, a *Manchester Guardian* review of *Brotherman*, shortly after its publication, declared it to be a predictable example of "Negro novels, even if they are set in Jamaica instead of Harlem."[33] Reviewers in Jamaica adjudged the French paintings "remarkable" (Edna Manley), which might be another way of saying that his work was pleasurably exotic because the subject matter, which included scenes of Paris, was not predictable in the context of Jamaica: Harry Milner liked the departure from Mais's earlier fascination with "Modigliani [and] African sculpture."[34] An April 20, 1955, notice on page 14 of the *Jamaica Daily Gleaner*, "Roger Mais Exhibition," has a photograph of Edna Manley attending the event, and notes that while Mais was too ill to attend, he was represented by Albert Huie. This notice and the Milner and Manley reviews refer to seventy paintings consisting of eight oils, including *The Accompanist* and *Madonna*; two pastels; and "the most remarkable watercolours produced in this country for a very long time," according to Edna Manley, who categorizes the watercolors into three groups: buildings, "atmospheric naturalism," and a third group marked by "explosions of color." The subjects of the paintings include Montmartre, the River Seine, Notre Dame, and two nudes.[35]

This description and the Jamaican responses suggest that his paintings are unconnected stylistically to the twelve illustrations with captions consisting of phrases from the novel and the uncaptioned frontispiece that constitute his illustrations for *Brotherman*. But if this is the case, of course, we would have to conclude that his time in France makes no difference to the way we read his novels—that the *site* of composition or proofreading is insignificant. Mais's letters to his family, however, suggest that his experiences in England and particularly in France did influence his work and raise the question: how would such "difference" or "influence" be quantified? I wonder if it might not alter our reading of both novels' portrayal of the commitment to truth in art or healing in the face of small-mindedness or betrayal when we consider that he prepared the final edition of *Brotherman* in Paris or was writing what would appear to be the initial drafts of *Black Lightning* in the south of France. I have argued elsewhere that it is productive to read *Brotherman* in terms of a deep ambivalence about sexual energy, as the depiction of a leader who, acutely conscious of others' expectations, invests in an asceticism meant to be disciplined and restorative, even if others interpret it as masculine abnegation and failure.[36] If Brotherman is trying to figure out if sensuality will drag him down, my interpretation of some of Mais's responses to his mother's letters is that his creator is as well.

In Mais's own life, the claims of the Caribbean and European Others are equally unsettling, and require him to prove his artistic distinction or his masculinity. His experience as a colonial Jamaican, *in Jamaica*, anticipates existentialist ideas being worked out in Europe: the consciousness of the other's look that makes an "other" of the self, a look that both frees and harms, requiring mutual submission and recognition in the process of confronting alienation and pursuing freedom, is an essential element of his life well before he sails for Europe.

The claim here is not that Mais's year in France accounts for these themes in his work, but that his time there certainly provides an important lens for thinking about his novels, which have tended to be discussed in terms of Jamaica or a Jamaica/England axis. We can position his life and work in relation to a historical period and geographical location marked by an explicit theorization of the gaze and the claims of the other. The letters written during his time in France press us to consider the continuing claims of the family on the migrant, beyond, say, nostalgia or moral and intellectual constriction. Women in particular turn out to be foundational to the artist's cultural achievements. The much-vaunted *break* required to escape the noose of the middle-class family and usher in the authentic folk turns out be somewhat romantic: an excision required, perhaps, for the ideal of the brilliant, autonomous writer. Mais's family certainly continues to exert a claim that is both generative and traumatic. One way in which this claim is apparent is in the debilitating regard of the other that is seen as so key in existential terms to the making of the self. Caribbean streets and homes generate the look that is usually discussed only in terms of the racialized gaze in the metropolitan city: *Look, a Negro! Maman, a Negro!* Similarly, locations such as Kingston are the source rather than the destination of the remittance, in today's terminology. As we have seen, Mais's family members are aesthetic interlocutors, key financial patrons, mediators with Caribbean-based power brokers, as well as loving and infuriating sources of sustenance.

Notes

1. Hearne to Mais, March 13, 1954, Roger Mais Papers, the Special Collections of the West Indies Collection, UWI Library, Mona, Jamaica. Further references to Mais's letters will be in the text, with the recipients sometimes identified with the following abbreviations: "M" for his mother, Mrs. E. C. Mais; "JT" for his sister, Mrs. Jesse Taylor; "S" for Max Schwermer; "RM" for Roger Mais. My major sources throughout this essay are the Roger Mais Papers, and Daphne Morris's wonderfully meticulous study, "Roger Mais: The Evolution of a Novelist" (Ph.D. diss., University of the West Indies, Mona, 1987). I am grateful for the assistance of Frances Salmon of Special Collections.

2. Norman W. Manley, introduction to *The Three Novels of Roger Mais* (London: Jonathan Cape, 1966); Alison Donnell, *Twentieth-Century Caribbean Literature: Critical Moments in Anglophone Literary and Critical History* (London: Routledge, 2006), 50.

3. George Lamming, *The Pleasures of Exile* ((1960; repr., Ann Arbor: University of Michigan Press, 1992), 42.

4. David Scott, "The Sovereignty of the Imagination: An Interview with George Lamming," *Small Axe* 12, no. 3 (September 2002): 118.

5. For a detailed account of his interaction with US agents and editors, and of writers who served as models for his short fiction, see Morris, "Roger Mais," 5.

6. See John Hearne, "Roger Mais: A Personal Memoir," *Bim* 6, no. 23 (December 1955): 143; Fred Wilmot, "One Man's Opinion," *Public Opinion* (July 26, 1952): 4; Roger Mais, "Why I Love and Leave Jamaica," *Public Opinion Roger Mais Supplement* (June 10, 1966): 7.

7. Scott, "Sovereignty of the Imagination," 118, 119.

8. Ibid., 119.

9. Jean D'Costa, "Roger Mais's Jamaica: 11 August 1905–15 June 1955," *Jamaica Journal* 29, no. 3 (2006): 6–13.

10. Lamming, *Pleasures of Exile*, 41. Rob Nixon and Belinda Edmondson tease out the nuances of "exile," "expatriate," and "immigrant" in relation to Caribbean writers in the 1950s and 1960s. See Rob Nixon, *London Calling: V. S. Naipaul, Colonial Mandarin* (New York: Oxford University Press, 1992); and Belinda Edmondson, *Making Men: Gender, Literary Authority, and Women's Writing in Caribbean Narrative* (Durham, N.C.: Duke University Press, 1999).

11. Sylvia Wynter, "Reflections on West Indian Writing and Criticism: Part 1," *Jamaica Journal* 11 (December 1968): 26.

12. Scott, "Sovereignty of the Imagination," 101.

13. See Carol Tulloch's discussion of photographs of older women and women with children, and of single women, in the English media's coverage of West Indian migrants to London in the 1950s. Carol Tulloch, "Strawberries and Cream: Dress, Migration and the Quintessence of Englishness," in *The Englishness of English Dress*, ed. Christopher Breward, Becky Conekin, and Caroline Cox (Oxford: Berg, 2002), 61–76. See also Donette Francis's discussion of one such female migrant, Joyce Gladwell, in this volume.

14. Gautam Premnath, "*The Lonely Londoners* and Its Readers" (paper presented at the Modern Language Association Convention, Los Angeles, January 8, 2011).

15. Annie Paul, "Once There Were Humans [interview with Peter Abrahams]," *Chronic Books: Chimurenga Chronicle Review of Books* (May 18–24, 2008): 38–41.

16. The May 1944 issue of *Negro Story*, edited by Alice C. Browning and Fern Gayden, includes Wright's "Almos' a Man," and Mais's "World's End." See Bill Mullen, "Popular Fronts: 'Negro Story' Magazine and the African American Literary Response to World War II," *African American Review* 30, no. 1 (Spring 1996): 10.

17. Michel Fabre, *The Unfinished Quest of Richard Wright*, trans. Isabel Barzun (1973; repr., Urbana: University of Illinois Press, 1993), 219–220; George Lamming, *In the Castle of My Skin* (1953; repr., Ann Arbor: University of Michigan Press, 1991), ix–x.

18. See *Les Temps Modernes* 9, no. 100 (March 1954): 1575–1609; 9, no. 101 (April 1954): 1820–1866; 9, no. 102 (May 1954): 2007–2045. The final installment appeared in 9, no. 103 (June 1954): 2154–2193, an issue that included a translation of Faulkner's *Mississippi*. The translations of *Castle* are entitled "Les îles fortunées" and are by Colette Audry and Henriette Etienne.

19. Hazel Rowley, *Richard Wright: The Life and Times* (New York: Henry Holt, 2001), 415.

20. Fabre, *Unfinished Quest*, 383.

21. Rowley, *Richard Wright*, 478–479, 584 n.40.

22. Morris, "Roger Mais," 32–40.

23. That is, *The Hills Were Joyful Together* and *In the Castle of My Skin*, respectively. The article is on page 32 of the issue; a clipping of the article is in Mais's papers.

24. October 28, 1952, quoted in Morris, "Roger Mais," 50.

25. Frantz Fanon, *Black Skin, White Masks*, trans. Richard Philcox (1950; repr., New York: Grove Press, 2008), 93.

26. Morris, "Roger Mais," 53.

27. On this and the following two paragraphs, see Fanon, *Black Skin, White Masks*; George Lamming, "The Negro Writer and His World," in *Conversations: Essays, Addresses, and Interviews, 1953–90*, ed. A. Andaiye and Richard Drayton (London: Karia Press, 1992), 36–45; Toril Moi, *Simone Beauvoir: The Making of an Intellectual Woman* (London: Blackwell, 1994), 204–213; David Macey, *Frantz Fanon: A Life* (London: Granta Books, 2000), 154–198; and Jean-Paul Sartre, "Black Orpheus," in *"What Is Literature?" And Other Essays*, trans. John McCombie (Cambridge, Mass.: Harvard University Press, 1988), 291–330.

28. Sartre, "Black Orpheus," 294.

29. See Moi, *Simone Beauvoir*, for a discussion of this aspect of Beauvoir's thought.

30. Lamming, "Negro Writer and His World," 36–45.

31. Scott, "Sovereignty of the Imagination," 121–122.

32. Ibid., 119, 127–128; Orlando Patterson in conversation with David Scott, Caribbean Epistemologies Seminar, CUNY Graduate School, May 4, 2012.

33. The review is dated June 15, 1954, and is a clipping in Mais's papers.

34. Edna Manley, "Pictures by Roger Mais," *Daily Gleaner*, April 28, 1955, 8; Harry Milner, "A Success and a Revelation," *Daily Gleaner*, April 22, 1955.

35. Manley, "Pictures by Roger Mais."

36. Faith Smith, "*Brotherman's* Ascetism," *Caribbean Quarterly* 59, no. 2 (2013): 10–24.

Marie Chauvet and the Writer's Exile from the Postcolonial Public Sphere

RAPHAEL DALLEO

The story often told in Anglophone Caribbean studies about the 1950s and 1960s generation—that the writers were mostly men, that they wrote from outside the region, and that their work was the origin of true Caribbean literature—does not hold up when viewed in regional perspective. Seen in this broader context, the 1950s and 1960s are still pivotal years in the history of Caribbean writing; however, these years appear more conflicted and their legacy contradictory when we look past the Anglophone Windrush writers. Marie Chauvet, as a female novelist who wrote from her native Haiti throughout the 1950s and 1960s, seems the biographical antithesis of the group of male writers who wrote from exile in London. Yet her writing contains significant parallels to the work of her Anglophone contemporaries. Exploring the ways her work connects to that of the Windrush writers places the generation into a broader regional context. In the process, Windrush tropes like exile can be understood not just as a literal movement into the metropole or a transcendental metaphor for colonial Caribbean reality, but as a writerly response to changes in Caribbean social structures occurring throughout the region in the years following World War II. The 1950s and 1960s become crucial years in Caribbean literary history not as a pure postcolonial beginning, nor as an entirely anticolonial apogee, but as a heterogeneous moment in which anticolonial optimism and postcolonial crisis collide.

West Indian literary histories of Windrush focus on a set of Anglophone male writers such as George Lamming, Samuel Selvon, or Edward (Kamau) Brathwaite, who are seen to articulate the kind of anticolonial nationalism associated with the political movements in the region that helped bring about independence from Britain during this period. However, most of the residents of the region did not experience a change in flag during this period; islands like Cuba, Martinique, and Puerto Rico are thus left out of a narrative that focuses on the end of British empire. But the changes that took place in Caribbean writing in English during the 1950s and 1960s were not isolated phenomena. Haiti, in particular, with its much earlier 1804 independence from

France, is not often thought of as experiencing a parallel history to the Anglophone islands. Nonetheless, critics of Haitian literature position the post–World War II years as a crucial moment of transition and transformation for Haitian writing, just as critics of Anglophone writing focus on these years as initiating a new literature. Martin Munro, for example, chooses the student revolution overthrowing US-aligned president Elie Lescot as initiating "the post-1946 Haitian novel," while J. Michael Dash discusses "the emergence of the postmodern" in the 1960s.[1] Drawing Haiti into the discussion of the postwar Caribbean shows how writing from the Windrush era can be understood not only in terms of its response to impending independence—the picture that might emerge if we only consider Caribbean literature in English—but also as part of a redefinition of the writer's social role that occurred throughout the region and resulted from broader socioeconomic transformations of which changes in political status are only one symptom.

Marie Chauvet's work features prominently in periodizations of Haitian writing from this period. It is Chauvet's *Amour, Colère, Folie* (1968) that Dash references as "the full-blown emergence of a postmodernist poetics"; in Dash's reading, Chauvet is prototypically postmodern because of her "irreverent stand against all totalizing and centering systems."[2] For Dash, as well as other critics like Joan Dayan, Chauvet represents the onset of postmodern Caribbean writing because of her ability to "hold up to ridicule" and "mock" the "wretched pointlessness . . . of literary commitment" articulated by previous generations of Haitian writers like Jacques Roumain.[3] At the same time, other critics read Chauvet quite differently. Marie-José N'Zengou-Tayo, in her brief overview of the idea of the committed intellectual in Haitian literary history, argues that "Chauvet expresses her faith in the role of the intellectual and poet as an agent of change."[4] N'Zengou-Tayo contrasts Chauvet's work with Lyonel Trouillot's novels, which depict "the end of the leading role usually assigned to the politically committed intellectual in Haitian literature."[5] Chauvet is thus read as either the last modernist, clinging to the writer's public role, or the first postmodernist, whose writing moves past that model. I want to suggest Chauvet can be read in such opposing ways because unlike either Roumain in the 1930s and 1940s or Trouillot in the 1980s and 1990s, her career spans a transitional period in Caribbean writing. By looking not only at the 1960s *Amour, Colère, Folie,* but also at Chauvet's *La danse sur le volcan* (1957), I argue that whereas Roumain in *Gouverneurs de la rosée* (1944) can imagine a literary intellectual who combines specialized knowledge with the sensitivity to listen to and then speak for his or her people, and whereas Trouillot has moved away from celebrating the literary intellectual to take his protagonists from minor functionaries like the postal service employee in *Rue des pas perdues* (1996), Chauvet's novels navigate a space in between, where the idea of the committed intellectual still seems possible but is becoming increasingly in doubt.

Anglophone Caribbean writing from the 1950s and 1960s found itself in a similarly in-between space. George Lamming's essay collection *The Pleasures of Exile* (1960) captures this conflict especially acutely. On the one hand, *Pleasures* is perhaps the fullest expression of the intellectual's social role by a Windrush writer.[6] Lamming makes this case through a reading of colonialism and anticolonial opposition as discursive struggle, a formulation common to anticolonial works like V. S. Reid's *New Day* (1949) or Martin Carter's *Poems of Resistance* (1954). Lamming's version of the Haitian Revolution, from the chapter "Caliban Orders History," foregrounds the revolution as speech act. If slavery turns humans into objects, "fed, kenneled, and pushed around as ploughs may be polished,"[7] when the Haitian Revolution succeeds, for Lamming, "a new word had been spoken . . . the ploughs had spoken" (125). Lamming's emphasis is first on Toussaint as heroic figure—not to mention reader (125) and writer (140)—able to give form ("order") to the inchoate desires of those who are enslaved. Lamming further emphasizes the idea of revolution as closely tied to writing and imagination by focusing on C. L. R. James as chronicler of the revolution: "It is wonderful that this epic of Toussaint's glory and his dying should have been rendered by C. L. R. James, one of the most energetic minds of our time, a neighbour of Toussaint's island, a heart and desire entirely within the tradition of Toussaint himself" (150). *The Pleasures of Exile* thus posits the writer's challenge to colonial discourse as part of the tradition of antislavery and anticolonial radicalism. It is in this context that Lamming argues for the Windrush generation's "discovery of the novel" (37) as the most important event in West Indian history since emancipation, on the grounds that "the novelist was the first to relate the West Indian experience from the inside" (38) and "restored the West Indian peasant to his true and original status of personality" (39). If the Haitian Revolution can be thought of as a speech act on the part of the slaves, the later anticolonial revolution will similarly be enacted by changes in consciousness that Lamming hopes to help inspire.

As effectively as Lamming's *The Pleasures of Exile* articulates this idea of the committed intellectual whose writing is part of social transformation, his essay collection, published in 1960, is equally notable as a hinge between anticolonial certainty and postcolonial doubt.[8] Commentators on Lamming have generally focused their attention on the essays from *Pleasures* that articulate the anticolonial intellectual project, as in the sections on the Haitian Revolution or the rewriting of Shakespeare's *The Tempest* from Caliban's perspective.

But *Pleasures* is a complex collection that contains a number of often over-looked essays that cast doubt on a purely anticolonial reading. The first chapter, for example, curiously identifies a changing cultural context that already calls into question the efficacy of anticolonial rewriting: "Prospero may have thrown away his Book; but the art of radio will rescue his weariness from despair; immortalise his absence" (14). Lamming repeatedly returns to the rise of the radio in discussions of the BBC *Caribbean Voices* program and his account of covering the funeral of George VI for the BBC. In casting radio's popularity as tied to Prospero's departure from the island at the end of *The Tempest*, Lamming offers a novel way of thinking about the writer's social role. The anticolonial author has participated in a struggle over the word centered on the European canon, a discursive struggle that Lamming's engagement with *The Tempest* exemplifies. But in a world where the written word is less the vehicle of cultural imperialism than newer, more ephemeral media, the writer's social role is suddenly much less clear. In light of this changed social reality, one of the essays most obviously concerned with the writer's relationship to anticolonial struggle, titled "An Occasion for Speaking," ends with Lamming lamenting, "I have had it (as a writer). . . . I have lost my place, or my place has deserted me" (50). *The Pleasures of Exile* thus combines its careful theorization of the committed writer with repeated hints of the rising challenges to literary commitment.

Lamming's interest in the story of the Haitian Revolution was by no means unique among writers of this period. James, a Trinidadian, not only wrote the famous book of history, *The Black Jacobins* (1938), but also staged two plays based on Haitian history, *Toussaint L'Ouverture* (1936) and *The Black Jacobins* (1967). The Cuban Alejo Carpentier's *El reino de este mundo* (1949) depicts the Haitian Revolution, as do St. Lucian Derek Walcott's *Henri Christophe* (1949) and *Drums and Colors* (1958), Martinican Édouard Glissant's *Monsieur Toussaint* (1961), and Martinican Aimé Césaire's *La tragédie du roi Christophe* (1963). These works, all published or first performed between 1936 and 1967, show how Caribbean writers from this period used the story of one of the region's great revolutionary moments from the eighteenth century to imagine the transformations occurring around them with the end of modern colonialism in the middle of the twentieth.

Marie Chauvet's *La danse sur le volcan* was published during the late 1950s as part of this larger context.[9] Some of the most famous literary renditions of the Haitian Revolution from this period—the plays by Césaire, Glissant, and Walcott, for example—focus on the aftermath of the uprising and the challenges in building a nation-state after a revolution. Chauvet, on the other hand, sets her story in the lead-up to the revolutionary action, focusing attention on the changes in consciousness that make this moment possible; like Lamming's *Season of Adventure* (1960), *La danse sur le volcan* explores how these changes in consciousness affect and are effected by artists as they find ways to articulate the oppositional impulses of the oppressed. Chauvet chooses as her protagonist a historical figure, Minette, a free person of color who broke through the color line and became the first person of African descent to be allowed to appear on stage in Saint-Domingue during the late eighteenth century. Other historical characters like Léger-Félicité Sonthonax and Alexandre Pétion also appear in the novel, but the story focuses much less on these political figures than on how the events leading up to the revolution are felt by artists like Minette.

Chauvet, like Lamming, creates a role for herself as anticolonial artist by positing language as central to revolutionary struggle. The novel shows how planter control of society is enacted through discursive means, whether in newspapers and the theater or state-sponsored spectacles like public whippings. To maintain its discursive monopoly, white society makes public space virtually inaccessible to those of African descent. Even as a free woman of color, Minette finds the institutions of the public sphere unavailable to her: she is excluded from the events of high society, she cannot even afford entry into events held in the public square (74), and the novel notes that the most important newspaper, the *Gazette*, "never mentioned Negroes and mulattoes" (69). The early plot involves Minette's efforts to break into the white-controlled world of public discourse: when she gives her first performance, she is described as the "first of her race to leap over the insurmountable barrier of prejudices" (37). The artist's contribution is thus cast as symbolic equivalent of the revolutionary struggle just beginning to take place.

Throughout *La danse sur le volcan*, the most basic attempts at resistance or defiance on the part of enslaved people are similarly framed as attempts to speak: "even though they knew their own revolt lacked the strength and organization to be successful, the slaves sought to give it expression" (320) through poisoning and suicide. Yet so much of this oppositional energy is undirected as long as the owners control the plantation public sphere. In the early part of the novel, enslaved people appear physically only as they are displayed for sale or publicly punished. After one mild uprising, random blacks are chosen and then "led to the public square and hanged from lampposts after the mere semblance of a trial" (100). These sorts of tortures are repeatedly called "spectacles" (45, 330) in which slaves and free people of color are "explicitly invited to attend" (331). Minette understands that these events have a pedagogical purpose to intimidate, as they are "deliberately staged . . . to remind her, should she ever forget it, of how the back of a slave looked after being lashed with a whip" (45). The public whippings, the display of the body parts of the tortured, and the screams of the victims of this violence are all meant to convey this message about power and control of both the physical and symbolic realms.

Chauvet's novel shows how Minette's transformation into ally and eventual spokesperson for enslaved people requires her to see the alternative lessons that can be learned from these kinds of performances. Her new way of see-ing develops out of a process of learning to interpret the speech acts of the oppressed that colonial power has tried to designate as outside of what will be considered legitimate discourse. Throughout the novel, enslaved people struggle to speak back, even if their forms of expression are forced under-ground by the colonial system. Early in the novel, enslaved people hardly appear and are almost completely silenced; yet they are able to influence Minette and help change her consciousness through transmitting the neces-sary messages. The enslaved man whom Minette sees being whipped speaks to her without words: "the slave turned his head toward them and stared at Joseph. He hardened his muscles defiantly as though he were making an effort to break the chains, a gesture whose meaning did not escape the colonist. His whip whistled in the air as it lashed across the slave's face. Minette uttered a cry of horror which was lost in the tumult of noise made by the crowd and the clanking of the chains" (44). In this passage, the enslaved person manages to send a clear message of resistance that forms part of Minette's early education. But we also see in the slave-owner's use of violence an attempt to silence this message. In this context, the enslaved population is almost entirely without dialogue in *La danse sur le volcan*, even as their presence is felt in the distant drums (111) and *lambi* (68, 195, 225), sounds that imply threat and rebellion but can only appear to Minette as disembodied noises.

These noises and signals may appear to be virtually incomprehensible, but they communicate the correct message to Minette. After witnessing the slave's whipping, rather than learning the lesson meant to be enforced by colonial spectacle, she instead sympathizes with the victim, and "Minette's view of slavery underwent a sudden and profound change" (45). A little later, seeing slaves being sold makes her imagine that "it would be nothing, nothing at all to plunge a knife into some necks, to poison, to set mansions and plantations to the torch" (115). In this context, the trajectory of *La danse sur le volcan* is Minette's coming to consciousness as she develops the language for under-standing and combating the inequalities of her society.

While seeing the suffering of those who are enslaved profoundly affects Minette, it is only later that she develops a language for articulating her new worldview, and that process is central to the novel. Two characters in particular help her move from simply responding emotionally to what she witnesses, to having the proper anticolonial framework for understanding what these incidents mean. The first character who helps Minette develop this new language is Joseph Ogé (whom we learn later in the novel is the brother of historical figure Vincent Ogé, an early revolutionary leader). Joseph is a fugitive fleeing law enforcement on the island because of his activities in "teaching some young slaves to read" (15); he brings this pedagogical aspect of anticolonialism to his relationship with Minette, introducing her to Enlightenment ideas about freedom through writers like Rousseau (28) and Abbé Raynal (73). It is from him that she first learns the language for what she sees around her: "'I don't want to be . . .' Minette paused as if searching for a word . . . 'exploited. You taught me the meaning of this word and I have a horror of it now'" (72). Although she has difficulty finding the right word, she manages to. At this point, she acknowledges it as Joseph's word, but it becomes her own as her consciousness develops.

The other character who helps Minette find a new language is Zoé, a darker-skinned free woman. Learning Minette's age, Zoé observes, "when I was fifteen I already understood many things" (96); she takes it upon herself to help give Minette this same understanding. As Zoé begins—"Your mother was born in slavery and your own freedom is only the result of sheer chance"—Minette realizes that she is being taught: "Minette got the impression that what Zoé was saying now was something that she had repeated hundreds of times to hundreds of other persons with a specific aim in view" (97). What Minette learns from Zoé is another way of articulating what she already unconsciously knows. Zoé continues by generalizing from individual experience to larger structural causes: "My parents were slaves in Martinique. It is a country that very much resembles Saint-Domingue as far as suffering and injustice are concerned" (97). Minette zeroes in on the word "injustice"; just a few pages later, when she is not offered a contract like the theater's white performers, she protests, "It's unjust, unjust!" (121). This word becomes a mantra for Minette as she encounters the inequalities of plantation society.

Minette's development from isolated artist to committed intellectual thus comes as she learns from the physical suffering enslaved people endure, but requires that her conceptual vocabulary for making sense of those experiences also undergo transformation. Once she has acquired this new language, she is able to play her part in the unfolding revolution. Toward the end of the novel, Joseph's tongue is removed by planters seeking to literally silence him, and Minette must step into his place when his muteness threatens to leave the uprising dangerously without articulation. After whites betray the agreement they have signed granting the *affranchis* (free people of color) rights, a crowd gathers outside the theater shouting in protest and building toward action. Minette notices Joseph's arrival and that "his inability to speak made his eyes bulge.... To think that he had once dreamed of galvanizing crowds to action with his words! The movement had come, the moment for which he had waited all his life. Great rebellious stirrings were in motion and he could not talk to his own people! Instead, hatred was their guide" (352). Minette realizes that Joseph is trying to communicate the overwhelming advantage the police have over this small and unguided uprising, that he wants to "stop the crowd before it went to its certain death" (352). With Joseph unable to take over the spokesperson role, Minette is forced finally to put her voice in the service of her people and connect her status as artist with the broader social movement: she begins to sing "a passage ... which Joseph had recited eloquently in the past" (352), which leads the crowd to "beg[i]n singing ... in chorus" (353). United in this way, the crowd registers their protest against what has happened but avoids "hav[ing] themselves massacred by the National Guard like so many sheep" (352). *La danse sur le volcan* culminates in Minette consolidating the identity of political artist, just as the novel also ends with the revolution about to achieve the end of slavery and colonialism in Haiti.

La danse sur le volcan thus parallels the exploration of the relationship of the intellectual or artist to revolution seen in Windrush texts like *The Pleasures of Exile, Season of Adventure, New Day,* or *Poems of Resistance*. In depicting revolution as discursive struggle and imagining the need to transform Caribbean consciousness as a prerequisite to social transformation, these works position literature and the writer as crucial to decolonization. *La danse sur le volcan*, written in the 1950s in the aftermath of the US occupation, inhabits this anticolonial space where Chauvet can explore the possibility of the intellectual creating links to social movements, and in the process expands our understanding of Caribbean literature of decolonization beyond the English-speaking islands.

Reading Chauvet in the context of her Anglophone peers not only shows how her figuring of the Haitian Revolution echoes the anticolonial aspirations of the period. The development of Chauvet's work into the 1960s also connects to the concerns of Windrush through her increasing attention to the writer's disconnection and internal exile. Yet exile in Chauvet's work is not associated with physical migration to the metropole, nor is it an abstract metaphysical feeling of unbelonging. In 1960s Haiti, internal exile becomes the status of the writer persecuted by the postcolonial political regime. Dash frames the new status of intellectuals in Haiti in terms of their expulsion from the postcolonial public sphere: "like Plato, François Duvalier banished intellectuals from his republic."[10] The exile that would become a defining trope of the Windrush generation thus comes in non-Anglophone islands like Haiti to stand for the status of even the writers who stayed in the region but found themselves pushed out of the public sphere. Although *La danse sur le volcan* already foreshadows this possible future with the removal of Joseph Ogé's tongue, *Amour, Colère, Folie* depicts a world in which the powers that be see poets as threats and rivals, and writers have become internal exiles.

Like *The Pleasures of Exile*, Chauvet's writing straddles the optimism of the years immediately following World War II and the loss of faith in literature's revolutionary power that begins to become visible in the 1960s. From the heroic intellectual project sketched out in *La danse sur le volcan*, Chauvet's later trilogy, *Amour, Colère, Folie*, depicts the crisis of the idea that literature can have a public role in the region's social movements.[11] Each of the novellas in *Amour, Colère, Folie* revolves around the impotence and degradation suffered by characters who hope to be writers and heroic actors but are condemned to complete failure in their attempts. In all three sections, these aspiring literary intellectuals come into conflict with a militarized secret police supported by complicit doctors, lawyers, and government functionaries. The solidarity between sensitive writers and the folk hoped for by the anticolonial generation is no longer possible in this new context.

The final section of the trilogy, "Folie," makes the new status of the writer most overt.[12] "Folie" revolves around a group of male poets trapped in a room together with the forces of repression and dictatorship just outside of their door. They can no longer write, and they can no longer intervene in the world around them. "Folie" shows a total inability for writing and meaningful action to be united and represents the final alienation and expulsion of writers from the postcolonial public sphere. The story is delivered entirely through the monologue of one of the poets, René, whose narrative rapidly descends into the title's madness. While the narrators of each novella in the trilogy all show themselves to be writers and intellectuals disconnected from their societies, the poets from "Folie" appear the most delusional in their longing to matter. This last part of Chauvet's trilogy presents the culmination of the crisis of the author as heroic actor.

The poets of "Folie" imagine their project—of standing up to oppression and inspiring their people to join them—through invoking the Haitian Revolution. Toward the beginning of René's monologue that makes up the novella, he proclaims: "By the glory of our forebears, I'm going to do it, kick the door open and walk up to them. Dessalines! Pétion! Toussaint! Christophe! I call on all of our indomitable heroes for help" (290). René names the men of action who fascinated male anticolonial writers like Lamming, James, Walcott, Carpentier, Césaire, and Glissant in their renditions of Haitian history from the

1950s and 1960s. René has written verse about these Haitian heroes (322), yet as his monologue continues, the reader begins to see the incongruity of René considering himself as inheritor of this tradition. *La danse sur le volcan* showed Chauvet carefully thinking through the ways that art parallels but is distinct from the kinds of action taken by figures like Pétion or Toussaint; René's hubristic dreams—"This Haitian province . . . I will free you from the devils' claws!" (295)—conflate these different forms of action and in the process ignore the unique contributions literature can make to social struggle.

Chauvet's trilogy, written amid the decline of anticolonialism, shows how nostalgic conceptions of the writer continue to exist even when they do not fit the new reality in which those whom the writers imagine as the folk may not need or even want the salvation the poet offers. The novella illustrates the narcissism of René's political aspirations by paralleling them with his desires to save his neighbor, Cécile, who appears to be mostly unaware of him but to whom he nonetheless promises, "I will fly to your rescue" (295). The idea of figuring the folk or homeland as a woman in need of masculine salvation is a typical anticolonial trope, as Dionne Brand explains in her essay "This Body for Itself": in the work of Lamming, Roumain, and Earl Lovelace, she argues, we see "the woman as country, virginal, unspoiled land, as territory for anti-colonial struggle."[13] "Folie" depicts its poets conceiving of their relationship with their community in precisely these gendered and hierarchical terms, and identifies the failure of their project in this conception. While *La danse sur le volcan* requires Minette to learn from the oppressed, "Folie" contains no such learning process for René or the other poets.

As much as "Folie" lays bare the poet's self-centered desire to lead the people, it allows René to be self-reflective enough to ask himself, "when did I leave the common people behind?" (322). In emphasizing historicity in this way—the sense that a time of literature's connection to the public is something lost—"Folie" becomes less a condemnation of literary commitment than a melancholic depiction of its exhaustion. The anticolonial ideal—that artists like Minette can learn from the oppressed to cast off privilege and thereby align their writing with the revolutionary energies of the folk—is out of place in the world of "Folie." The distance from the people that writers in "Folie" feel is not privilege: these poor poets already occupy the lowest rung of society and have no privilege to cast off. Imagining themselves above a people in need of uplift misrepresents postcolonial reality. René and his friends have not left behind the people through upward mobility: in "Folie," they live in a rat-infested shack, isolated and impoverished. Rather than the satirized anti-colonial intellectual who becomes part of the power structure seen in work by Lamming or V. S. Naipaul, "Folie" critiques both the pompous idea of writer as leader as well as the alternative notion that marginality will provide a better space from which to construct an oppositional identity.

In "Folie" the authorities who order the arrest and eventual execution of the poets take this same heterogeneous view of writing, fearing that authors are a threat even while knowing that they are powerless in the new context. The commandant accuses René and his friends of "inciting a mob" (363) and "inciting the crowd" (370), but within the story the poets are never in contact with anyone outside of their home (and their inability to publish their poetry is part of this failure to reach a public [290]); the doctor who oversees the torture of these prisoners recognizes the madness of this accusation, diagnosing that "these men are not in full possession of their faculties. Torturing them will be a complete waste of time" (371). The commandant's paranoia that these poets could incite the people shows the persistence of the anticolonial ideal of writer as leader, but the story demonstrates that for the poets as well as the commandant, this view is delusional in light of a new context in which writing can no longer mobilize a national public.

Chauvet's work fits into the region's larger trends, moving from an anticolonial discourse optimistic about its ability to construct productive ties between writers and social movements to a postcoloniality where literary intellectuals found themselves exiled from the public sphere. Despite the uniqueness of Haitian history, Chauvet narrates the development of the committed intellectual in the context of a struggle against colonial domination in *La danse sur le volcan*, then, in *Amour, Colère, Folie* places the breakdown of that authorial identity in the aftermath of the twentieth-century US occupation and alongside the rise of local totalitarianism. Chauvet's writing thus connects Haitian literary history to the regional story of anticolonial opposition and postcolonial crisis that dominates the work of Anglophone Caribbean writers like Lamming. Viewing the Windrush generation through this kind of regional perspective shows how their work is not the product of a uniquely Anglophone experience, and that their writerly projects cannot be contextualized solely with the shifting political status tied to the end of British empire. Considering Caribbean literary history comparatively, across linguistic and national boundaries, makes clear that ideas of anticolonialism and exile represent writerly responses to the region's larger social transformations.

Notes

1. Martin Munro, *Exile and Post-1946 Haitian Literature: Alexis, Depestre, Ollivier, Laferrière, Danticat* (Liverpool: Liverpool University Press, 2007), 29; J. Michael Dash, *The Other*

America: Caribbean Literature in a New World Context (Charlottesville: University of Virginia Press, 1998), 17, 108.

2. Dash, *Other America*, 109, 110.

3. Ibid., 112. Dayan joins Dash in contrasting the postmodern distrust of master narratives seen in Chauvet's fiction with the "modernist" or "nationalist" work of her predecessors: according to Dayan, Chauvet "go[es] beyond the 'peasant novel' or proletarian visions of Roumain or Alexis" and thus "is scorned by those whose more 'political' agenda demands that they speak for and with the people." See Joan Dayan, *Haiti, History and the Gods* (Berkeley: University of California Press, 1998), 80.

4. Marie-José N'Zengou-Tayo, "The End of the Committed Intellectual: The Case of Lyonel Trouillot" in *Ecrire en pays assiégé/Writing Under Siege*, ed. Marie-Agnès Sourieau and Kathleen Balutansky (New York: Rodopi, 2004), 327.

5. Ibid., 332.

6. See Supriya Nair, *Caliban's Curse: George Lamming and the Revisioning of History* (Ann Arbor: University of Michigan Press, 1996), 8; and Sandra Pouchet Paquet, *Caribbean Autobiography: Cultural Identity and Self-Representation* (Madison: University of Wisconsin Press, 2002), 134.

7. George Lamming, *The Pleasures of Exile* (1960; repr. Ann Arbor: University of Michigan Press, 1992), 120. Subsequent references appear parenthetically in the text.

8. I elaborate on this reading of *The Pleasures of Exile* in "Authority and the Occasion for Speaking in the Caribbean Literary Field: George Lamming and Martin Carter," *Small Axe* 20 (June 2006): 19–39.

9. Marie Chauvet, *Dance on the Volcano* [1957], trans. Salvator Attanasio (New York: W. Sloan, 1959). Subsequent references appear parenthetically in the text.

10. J. Michael Dash, "Blazing Mirrors: The Crisis of the Haitian Intellectual," in *Intellectuals in the Twentieth Century Caribbean*, ed. Alistair Hennessy (London: MacMillan Caribbean, 1992), 2:183.

11. Marie Chauvet, *Love, Anger, Madness* [1968], trans. Rose-Myriam Réjouis and Val Vinokur (New York: Modern Library, 2009). Subsequent references appear parenthetically in the text.

12. Dash focuses especially on "Folie" as embodying what he sees as Chauvet's postmodern critique of master narratives. Dash, *Other America*, 111–116.

13. Dionne Brand, "This Body for Itself," in *Bread Out of Stone* (Toronto: Coach House Press, 1994), 35.

Beyond Windrush and the Original Black Atlantic Routes: Austin Clarke, Race, and Canada's Influence on Anglophone Caribbean Literature

MICHAEL A. BUCKNOR

The traditional Windrush focus on London-based Caribbean authors over-shadows other Afro-Caribbean diasporic routes of literary production in what Paul Gilroy calls "Black Atlantic" circuits of exchange, a focus that, con-sequently, obscures from critical view a clear Canadian influence on Carib-bean literary development. Given that Caribbean literary history has been linked with global circuits of exchange and ideological coalitions from its early Windrush accounts, Paul Gilroy's "Black Atlantic" conception is a use-ful frame for tracking the transnational flows of "black" Caribbean cultural production.[1] Yet as Barbadian/Canadian cultural critic Rinaldo Walcott has argued, "discourses of black diaspora(s) and the Black Atlantic" have largely left Canada out of their consideration of these exchange routes.[2] Like Walcott, other critics such as Diana Brydon, George Elliott Clarke, and Peter Childs and Patrick Williams[3] are correct in criticizing Gilroy's occlusion of Canada in his Black Atlantic routes. However, I also agree with Walcott's further inter-vention that these black transnational concepts are useful despite this limita-tion because they force us to examine Black Atlantic movements "beyond the original dispersal."[4] Indeed, Gilroy himself implicitly invites the application of his concept to other routes when he admits that "there are also many omis-sions," for he has "scarcely more than put down some preliminary markers."[5] My use of the term "beyond" in the title of this essay, then, is therefore not a bracketing or displacement of either Windrush constructions of West Indian literature or the Black Atlantic/diasporic constructs. Instead, it is more of an expansion, and also a complication, of these conceptualizations. Though Gil-roy's trade routes set up historical points of reference in his Black Atlantic circuits of exchange that do not include Canada—Africa, America, the Carib-bean, and Britain are his orienting points—his oceanic metaphor suggests the geographically fluid nature of transnational circulations of ideas and cultural products, thus creating the possibility for an even more extensive vision than his own geographic coordinates might imply.[6]

By rerouting Gilroy's transnational cultural flows to Canada and by exposing the coalitions around race theorized in works such as Michelle Ann Stephens's *Black Empire: The Masculine Global Imaginary of Caribbean Intellectuals in the United States, 1914–1962,* I hope to signal the complexly transnational formations of Caribbean literary production. Though literary histories usually require some kind of beginning point, such origins are always under review, contingent on new archives of history and based on numerous interactions across multiple locations. I use the example of Austin Clarke, a Barbadian-born author resident in Canada, to show the ways in which ideology, literary community, and multiple diasporas lead to circulations beyond Gilroy's transnational checkpoints and beyond conventional constructions of Anglophone Caribbean literature. This essay demonstrates that, while traditional Windrush accounts remind us of the significant role metropolitan visibility played in the international promotion and reception of this literature, metropolitan locations *outside* of England also made important contributions to this process. Clarke's interaction with his Windrush compatriots such as Samuel Selvon and Andrew Salkey, his pioneering "invasion" of the "ivory towers" of Canadian publishing, and his strategic positioning at the Canadian Broadcasting Corporation (CBC) as "spokesperson" for issues of race and the civil rights movement all highlight the formative role that Clarke and Canada played in the development of West Indian literature, especially with regard to notions of blackness.

There is no doubt that London and the Windrush writers have been prominent in accounts of Caribbean literary history, overshadowing Canada's role in the development of that literature. George Lamming, who arrived in London with Selvon in 1950, feels no compunction in declaring in his 1960 *The Pleasures of Exile* that the decade of the Windrush period was the time in which "the West Indian acquired recognition as a writer," with the corollary assumption that Britain was the place where literary coronation was first conferred.[7] By 1966 it is already a taken-for-granted idea that London has been central to Caribbean literary production: Kenneth Ramchand, in *West Indian Narrative,* feels no need to elaborate on the significance of this location for Caribbean literature's development, simply remarking that "the fact that the majority of West Indian writers make their headquarters in London has been discussed and speculated upon at length."[8] This view is so dominant that as recently as 2003, in *West Indian Intellectuals in Britain,* Bill Schwarz could still matter-of-factly position "literary London" as the womb space for West Indian literature: "the emergence of the West Indian novel, as a form, coincides with the great migration of the 1940s and 1950s" to London.[9] Whether conceived as "headquarters," birthplace, or site of legitimization, London has consistently been defined as the preeminent space for the considerations of the development, if not also the emergence, of Caribbean literature. Indeed, there is a great deal of merit in this privileging of London and the Windrush period in Caribbean literary history, since, as Philip Nanton reminds us, at the time there was a "surge of creative output," and West Indian writing was able to clear a space on the world literary map.[10] Anne Walmsley's history of the Caribbean Artists Movement provides an account of some of the advantages that London afforded Caribbean writers in the post–World War II period. Importantly, she identifies publishing and earning opportunities, broadcasting exposure through the BBC, the supporting environment of a thriving artistic community, and the agitation of political organizations dedicated to issues of race as contributing factors that made London a crucible of Caribbean literary development at the time. In fact, many writers had come with the hope, she claims, "that in Britain they would obtain training and experience, a responsive audience, and opportunities to live by the practice of their craft."[11] If these are in fact the conditions for the development of Caribbean literary production, then Austin Clarke was helping to develop similar enabling spaces in Canada.

Even with this London-centric focus, the writers and editors at the time sought to qualify the idea of the centrality of London to Caribbean literary development, either by revising the creation myth of West Indian literature or by invoking concepts of border crossing and transnationalism. Ramchand's 1966 acknowledgment of the nurturing role of London during the Windrush period of literary migrations, for example, is qualified by his pointing out that this burgeoning of West Indian creativity should be seen as a continuation of the work of earlier writers such as the Jamaican/American Claude McKay and the Trinidadian/British/American C. L. R. James. As Ramchand observes in introducing part three of his anthology, "the preceding extracts from James and McKay should help to dispel the idea that West Indian writing only begins in the 1950s or that it lacks continuity."[12] Also, while on the one hand, in his 1960 introduction to *West Indian Stories* Salkey admits that "England has been a sort of necessary common denominator, a link holding all its constituent parts together" (10), on the other hand, he also claims that "England *and* the West Indies must be held jointly responsible for the results of West Indian literary endeavour."[13] In fact, both Walmsley in *The Caribbean Artist Movement* and John Clement Ball in *Imagining London: Postcolonial Fiction and the Transnational Metropolis* challenge the idea of metropolitan centrality when they corroborate the transnational nature of that literary production:

both critics focus our attention on the important role that little magazines in the Caribbean played in encouraging young writers, as well as the ways in which these journals facilitated a process of intellectual exchange between the Caribbean and the BBC's *Caribbean Voices* program in London.[14] According to Walmsley, "by 1946, the programme had become an almost exclusively literary magazine, drawing its material from the whole of the West Indies via Cedric Lindo, a Jamaican journalist."[15] For Ball, "the London that called the West Indies on *Caribbean Voices* became, over time, less hegemonic, more thoroughly decentred, more like a node in an intricate web of transnational relationships."[16] In this regard, Salkey's ambiguous positioning of London as the linchpin that holds everything together and, at the same time, merely one link in a chain of creative production might be read as an intimation of the complex, transnational circuits of exchange that actually facilitated the development of Caribbean literature.

Following on this kind of thinking, then, I wonder if the very contradictions, hesitations, and qualifications around the construction of Caribbean literary history in relationship to the Windrush generation might offer us a space to map alternative routes and even parallel sites of Caribbean literary production. So, while for Ramchand, "Britain . . . was the natural resort for the 'English-speaking' West Indian in search of a market and an audience," there would seem to be a place in our literary history to consider other diasporic routes such as Canada, especially when similar conditions obtained there for the burgeoning of a Caribbean literary tradition.[17] It seems odd that even for a Canadian critic like Ball—who is keen to dislodge the idea of London's centrality to Caribbean literary history and who also makes productive use of Gilroy's Black Atlantic model of exchange to show the cultural circuits between Britain and the Caribbean—the role of Canada in the development of Anglophone Caribbean literature nevertheless remains off-limits. While Ball joins other critics such as Alison Donnell and Sarah Lawson Welsh in beginning the work of reconceptualizing the place of London in Caribbean literary development by way of a network metaphor, Canada has yet to be factored into this circuit of exchange.[18] As Ball persuasively argues: "To see *Caribbean Voices* as a network—[that is] as a complex set of dynamic relations among a multicultural London and many different West Indian islands—is to complicate not only traditional views of London as centre or capital of West Indian literature, but the very idea of there being a centre at all."[19] Expanding Ball's concept of the network can provide a way to expose the ripples of Canada's transnational outflows via its diasporic communities. Building on the work of Rinaldo Walcott, who has suggested that conceptualizations of black diasporic routes need to take a detour to Canada, I want to make use of Gilroy's and Stephens's transnational theories as a way to track Canada's channels of influence on Caribbean literary history.

Gilroy's conception of the Black Atlantic is useful not only because it opens up the possibilities for seeing new routes of transnational circuits of exchange but also because issues of race—and specifically identity politics around blackness—featured significantly in the mutual transformation processes between the literary and the social in Anglophone Caribbean literature. Gilroy's Black Atlantic takes as its grounding principle "the image of ships in motion across the spaces between Europe, America, Africa and the Caribbean," and this conceptualization focuses attention on, among other things, "the *circulation* of ideas and activists."[20] An investigation of Clarke's literary activities in Canada suggests that the ideas (around publishing, broadcast exposure, literary community, and political activism) that led to literary success in London were also rerouted to Canada. This kind of circulation provides support for Gilroy's rejection of the idea of the containment of cultural flows within the borders of the nation and posits instead a transnational circuit of exchange. Although critics such as David Chariandy have correctly questioned the binary opposition between the national and the transnational in Gilroy's work, I want to suggest that the idea of transnational cultural exchange appropriately accounts for the circulating winds under the creative wings of West Indian literature.[21] For Gilroy, "the history of the Black Atlantic . . . continually crisscrossed by the movements of black people . . . engaged in various struggles towards emancipation, autonomy and citizenship provides a means to reexamine the problems of . . . historical memory."[22] Some of the "crisscrossing movement" and "struggles towards emancipation" involved the migration of black people from America to Canada via the Underground Railroad, the pilgrimage of Maroons from Jamaica to Canada's Nova Scotia and later back to Sierra Leone, as well as Caribbean people's post–World War II travel to Canada for work and study.[23] Beyond the movement of people, there was also the airmail travel of letters between a community of writers from the Caribbean, settled all over the world, who reviewed each other's work; organized publication projects; facilitated further travel and visits to each other for talks, readings, and writer-in-residence programs; and formed author organizations. To a large extent, they created through correspondence a transnational literary society (albeit predominantly male). Conceived then as a "webbed network," the Black Atlantic model allows us to see the ways in which "black survival depends on forging a new means to build alliances" that "involves processes of political organization that are explicitly transnational and international in nature."[24]

Stephens develops Gilroy's idea of "political organization" further in her work, demonstrating how coalitions around race led to border overflows of ideology. Though, like Gilroy, her work fails to include Canada in the black intellectual global enterprise—her book focuses on the Caribbean/American figures Marcus Garvey, Claude McKay, and C. L. R. James—her ideas can productively be applied to Canada (and the post–World War II period as well). Stephens observes that in the post–World War I period black intellectuals "attempted to construct an oppositional form of black nationalism and political representation in an international imperial world that did not yet recognize black colonial subjects as national peoples." Consequently, she argues, "black subjects could strengthen their individual nationalist struggles and aspirations through . . . transnational race-based networks."²⁵ Stephens builds on the work of Michael Hardt and Antonio Negri's 2000 book *Empire*, which argues that "new forms of Empire bear more of a resemblance to the structures of premodern empires than to modern states created in and emerging from imperialism."²⁶ The model of premodern empire is one that, for Hardt and Negri, "establishes no territorial center of power and does not rely on fixed boundaries or barriers," while it also "incorporates the entire global realm within its open, expanding frontier" and "manages . . . plural exchanges."²⁷ For Stephens, the diasporic Caribbean intellectual figures of Garvey, McKay, and James are shown to understand how multiple forms of empire provide the "context shaping all black travels, displacements, and even engagements with various forms of internationalist discourse."²⁸ Like Ball, Stephens suggests (following on Walter Mignolo's views of what he calls "other-thinking") that in the interactions of empire, just as in the colonial relationship, a border-thinking emerges in which "the world views [*sic*] of colonial subjects and intellectuals also migrate and then have a shaping impact on the broader geopolitical world around them."²⁹ It is in this context of ideological border overflows—the spillage of ideas and political mobilization beyond national borders—that Gilroy's "circulation of ideas and activists" can be accommodated, giving us a better understanding of how the transnational flow of ideas surrounding race also featured in the development of West Indian literature. Recognizing the power of ideological solidarity around race stimulated by Clarke's movements through Toronto, London, and Harlem, as well as his engagement with central players in the civil rights movement, illuminates the ways in which such transnational circuits of ideology led to Clarke's visibility in Canada, and thus the ways in which Canada, too, occupies an important place in the global story of postwar Anglophone Caribbean literature.

Austin Clarke—who went to Canada to study in 1955, five years after Lamming and Selvon journeyed to England, and who, prior to his departure to Canada, worked with Frank Collymore on *Bim*—is an important figure for considering how the variegated flows of cultural circulation contributed to the emergence of West Indian literary production. It is worth noting here that little magazine exchanges between Bridgetown, Kingston, Port of Spain, and Georgetown accounted for a regional circuit prior to and during the London publication surge, such that the latter could not have happened without an instigating literary circulation in the Caribbean. As Bill Schwarz observes, "the journal *Bim* . . . [produced in Barbados] effectively functioned as the resource for the BBC's *Caribbean Voices* from 1943 to 1958."[30] Walmsley, moreover, argues that the program "was also in effect a fledgling school in creative writing, and a broad-based literary club."[31] Importantly, a young Clarke, as a student of Collymore's at Combermere School in Barbados, was fully aware of *Bim* and also listened to the BBC program on many Sunday evenings.[32] In his memoir of his friendship with Samuel Selvon, Clarke writes: "Samuel Selvon of Trinidad was one voice I heard over the radio. His works had appeared earlier in . . . the small, tidy, impressive and clairvoyant pages of *Bim*."[33] For Ball, this diasporic exchange between the Caribbean and Britain through airmail correspondence and radio airwaves removed the center of activity away from the geographically bounded space of London to a more open, dynamic network of exchange not locked into national borders: "it was in the open, wireless air over the Atlantic that the BBC linked distant places into one dynamically related, decentred literary and cultural space."[34] Clarke, both before and after his migration to Canada, was undoubtedly an important part of this space.

To extend Ball's idea, it is useful to look at correspondence also going to and from London, Canada, the United States, the Caribbean, and the rest of the world—indeed, wherever these literary friends found themselves. In the Austin Clarke archives, for example, I have found correspondence between Clarke and his fellow Barbadians Edward (Kamau) Brathwaite and George Lamming, the Guyanese-born Jan Carew (who held a Canadian passport), the Jamaicans James Berry and Andrew Salkey, and the Trinidadian Samuel Selvon (who spent his last years in Canada), among many others. The earliest correspondence is from the early 1960s, around the time of the flourishing of West Indian writing in London. As Walmsley notes, "the writers and artists who had come to Britain from the Caribbean had by the 1960s established themselves professionally."[35] Clarke, having arrived in Canada in 1955, had by 1963 published a short story in *Bim* and had his work featured in a prominent Canadian journal, the *Tamarack Review*. In 1964 he won a short story competition in Canada and, after the publication of the story in *Saturday Night*, was nominated in 1966 to be included in a survey of Canadian literature.[36] By 1965 he had published two novels, *Survivors of the Crossing* and *Among Thistles and Thorns*, cementing his meteoric rise as a West Indian author in Canada. Significantly, in 1965 Clarke made his own crossing of the Atlantic from Canada to England, during which he consolidated important literary friendships and connections with his British-based compatriots. He visited London to launch his second novel *Thistles*, published by Heinemann. Part of that trip involved his assignment, as a freelance radio broadcaster for the CBC, to do a "three-part series on West Indian immigrants in London."[37] While there, he was invited to participate in a discussion with V. S. Naipaul and Anthony Burgess on the BBC program "The World of Books," and he also gave an invited talk at the West Indian Students Centre: he thus spent much of his time in London interacting with a host of Caribbean students and writers. He was also featured in the *Times Literary Supplement* along with Selvon, Lamming, and Naipaul, as the "new wine" of postcolonial writing.[38] The idea that West Indian writers were invigorating writing in English suggested in this influential British periodical is echoed in a Canadian magazine, *Saturday Night*, in a review article entitled "Caribbean Renaissance" featuring Clarke's second novel. In this review, Kildare Dobbs goes further to suggest that what was happening to the literary scene in London was now also taking place in Toronto through Austin Clarke: "Hitherto England, that's to say London, has had the benefit of this second literary renaissance by providing writers like George Lamming, V. S. Naipaul and others with a livelihood and audience. Now, to a certain extent, Canada is sharing those benefits."[39] I emphasize all of this to show that the routes of the Black Atlantic definitely included Canada through Austin Clarke.

From Clarke's extensive archive of correspondence, it is clear that Clarke maintained a strong alliance with other Caribbean writers and editors and was part of a transnational literary community that helped to provide support for each other. If one can imagine a time without cell phones, where letters operated much like text or Blackberry messages, then one can see how letter writing became an important circuit of exchange and support. On September 28, 1965, for example, Andrew Salkey writes to Clarke and sends him Jan Carew's address in Spain, and by October 26, 1965, Carew is already replying to a letter sent by Clarke.[40] What is even more remarkable is that there was a constant flow of exchanges between West Indian writers in London and Clarke in Toronto—and when they moved to other parts of the world or returned to the Caribbean, the contact remained. On one occasion when Edward (Kamau) Brathwaite, who was then living in Jamaica, was visiting Nairobi, his wife, Doris, replied on Brathwaite's behalf, filling Clarke in on developments with *Savacou* and welcoming Clarke's contribution to *Savacou* in the form of a short story.[41] They shared publication news of their own or of other West Indian writers with each other: Jacques E. Compton informs Clarke in his letter of October 23, 1966, of John Figueroa's publication of *Caribbean Voices* Volume 1; Jan Carew writes to Clarke on April 25, 1966, about his editing trip to Ghana for work on the *African Review*; and Andrew Salkey informs Clarke of George Lamming's Barbados number of *New World Quarterly* in a letter of August 30, 1966. On April 2, 1964, Brathwaite, writing from Jamaica, offers congratulations to Clarke on the publication of his stories in *Bim*, one of which Brathwaite staged in St. Lucia: "First thing, let me congratulate you on your work. . . . These stories in *Bim*, esp the first one in dramatic monologue. Had this performed . . . when I was in St. Lucia last year. They loved it madly. Looking forward to your novel."[42] He also encourages Clarke to link up with Paule Marshall "if/when in NY."[43] There were also reviews of Clarke's work by fellow Windrush writers. In 1965 Derek Walcott, for example, writes a very encouraging review of Clarke's second novel in the Trinidad and Tobago *Sunday Guardian*. Though critical of Clarke's first novel, he lauds Clarke's *Bim*-published stories for his talent for dialogue and says of *Thistles*: "what gives Mr. Clarke's awkward but passionate work an original distinction is the strange sense of elation underlying his character's suffering."[44] Salkey, too, reviews *The Meeting Point* for the BBC in May 1967 and informs Clarke that the recording "will be heard throughout the nine radio stations in the West Indies."[45] The letters of the 1960s (and later the 1970s) flesh out Clarke's growing importance in the network of Windrush writers, his participation in the regional circuits via *Bim* and *Savoucou* (this latter edited in Jamaica), his recognition by fellow authors, and his role in consolidating a transnational community of writers.[46]

This transnational consolidation is even more evident when we examine the CBC portion of Clarke's archives, in which he plays a central role in broadcasting the work of other Windrush writers on the Canadian airwaves. Like most writers of the time, Clarke had to make a living by means other than his literary output, something he does mainly through journalism and freelance work for the CBC. In this role, there is ample evidence that he ushered, facilitated, and actively recommended the use of his work and those of other West Indian writers on CBC artistic programs via interviews, readings, reviews, and radio plays. Such networking was so successful that by 1970, Robert Weaver, radio network supervisor, complains in a letter to Clarke that "we [CBC] are becoming increasingly swamped with material for the West Indies programs."[47] It should be noted too that the CBC had offices in London and New York and thus had ways of making transnational broadcasting arrangements. A representative of Faber and Faber, publishers of Wilson Harris, writes to Clarke in care of the CBC's office in London about the timetable for broadcasting a program on Harris: "perhaps you would be good enough to let me know when you plan to broadcast the programme on Wilson Harris?"[48] In 1964 Weaver delays accepting more tapes from Clarke because, as he explains: "I already have on hand two short stories, one by Selvon and the other by Ismith Khan, which were both recorded through our London office using a West Indian actor now resident in England."[49] Carew promises to send to him "a half hour radio play THE FIVER-MAN" for broadcast on the CBC instead of *University*, which was the "biggest success ever in the Guyanese theatre."[50] During all of this time, Clarke's own short stories and novels are being read and reviewed constantly on the CBC. For example, Clarke's story "They Heard a Ringing of Bells" was read on a program entitled "Anthology" in early 1964, while *Thistles* was reviewed on the evening of September 22, 1965, on the CBC.[51] That Weaver could talk about West Indian programs as part of the CBC offerings indicates that the CBC played a similar role to the BBC's *Caribbean Voices* program, and, as should be clear by now, Clarke was at the center of this media focus.

The lively history of connection among this old boys' club of writers—some of whom had gone to school together—was further cemented by the ways in which issues of race, a sense of dislocation in a postcolonial "imperial" metropole, and an activist sensibility all helped secure their commitment across waters in both a literary and a social cause. Given the context of their artistic production, and given that, as Lamming reminds us, these artists discovered a sense of their West Indianness in London—in a way becoming West Indian and, as Schwarz points out, also "becoming black"[52]—it is important to factor their activism around race into the discussion. In 1964 James Berry invites Clarke to contribute to a new literary journal, *SOL*, that has as its mandate the consideration of the "role of the writer in contributing to the progress of the black man and the rest of humanity."[53] Clarke is also invited around that time to do a ten-session series on "Black Literature" as in-service training for the Bridgeport Board of Education. In 1967 Carew invites him to serve as one of two vice-chairmen of the Third World Writers and Artistes in the Americas. One of the immediate objectives was "to achieve a more effective liaison between writers and artists from the Spanish, Portuguese, English, Dutch and French speaking countries in the Western Hemisphere who at a very fundamental level face the same cultural, economic and political challenges."[54] These objectives of the organization support Stephens's argument that "more than an anticolonial politics, and more than the organizing of an international black working class, black transnational intellectuals were fundamentally engaged in finding ways to represent a multiply [*sic*] national global black community."[55]

These invitations to join black activist projects indicate Clarke's central role in the race politics of the 1960s, which in turn played an important part in his public profile as a writer: Clarke participated widely in public discussions of race and played a huge role in bringing issues of race to the Canadian public through his interviews of significant figures in the civil rights movement. Commissioned by the CBC to interview James Baldwin, he ended up gaining access to Malcolm X when Baldwin proved inaccessible. By the mid-1960s he was able to claim that, save for Martin Luther King Jr., he had interviewed "all the main personalities" in the civil rights and Black Power movements.[56] These included Malcolm X, Stokely Carmichael, Roy McKissick, Leroi Jones, Larry Neal, Paule Marshall, Louis Farrakhan, and Max Roach, among others. In this regard, Clarke emerged as a spokesperson for issues of race and the civil rights movement in Canada, whether as interviewer or guest on radio programs (and later on television), and this public profile definitely assisted in bringing his work to the attention of the Canadian literary establishment. His activism and journalism on issues of race that helped to put the agenda of racial justice in the public domain were also clearing a space for the greater acceptance of the creative writing of people of color in Canada. His activism resulted in letters to the editors of newspapers and even letters sent to him personally. For example, a former professor at the University of Waterloo who had followed Clarke's interviews in Harlem wrote a letter to Clarke from British Columbia the same afternoon he heard a discussion between Clarke and someone he identifies as "that Christian man." He writes inter alia: "I've been meaning to write to you anyway to tell you I enjoyed that series . . . when you did a lot of interviews in Harlem. . . . I have enjoyed your radio talks and, when the revolution comes, spare at least one white man, to be precise—me."[57] In a review by Pat Pearce entitled "Study of Harlem: A Shocking Hour," she acknowledges that the programs on Harlem done by Clarke were helping white Canadians to understand the issue of race both in the United States and in Canada.[58] As early as 1965 Clarke is being hailed as "Canada's Leading Negro Author," as one reviewer headlined his article.[59] Clarke's political activism, bolstered by his Caribbean counterparts in England and the United States, was able to begin chipping away at the walls of division around race. Henry Boyle, CBC features supervisor, summarizes Clarke's race work in journalism thus: "I have used Austin Clarke as an interviewer and writer on several occasions and found his work to be outstanding. He is particularly sensitive and yet objective. He prepared two one-hour programmes on Harlem prior to the outbreak of troubles. He has done an hour of the coloured situation in England. He has prepared for your use in January, an hour programme on Poets in Canada."[60] Though he was sometimes accused of reinforcing the very racial views he interrogated, Clarke nevertheless profiled the issue and helped to create a space for conversations and mutual exchanges that contributed to the process of breaking down the ideological walls of racism. Moreover, this activism around race also put a spotlight on Clarke and solidified his image as a black Canadian writer. So prominent is this image that Rinaldo Walcott has argued that in part due to the achievements of writers such as Clarke, "the hypervisibility of Caribbean blackness makes 'indigenous black Canadians' invisible."[61]

What Clarke's journey as a writer exposes is that Toronto provided parallel metropolitan mechanisms for West Indian publishing to those developing in London. Progressing in an alternative but structurally similar context, Clarke's literary emergence laid the groundwork for the Canadian publishing success of those who followed in the 1980s and 1990s, including Dionne Brand, Olive Senior, Neil Bissoondath, and Cyril Dabydeen, among others.[62] Arguably, this later, late twentieth-century renaissance of West Indian publishing in Canada shifts the major publishing locale of transnational publication from England to Canada, and much of this is surely related to Clarke's own literary success in Canada. Yet his work was not limited to a Canadian metropolitan scene. By the time his second book, *Among Thistles*, had come out, it was reviewed throughout the length and breadth of Canada (Ottawa, Fredericton, Montreal, Calgary, Vancouver, Toronto), the United Kingdom, Africa, and the Caribbean. I was stunned by the number of reviews found, suggesting that between the marketing strategy of his publisher and his public profile, his work was being introduced to a wide reading public from England to Canada (and of course from earlier, through *Bim*, it was also being received in the West Indies). Considered the granddaddy of Caribbean/Canadian writing, he ought to find a place within the history of the Windrush-attributed upsurge in West Indian writing. His singular position in the middle of this circuit of exchange highlights how Canada should be considered an important nodal point in Gilroy's Black Atlantic and, relatedly, the postwar development of West Indian literature.

Yet what can we gather about Canada's positioning within our understandings of cultural production with regard to the hegemony of metropolitan locations and the politics of erasure? There is clear evidence in the historical account of Anglophone Caribbean literature that Canada and Clarke slip between the cracks of literary constructions. The question of Canada's borderline national profile has been considered by many thinkers, including Russell Brown, George Grant, and Marshall McLuhan.[63] The view has often been posited that a less aggressive nationalism is evident in Canada, a trait that allows the nation to fade into the background, sitting quietly between the Old World empires of Europe and those of the New World in North America. As W. H. New argues, "For most of its history, Canada has been an Atlantic and an

American Society, looking east to Europe and south to the States for imperial roots and continental desires—so much so—that . . . these two borders came to seem normative angles of cultural disposition."⁶⁴ McLuhan's consideration of the "linking effects of new communications media," as Ball describes it, allows us to see how local and global can interact in what New says is a Canadian way of "seeing the connection between the local and the large, and of constructing the border between them as a field of negotiating relationships."⁶⁵ In this light, we might think of Caribbean/Canadian writing—and its role in the dynamic development of Anglophone West Indian literature—as a demonstration of the ways in which this particularly Canadian cultural overflow into diasporic space dismantles the sites of power and epistemological structures normally attributed to Windrush literature. Ball has convincingly argued that London's power base was always under adjustments from its cultural rivulets. The idea of who is global and who is local, who is large and who is small, and who is center and who is margin becomes reconceptualized if we think of the border as a "sea" of negotiated relationships. While McLuhan talks about the "new communications media" as facilitating this connection across geographical locales and power bases, I want to suggest that even with the old communication methods of letter writing, a community of cultural architects and activists was being constructed. Such a community recalls Gilroy's very suggestive concept of "diasporic intimacy," which, though he does not fully develop it, is seen as "a marked feature of transnational Black Atlantic creativity."⁶⁶ For Gilroy, "the contemporary black arts movement" has "created a new topography of loyalty and identity" in which the preeminence of the nation is displaced.⁶⁷ This new topography can usefully describe this band of letter-writing men, in which a community of interest other than the nation was most operative. While I am not convinced that the nation is eclipsed in transnational circuits, the relationship between transnational subjects and the nation nevertheless works to de-emphasize the strictly national orientation often emphasized in the postwar period of decolonization and independence. Further, the personal communication network of Clarke and his fellow writers speaks to the ways in which the power positions of not just the local and global but also the private and the public intersect and become reformulated in the open seas of transnational cooperation. The historical construction of Anglophone Caribbean history, when reconceptualized through the matrix of cultural networks and circuits of ideas, extraterritorial communities, political allegiances, and the affect of artistic friendships, dislodges the familiar literary creation myth and reveals an important component of literary production that has largely been erased. This re-visioning of literary histories displaces London as the single geographical ur-space of creative production, exposing the inflows and outflows of cultural production among numerous nations, including Canada, and forcing recognition of the discursive mutations of political activism and the fluidity and dynamism of human cultures. To understand the confluence of diasporas through these main sites of cultural production—Britain, America, the Caribbean, and Canada—is to understand how national geographical borders are continuously overrun by flows of cultural exchange, ideological agitation, and personal affect via the literary production circulating across and within the Black Atlantic.

Notes

1. Though the Caribbean is not limited to its African identity, the production of its literature benefited from the advocacy on issues of race by way of the Black Power movement.

2. Rinaldo Walcott, *Black Like Who? Writing Black Canada.* (Ontario: Insomniac Press, 1997), 17. See also Diana Brydon, "Rerouting the Black Atlantic," *Tapia 5* (Spring 2001): 94–100. In this review essay, she concludes: "Although Gilroy's focus fell on rethinking the relations of the Caribbean, the United States, and Africa from the perspective of black Britain, his theorizing of the Black Atlantic invites the expansion of his thesis into other domains" (95).

3. See, for example, Brydon's "Rerouting the Black Atlantic," 95; Peter Childs and Patrick Williams, eds., *An Introduction to Postcolonial Theory* (London: Prentice-Hall/Harvest Wheatsheaf, 1997), 83; and George Elliot Clarke, *Odysseys Home: Mapping African-Canadian Literature* (Toronto: University of Toronto Press, 2002), 9.

4. Rinaldo Walcott, "Migration: Returns and Redirections in Caribbean Diaspora Literary Politics, 'Tom Say,'" in *The Routledge Companion to Anglophone Caribbean Literature*, ed. Michael A. Bucknor and Alison Donnell (New York: Routledge, 2011), 500.

5. Paul Gilroy, *The Black Atlantic: Modernity and Double Consciousness* (Cambridge, Mass.: Harvard University Press, 1993), xi.

6. For other influential versions of this kind of thinking, see also Brent Hayes Edwards, *The Practice of Diaspora: Literature, Translation, and the Rise of Black Internationalism* (Cambridge, Mass.: Harvard University Press, 2003); and Michelle Ann Stephens, *Black Empire: The Masculine Global Imaginary of Caribbean Intellectuals in the United States, 1914–1962* (Durham, N.C.: Duke University Press, 2005).

7. George Lamming, *The Pleasures of Exile* (1960; repr., Ann Arbor: University of Michigan Press, 1992), 211.

8. Kenneth Ramchand, *West Indian Narrative* (London: Thomas Nelson and Sons, 1966), 224.

9. Bill Schwarz, *West Indian Intellectuals in Britain* (Manchester: Manchester University Press, 2003), 9.

10. Philip Nanton, "Political Tension and Caribbean Voices," in Bucknor and Donnell, *Routledge Companion to Anglophone Caribbean Literature*, 585.

11. Anne Walmsley, *The Caribbean Artists Movement 1966–1972: A Literary and Cultural History* (London: New Beacon Books, 1992), 8.

12. Ramchand, *West Indian Narrative*, 55.

13. Andrew Salkey, ed., *West Indian Stories* (London: Faber and Faber, 1960), 10. Salkey is here using the term "West Indian" to refer to the Anglophone Caribbean.

14. John Clement Ball, *Imagining London: Postcolonial Fiction and the Transnational Metropolis* (Toronto: University of Toronto Press, 2007).

15. Walmsley, *Caribbean Artists Movement*, 6.

16. Ball, *Imagining London*, 108.

17. Ramchand, *West Indian Narrative*, 57.

18. Alison Donnell and Sarah Welsh, eds., *The Routledge Reader in Caribbean Literature* (London: Routledge, 1996), 214. This idea appears in their introduction to the "1950–1965" section of the volume.

19. Ball, *Imagining London*, 108.

20. Gilroy, *Black Atlantic*, 4.

21. David Chariandy, "Postcolonial Diasporas" *Postcolonial Text* 2, no. 1 (2006), http://postcolonial.org/index.php/pct/article/view/440/839.

22. Gilroy, *Black Atlantic*, 16.

23. Ibid.

24. Ibid., 28–29.

25. Stephens, *Black Empire*, 3.

26. Quoted in ibid., 10.

27. Ibid., 11.

28. Ibid., 12.

29. Ibid., 13.

30. Schwarz, *West Indian Intellectuals*, 13.

31. Walmsley, *Caribbean Artists Movement*, 11.

32. Collymore was one of the first editors of *Bim*. See Edward Baugh, *Frank Collymore: A Biography* (Miami: Ian Randle, 2009).

33. Austin Clarke, *A Passage Back Home: A Personal Reminiscence of Samuel Selvon* (Toronto: Exile Editions, 1994), 12.

34. Ball, *Imagining London*, 109.

35. Walmsley, *Caribbean Artists Movement*, 30.

36. Letter from H. Gordon Green to Clarke, May 12, 1966 (Box 37). This letter is held in the Austin Clarke Archives in the library at McMaster University. Letters and other documents will be cited by date and, when applicable, box number.

37. Clarke, *Passage*, 18.

38. See "Old Bottles for New Wine," *Times Literary Supplement*, September 16, 1965, 793.

39. Kildare Dobbs, "Caribbean Renaissance," *Saturday Review* 80 (1965): 59.

40. See letters from Jan Carew to Clarke in Box 36 and letters from Andrew Salkey to Clarke in Box 42.

41. See handwritten letter from Doris Brathwaite to Clarke dated March 14 (without a year), but it is most likely 1972 based on Brathwaite's reference to Doris's letter in his May 25, 1972, letter (Box 35).

42. Brathwaite to Clarke, April 2, 1964 (Box 35).

43. Ibid.

44. Derek Walcott, "A Bajan Boyhood," *Sunday Guardian*, September 5, 1965, 8, 11.

45. Salkey to Clarke, August 5, 1967, with review attached (Box 42).

46. Clarke's growing image in the Caribbean is humorously affirmed when a female by the same name (Austin Clarke) writes to Clarke from the University of the West Indies in Trinidad to explain that she has had to respond to questions about her "literary activities" but "had to confess regretfully" that she was not the author. See Clarke to Clarke, April 13, 1964 (Box 36).

47. Robert Weaver to Clarke, October 16, 1970 (Box 36).

48. Wilson Harris to Clarke, July 8, 1965 (Box 37).

49. Weaver to Clarke, October 6, 1964 (Box 36).

50. Carew to Clarke, September 19, 1966 (Box 36).

51. Carew to Clarke, February 14, 1964 (Box 36); Transcript of review for broadcast on September 22, 1965 (Box 36).

52. See Lamming, *Pleasures of Exile*, 214; Schwarz, *West Indian Intellectuals*, 13.

53. James Berry to Clarke, February 27, 1964 (Box 35).

54. Carew to Clarke, November 10, 1967 (Box 36).

55. Stephens, *Black Empire*, 49.

56. Clarke, *Passage*, 44.

57. Jackson Van Deering to Clarke, November 25, 1963 or 1964 (Box 37).

58. Review, "Television and Radio," *Montreal Star*, October 28, 1963.

59. Review, "Canada's Leading Negro Author Writes About His West Indies," *Victoria Colonist*, October 3, 1965 (Box 34).

60. Henry Boyle testimonial letter, December 13, 1965 (Box 36).

61. Walcott, *Black Like Who?*, 39.

62. By 1998 I could argue that a new subfield of study had emerged—that of Caribbean Canadian writing. See Michael Andrew Bucknor, "Postcolonial Crosses: Body-Memory and Internationalism in Caribbean/Canadian Writing" (Ph.D. diss., University of Western Ontario, 1998).

63. See Russell Brown, *Borderlines and Borderlands in English Canada: The Written Line* (Orono, Me.: Canadian-American Center, 1990); George Grant, *Lament for a Nation: The Defeat of Canadian Nationalism* (Ottawa: Carleton University Press, 1978); and Marshall McLuhan, "Canada: The Borderline Case," in *The Canadian Imagination: Dimensions of a Literary Culture*, ed. David Staines (Cambridge, Mass.: Harvard University Press, 1977), 226–248.

64. W. H. New, *Borderlines: How We Talk About Canada* (Vancouver: UBC Press, 2011), 6.

65. Ball, *Postcolonial London*, 43.

66. Gilroy, *Black Atlantic*, 16.

67. Ibid.

Federated Ocean States: Archipelagic Visions of the Third World at Midcentury

MICHELLE A. STEPHENS

In 1955, while living as an expatriate in France, the American author Richard Wright traveled to Bandung, Indonesia, to participate in, as he would describe it, "a meeting of almost all of the human race living in the main geopolitical center of gravity of the earth."[1] Geographically, Bandung is located in Java, one of the larger islands in the archipelagic complex of 13,677 islands that make up the country of Indonesia.[2] Geopolitically, however, Wright was describing the now famous Bandung conference that took place April 18–24, 1955. Bandung has since become a marker for the emergence not only of Third World nationalisms but also for the idea of the Third World itself as a newly visible, politicizing area of the globe during the era of decolonization.

Why is it useful to think about the Windrush generation in light of such geopolitical developments as the "color curtain" Wright describes in evidence at midcentury in Bandung? First and foremost, leading Windrush writers such as George Lamming, Negritude writer Aimé Césaire, and midcentury African American writers such as Richard Wright and James Baldwin were all engaged with the Bandung conference as it applied to the black and colonial world. At the Congress of Negro Writers and Artists in Paris in 1956, many of them sought to bring the Bandung conception of a decolonizing, African and Asian "Third World" to the literary and cultural identity of the black world more broadly. For the most part, however, in defining what it meant to be part of a decolonizing "Third World," these writers remained tied to a vision of a liberated black identity grounded in the Western conception of the nation-state, and tied to a geopolitical arrangement of the world along the continental lines of Europe, Asia, Africa, and America. As such, these black male writers and intellectuals also saw themselves primarily engaging the relationship of various black and ex-colonial subjects to their colonizing European metropoles.

Two contrasting midcentury visions of the Third World, C. L. R. James's notion of West Indian federation and Indonesia's conception of itself as an archipelagic nation or "ocean state," rested on a very different metageography.

Figure 1. Flag of the West Indies Federation. (Wikimedia Commons)

This geography was located very much within the political imaginaries of these island societies as they strove to see and actualize their own links—those internal to their archipelagoes—rather than older links shaped by metropolitan, continental concerns. During the 1950s, both the site of the Bandung conference itself and the West Indies Federation, which actually operated between January 1958 and May 1962 in the Anglophone Caribbean islands, imagined and enacted alternative trans-island conceptions of political identity that could operate at both the national and international levels.

During this period, James was neither at Bandung nor a part of the immigrating Windrush generation. Instead, during the 1950s and 1960s he was in the United States and the Caribbean, actively thinking and writing about the place of island peoples in the decolonizing geopolitical world order and the contributions they could make to visions of world democracy. James's perspective was shaped by his earlier visit to the United States in 1939 on a speaking tour for the Socialist Worker's Party. During that year and into 1940, he addressed specifically the topic of "The Negro People and World Imperialism." James then chose to stay in the United States and went underground, joining a number of Trotskyist factions, living on the fringes, and developing a Marxist revision of the concept of integration.[3] His commitments to internationalist political ideologies led to his understanding that more than a commitment to nationalism for its own sake, black self-determination throughout the Americas would rest on a reconceiving of the state, more along the lines of the ancient Greek city-states in the archipelagic Aegean Sea.

While we tend not to place his work as central to understanding West Indian identity and literature in the 1950s, James's internationalism led him to the articulation of a structure of feeling endemic to the islands. Moreover, he elevated it to the level of a political and cultural philosophy by conceptualizing Caribbean identity and political unity in a federal, trans-island fashion similar to a developing midcentury concept of archipelagic nations (Philippines, Bahamas, Indonesia). His vision is important to reintegrate into our understanding of the 1950s and 1960s precisely because it corroborates scholars' emerging sense that nationalism, on the one hand, and exile and diaspora, on the other, are not the only frames within which to understand West Indian literature at midcentury. This notion of the archipelagic provides an alternative vision of Caribbean transnationalism.

Island visions that retained the relationality and mobility of the experience of exile but also the geographical and local groundedness in the Caribbean itself stand between nationalist and exilic or diasporic conceptions of West Indian identity that are often set against each other. Hence, as Kezia Page has recently argued, it should be possible to understand Caribbean diasporic identities less as alternatives to nationhood and more as mediating between island-nation and empire.[4] Page describes Caribbean subjects' transnational imaginaries as characterized by an "in-betweenity" that keeps their relationship with local conditions and geographies in the Caribbean in constant motion and tension with the immigrant's diasporic identity.[5] Archipelagic Caribbean and Third World subjectivities also inhabit spaces of liminality and imaginary "in-betweenness." Turning our attention to them further orients us toward "a rethinking of the Caribbean diaspora not in deterritorialized terms, but with attention to issues of regional sovereignty and national identity as much as issues of diasporan belonging."[6] Taking Page's starting point as salutary, a refocusing on the insular Caribbean can take us beyond discourses of both nation and diaspora in interesting ways.

As both geographical units and cultural and political formations, the archipelagic notions of federated islands and oceanic states add another dimension to the relationship between Caribbean nationhood and diaspora, between local Caribbean developments and the movements of Caribbean immigrants to England in the 1940s and 1950s. Just after the arrival of the SS Empire Windrush on England's shores in 1948, and just before the independence of the Anglophone Caribbean starting in the early 1960s with Jamaica and Trinidad, for a brief moment a different kind of transnational imaginary emerged, one forged in diaspora and yet profoundly located in an oceanic, island imaginary rather than a metropolitan, diasporic geography. This alternative imaginary was literally *trans*national in imagining a new way of conceiving the relations between Caribbean and other territories on an island-to-island, rather than an island-to-metropole, axis, turning "in-betweenity" itself into a geopolitical as much as a cultural value. This alternative imaginary, theorized most fully in and about the Caribbean by James, was part of a broader process of (geo-) political reconceptualization that first emerges at midcentury during the decolonization era. As contemporary scholar Mohamed Munavvar describes, this particular type of political imagination was formed around the idea of an "archipelagic principle" as an actual unit of international law.[7]

Until the middle of the twentieth century, Munavvar points out, as he tracks the development of a legal notion of the "archipelagic principle" in international law, almost all of the world's islands were either owned by another continental state or under colonial rule. Moreover, in colonial discourse the individual island was held up as the model and ideal for nationally bounded territorial sovereignty.[8] In this discursive context, islands were removed from their archipelagic and terraqueous contexts. Decolonization would serve as the catalyst not only for "ocean states" to begin "to appear on the political map of the world" but also on their own terms.[9] Starting in the 1950s, archipelagoes such as Indonesia, the Philippines, and, a bit later, the Bahamas began to define themselves as "ocean states" with a vision of their territory as lands and waters combined.

In 1957 Indonesia defined itself as one unit—an ocean state—made up of both land and water.[10] By 1960 both the Bahamas and the Philippines joined a discussion with the United Nations on the status of the waters in and around archipelagoes and their jurisdiction under international law. They compiled multiple arguments for their constituting, by law, a unified archipelagic identity combining land and sea—arguments based on geography, economic necessity, and national security. They also cited their need to build intrainsular relations, as well as interinsular highways from island to island. When the Indonesian delegate stated that "the Indonesian language equivalent for the word 'fatherland' . . . is 'tanah air' meaning 'land-water', thereby indicating how inseparable the relationship is between water and land to the Indonesian people," he deployed an additional linguistic justification for the idea of Indonesia as an ocean state.[11]

The Bandung meeting of Asian and African leaders, which was occurring simultaneously in Indonesia, posed a slightly different kind of threat to the continental nations resisting the idea of an archipelagic principle in international law. Less a new form of nationalism than a new way of conceiving internationalism, it was the Bandung conference that actually "prompted the economist Alfred Sauvy to coin the term 'third world.'"[12] Jean Lacouture's recounting of the genealogy of the term demonstrates Bandung's significance in a broader, midcentury, anti-imperial imaginary, one that included intellectual leaders of both the Indonesian and the Caribbean archipelagoes.

The genealogy of the term "Third World" refers back to the French Revolu-tion, to Emmanuel Joseph Sieyes's question, "What is the third estate?" posed in 1789. The Third Estate was traditionally the third social class with some political power, after the nobility and the clergy, but of the commons rather than the traditional ruling classes—in other words, the then-emergent mid-dle class. Sieyes's question prompted less a definition than a political decla-ration: "What is the third estate? Everything. What has it been hitherto in the political order? Nothing. What does it demand? To become something."[13] These phrases marked the moment when the French bourgeoisie demanded to become new subjects of history in a revolution that would ultimately lead to the end of one type of political order, monarchy, and the beginning of another, the nation-state.

Similarly, Bandung represented the emergence at midcentury of a new kind of political consciousness attached to a specific geopolitical imaginary, one that understood itself as linked by the historical legacy of colonialism. Walter Mignolo describes this as a consciousness generated from within colo-nial modernity but producing competing forms of knowledge, alternative imaginaries, and epistemologies. The division of the world into spaces "where coloniality of power is enacted" created decolonial sensibilities, competing forms of "subaltern knowledge" in which "*local* histories inventing and imple-menting global designs meet *local* histories, the space in which global designs have to be adapted, adopted, rejected, integrated, or ignored."[14] Bandung, as one of the signal events of decolonization, represented much more than a new form of nationalism, new entities joining the community of nations and demanding to be politically self-determined subjects in world history. The broader decolonial sensibility defining the period also offered other options for thinking about how the world's ex-colonial territories might organize their relations to and with each other, and to and with metropolitan, First World "centers."

In the very act of meeting together—and defining their meeting in interna-tional terms linked directly to the global history of empire, colonialism, and European and North American Others—the Bandung nations were propos-ing a new, geopolitical metageography. For Richard Wright, racial nationalism seemed to be the unifying ideological force at Bandung. If colonialism was a factor pushing these populations' destinies together from the past, Wright found that "class and racial and religious consciousness on a global scale" shaped the political and ideological principles undergirding their future.[15] The heretofore *nationally bound* forces of race and religion were becoming the very means for creating bridges between geopolitical entities defined as racially and culturally distinct, differentiated by their Asian and African continental identities as well as other, national-territorial designations.[16]

Wright's insight was that race and religion, as the forces relevant to the Third World's fashioning of a new political discourse, could cross not only state but also the continental lines of the area studies model organizing the world's metageography during this period. The "Third World," unlike the "third estate," was an intercontinental phenomenon—"*a racial and religious system of identification manifesting itself in an emotional nationalism which was now leaping state boundaries and melting and merging, one into the other.*"[17] Beyond the racial and religious nationalism of their leaders, however, for Wright, the peoples of the world represented at Bandung also constituted the human race itself, a new universal. These were the people Wright saw portrayed in the first novel of his West Indian contemporary, George Lamming's *In the Castle of My Skin*, as Wright described in his introduction to the first American edition.[18] At the start of the twentieth century, blacks from the West Indies and the American South shared the traumatic experience of being torn from the land, from the agriculturally based life-worlds of the peasantry, and thrust into the maelstrom of modernity. Now at midcentury, Bandung represented the promise that these populations could organize themselves into new, global, political assemblages. The moment "smacked of tidal waves, of natural forces," Wright proclaimed, his epic metaphors revealing the ways in which the type of political representation Bandung seemed to signify attached to real, geoformal and geopolitical formations that could overwhelm and flood the nationally and territorially bound order of the world prescribed by the old European, and the new American, empires.[19]

What was disturbing Wright at Bandung in 1955 was the question of *how*: What principle of unity could possibly organize a conversation that represented global diversity at the highest levels of magnitude? What kind of new political discourses were these people, originally left out of official national and world histories, creating at Bandung? What Wright and other decolonial writers of the period did not see was that the aspect of Bandung most disruptive to territorially bound nationalisms, at a deeply structural level, was the *geographic form* of the territory the conference was located in, rather than the ideological and cultural discourse within which the conference was framed. Indonesian leader Sukarno put it best in his speech when, commenting on the impossibility of Indonesia's own political form—that of an archipelagic state comprised of many islands, not a single, national, territorial unity—he essentially asked, "if a nation-state could be made of Indonesia, why could a transnational unity not be fashioned out of the Bandung nations?"[20] The intercontinental logic Wright saw in the transnationalism of Bandung was actually undergirded by an archipelagic political sensibility.

The Ocean States and C. L. R. James's Vision of Caribbean Federation

The political articulation of an "archipelagic principle" at midcentury thus represented the effort on the part of archipelagic communities to assert new forms of political organization organic to their insular condition in the discourse of the world's international courts and laws. When Indonesia and the Philippines brought grievances specific to their condition as archipelagic nations to an even more official, international "estates-general," the United Nations Conferences on the Law of the Sea, which met successively in 1958, 1960, and 1974, their central grievance was sovereignty over the waters internal to their total archipelagic territory, and the limiting of the rights afforded much larger maritime states, who invoked the freedom of the seas to justify their own extraterritorial control of, and travels through, archipelagic waters.

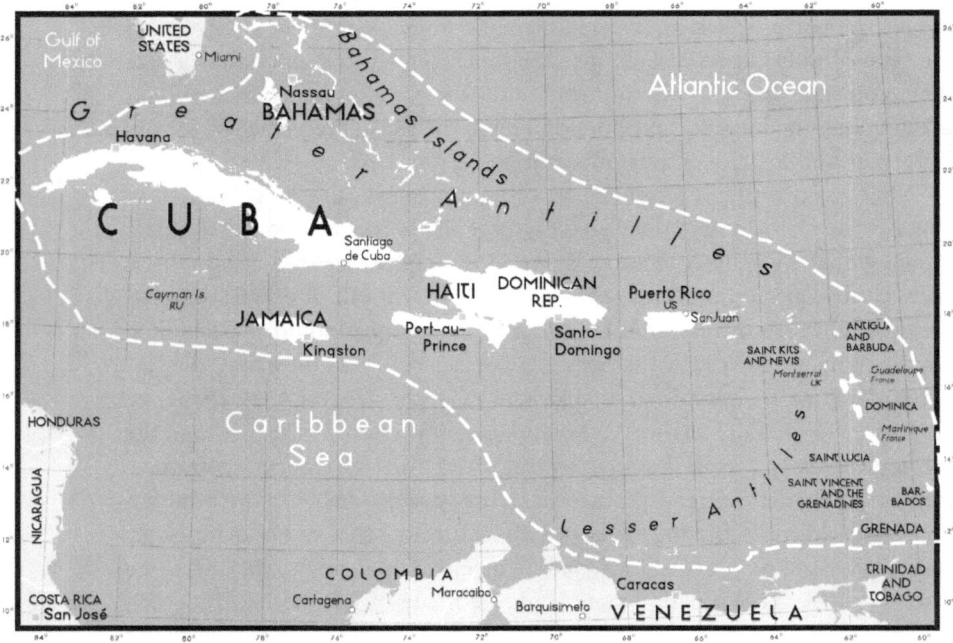

Figure 2. Mapping the Caribbean Islands as a biodiversity hotspot. (Certain images and/or photos on this page are the copyrighted property of 123RF Limited, its Contributors or Licensed Partners and are being used with permission under license. These images and/or photos may not be copied or downloaded without permission from 123RF Limited.)

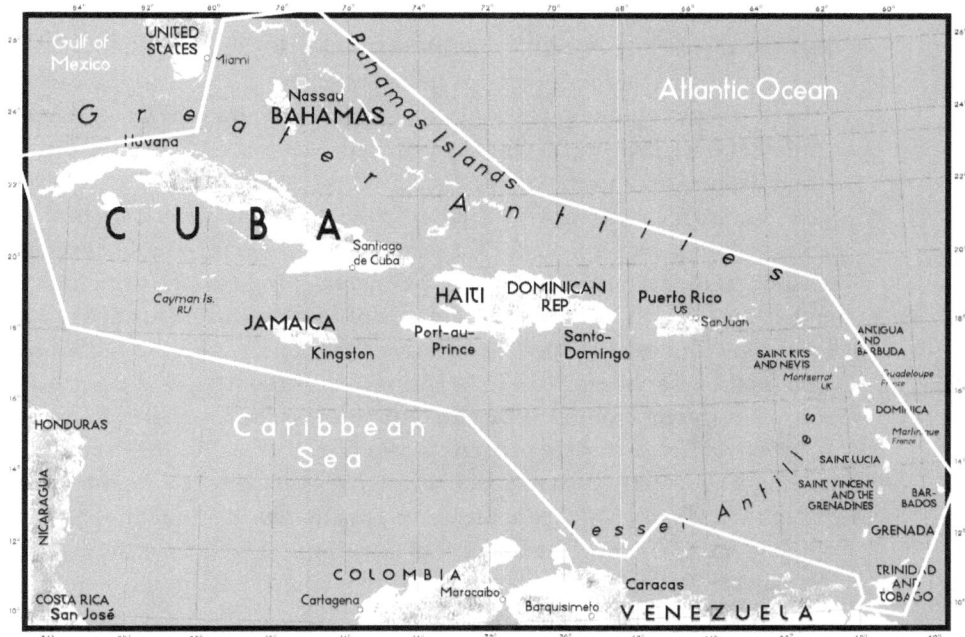

Figure 3. Mapping forest cover in the Caribbean. (Certain images and/or photos on this page are the copyrighted property of 123RF Limited, its Contributors or Licensed Partners and are being used with permission under license. These images and/or photos may not be copied or downloaded without permission from 123RF Limited.)

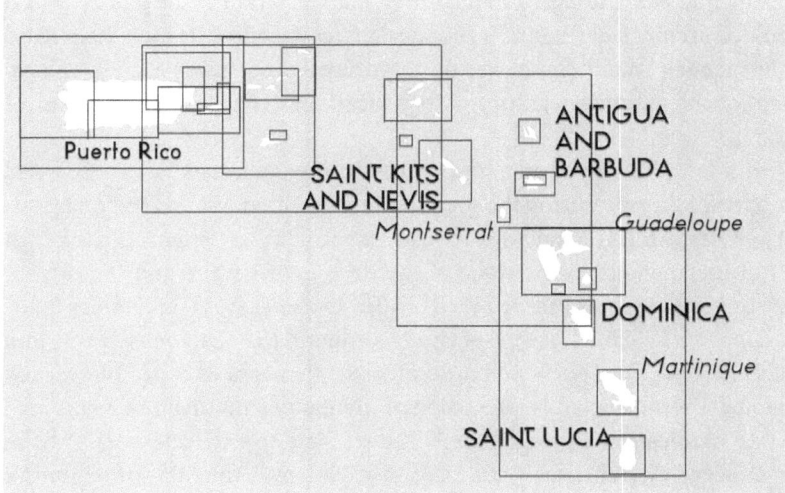

Figure 4. Nautical mapping of the Eastern Caribbean. (Certain images and/or photos on this page are the copyrighted property of 123RF Limited, its Contributors or Licensed Partners and are being used with permission under license. These images and/or photos may not be copied or downloaded without permission from 123RF Limited.)

During the debates at the United Nations, those countries that sought to organize themselves as ocean states—Indonesia, the Philippines, the Bahamas—faced direct opposition from those states that represented the world's greatest maritime powers at the time—the United Kingdom, the United States, the Soviet Union, and Japan. The key item in debate was the "baseline," that is, island nations' wish to encircle and mark off the island chains they believed were connected, within one baseline, as in the two maps of the Caribbean in figures 2 and 3. In the first, the Caribbean is conceived of as a biodiversity hotspot, in the second, as an area of forestation.[21] In both, the Caribbean is understood visually as a single ecological unit, each island as part of a linked ecosystem. This geographical perspective encloses and thereby unifies the islands of the Caribbean Sea within one baseline, in contrast to the organization and representation of the Eastern Caribbean on nautical charts, as imaged in figure 4. Here each island sits in its own box, a picture of the very vision the maritime powers encouraged. Purportedly a cartographic reinforcement of each island's territorial sovereignty, in actuality this nautical arrangement of the island chain provided a means of assuring, legally, the maritime states' free passage through archipelagic waters. They sought passage for more than "innocent" reasons, that is, for submarine and other military engagements as much as for commercial purposes.[22]

Munavvar's account of the international debates surrounding the "archipelagic principle," base lines, and ocean states offers the political proof that at midcentury, islanders were thinking of their existence very differently than mainlanders. He states boldly, "more than just a legal concept," the archipelagic principle was "the legal and territorial manifestation of the philosophical outlook of archipelagic states."[23] Indonesians' conception of their homeland as a terraqeous island chain was as important—and new—a geographical conception of national territory as the racial and religious nationalism of Bandung.

Within a nationalist frame, black writers who relocated to England and other parts of Europe during the 1940s and 1950s, either as West Indian immigrants or African American and African expatriates, experienced their own forms of melancholia in the wake of the decline of empire and the turn to exile.[24] In novels such as Richard Wright's *The Outsider* (1953) and James Baldwin's *Giovanni's Room* (1956), George Lamming's *The Emigrants* (1954) and Samuel Selvon's *The Lonely Londoners* (1956), elements of a profound existential angst were shaped by the colonial mentalities that Aimé Césaire had hoped to eradicate with Negritude.[25] The struggle to extricate oneself from Europe's legacies translates fictionally in each novel into the protagonist's struggle with some form of psychic shame. His path toward recognition is littered with his own affective and psychosexual baggage, a black affect of "*angst*: identity, self-awareness, and wholeness in a colonial, pluralistic society crippled by self-contempt and the psychic scars of slavery."[26]

The personal struggle playing out fictionally in these texts was debated publicly at another, Bandung-inspired, international meeting, the 1956 Congress of Negro Writers and Artists in Paris. In the debates between some of the most prominent black male writers of the period, there was a clear sense of the black male intellectual's responsibility for crafting the aftermath of decolonization. As Wright reported on Bandung, so too did James Baldwin, another African American writer, report on the different positions taken up at the conference. Three figures in particular held positions emblematic of a black male diasporic consciousness: Césaire, Wright, and Lamming.[27] Césaire focused on the decolonization of the black mind and the necessarily antagonistic relationship between such a mind and the colonial mentality that fostered it. Wright argued for the benefits of the intercultural encounter between colonizer and colonized, seeing the inheritances of the Enlightenment as valuable legacies left behind by the colonizer. Lamming translated both positions into literary terms, "insisting on the respect which is due the private life."[28] Baldwin thought that Lamming spoke as a "genuine writer," redirecting the discussion toward the affective and unconscious black life, a neglected space between political notions and cultural expressions of blackness. What all three speakers shared, however, as a common aspect of their black diasporic discourse was a continued engagement with the colonizer in Manichaean terms.[29]

Perhaps because James was stuck on an island owned by a new global hegemon, the United States, he was more attentive to the "future" of the world we live in, rather than the past of the colonial world the Third World was leaving behind. His reflections in *Mariners, Renegades and Castaways*, a work written during the limbo of his political exile on Ellis Island in 1953, are important for underscoring the different direction of his gaze from that of the exilic Windrush generation struggling to acclimatize themselves to life in the metropole. James's position, in a Black Atlantic conceived as an *oceanic* rather than a *diasporic* space, his *archipelagic* rather than *exilic* sensibility, allowed him to imagine different political alternatives for the future that would have Caribbean subjects interacting with each other in trans-island, transnational ways.

Assumed to be primarily a critique of American empire, *Mariners* positions a ship, the American *Pequod* from Melville's *Moby Dick*, as the setting for James's exploration of the strengths and limits of US democracy.[30] Paul Gilroy has highlighted the chronotope of the ship as important for understanding the history of the Black Atlantic.[31] Signifying diaspora, this chronotope finds its historical corollary in the *Windrush* passengers who sailed away from the Caribbean toward the exilic West Indian identities they created in the British metropole. However, in *Mariners*, rather than a figure for diaspora, the *Pequod* is a chronotope for an oceanic form of political organization shaped by an archipelagic sensibility—the island network as an ocean state.

If Melville's American "Nantucketers" owned the sea "as Emperors own Empires," then the Caribbean Sea lay at the heart of that maritime empire, its waters as available for the "free" passage of the United States as the waters of the Indonesian or Philippine archipelagoes.[32] "Islanders" were the peoples employed in this American imperial enterprise, but they could also play a role in defining the contours of their own postcolonial, maritime states. In other words, just as the peoples of the Pacific and Indian Oceans and the South Seas were doing this in the 1950s, James seemed to believe that the peoples of the Caribbean-Atlantic could strive to do the same.[33] In James's reimagining of the community created by the *Pequod*'s crew, we see a de-territorialized, oceanic rather than diasporic world, one that traveled in the wake of the ships of marine empires throughout modernity. That world, as James would reconstruct it in his imaginative rewriting of Melville's story, was a world of island men who "came from all over the world, were islanders from places like the Azores and the Shetland Islands."[34]

On the *Pequod*, the discourse of modern nationalism would work to keep archipelagic peoples isolated and divided from each other. Just as in the United Nations Conferences on the Law of the Sea, on Ahab's ship "nearly all the nations of the globe had each its representative," but they were organized in such a way that each was "not acknowledging the common continent of men [and] each Isolato liv[ed] on a separate continent of his own."[35] Isolationism was the dark side of national independence, creating the isolatoes of the modern world. In contrast, a federated *Pequod*, like the archipelagic ocean state, was both the literal and figurative means by which Melville's islanders and littoral peoples—the South Sea islander Queequeg; the Native American from Martha's Vineyard, Tashtego; and the African coastal tribesman, Daggoo; along with the rest of the crew—could chart a different course for democracy. James considered this a path their real-life Caribbean counterparts could follow.

James thought that by the 1950s, the ideal of the autonomous, sovereign nation-state as a political institution and idea had failed at achieving its core political goal of universal democracy.[36] He suggested that in the Americas one could produce a state created along different lines than those of Europe, but this state-form existed less in the continental United States than in the insular Caribbean. Melville's *Pequod* was leading us toward the image of Caribbean federation found in James's later writings on modern politics. In his dream of West Indian federation, James returned to a Greek notion of island chains shaped by the people's relation to water as much as land. This image of the island among waves appears as a symbol on the flag of the West Indies Federation (see figure 1).

James used the ancient world as his model for crafting a future vision of political utopia, and for him the virtue of the Greek city-states was precisely the way their size and status as *linked* microstates worked for them rather than against them. As James observes in comparing the Aegean and Caribbean worlds:

> The Greek City-States moved so far and so fast, and that is my hope for the development of the West Indies too. Those states were so small that everybody had a grasp of what was going on. Nobody was backward; nobody was remote; nobody was far in the country; and people in the West Indies are even closer because we have methods of transport that bring us very rapidly together.[37]

In this vision, forms of culture, democratic political practice, actual citizens, could travel easily between the states, crossing city-state lines. The Greek city-state offered James a utopian model of political freedom because it was a network made up of political units much closer in size to the physical realities of the Caribbean. Federation, he hoped, could turn the size of the islands, a potential weakness, into a strength, creating a new "national" community built not on territory but on the free movement of insular peoples, resources, and ideas across interinsular highways imagined as forming between individual territories that comprised the ocean states.

In the 1940s and 1950s James saw the beginning of two new political and economic processes—decolonization and globalization—that would drastically change world society in the second half of the century. When he said, "The Caribbean is now an American sea," he pointed to an emergent set of political relations resting less on the sovereign status of land than on the freedom of mobility across the world's waters assured to the powerful maritime states.[38] Noting the ways Europe was already being swept up by globalizing forces emanating from the United States, James pointed to the instability and vulnerability of the very notion of national sovereignty, and thus independence, in the face of a greater state's power.[39] With institutions such as Benelux and the European Common Market, the European nation-states were turning to forms of federation as a way of competing in a new, US-dominated world order, placing themselves in a geographical position to participate as more equal players in the global economy.[40] James's caution that "freedom from colonialism is not merely legal independence, the right to run up a national flag and to compose and to sing a national anthem," reflected his more layered understanding of the spectrum of political and economic sovereignty that would increasingly come to shape islanders' lives, both at home and abroad, in a globalizing world.[41]

Like the archipelagic principle articulated by the midcentury ocean states, James's vision of federation represented a more complicated way of thinking about maximizing the Third World's power and status in the wake of decolonization. Animated by the decolonial politics of Bandung, exiles of the Windrush generation such as Stuart Hall realized that federation posed a Caribbean vision of the Third World that went beyond the ideal of the autonomous, sovereign nation-state. As Hall describes:

> Up until 1954, I was saturated in West Indian expatriate politics. . . . We were passionate about the colonial question. . . . With the emerging postcolonial independence, we dreamt of a Caribbean federation, merging these countries into a larger entity. If that had happened, I would have gone back to the Caribbean . . . and tried to play a role there. That dream was over at the moment in the 1950s when I decided to stay [in Britain].[42]

At midcentury, federation provided a third archipelagic and oceanic vision between nation and diaspora, an intellectual trajectory and physical geography that ran island to island rather than island to metropole, something productively between independence and expatriation. It is this more sophisticated strain of nationalist thinking, one that might have been better positioned to address the rise of US power simultaneous with decolonization, that James's Windrush contemporary George Lamming lyrically describes in his 1960 essay "Ishmael at Home."[43] In a Caribbean "now very much at sea," the Caribbean Ishmael is left swimming in the wake of both the *Empire Windrush* and the *Pequod*, one sailing away from the Caribbean on its way to diaspora in the metropole, the other determinedly advancing toward the US Empire across the Caribbean Sea. In the face of this choice, James tried to articulate a Third World vision of emancipation that was organic to the Caribbean's archipelagic context. Federation represented a way of being at home among the waves, an oceanic transnationalism as mobile and migratory as a diasporic exilic consciousness abroad.

Notes

1. Richard Wright, *The Color Curtain: A Report on the Bandung Conference* (Jackson: University Press of Mississippi, 1994), 12.

2. Mohamed Munavvar, *Ocean States: Archipelagic Regimes in the Law of the Sea* (Boston: Martinus Nijhoff, 1995), 20.

3. See Michelle A. Stephens, *Black Empire: The Masculine Global Imaginary of Caribbean Intellectuals in the United States, 1914–1962* (Durham, N.C.: Duke University Press, 2005), 222–234.

4. Kezia Page, *Transnational Negotiations in Caribbean Diasporic Literature: Remitting the Text* (New York: Routledge, 2010), 3, 15.

5. Ibid., 1.

6. Ibid.

7. Munavvar, *Ocean States*, 5. As he defines the ocean state: "the archipelagic concept, the archipelagic doctrine, or the archipelagic principle . . . is about a group of islands and the waters surrounding them as a single entity for the purpose of delimiting the maritime zones of the island group as a single unit."

8. See Antoine Hatzenberger, "Islands and Empires: Beyond the Shores of Utopia," *Angelika: Journal of the Theoretical Humanities* 8 (April 2003): 119–128; and Philip E. Steinberg, "Insularity, Sovereignty and Statehood: The Representation of Islands on Portolan Charts and the Construction of the Territorial State," *Geografiska Annaler: Series B, Human Geography* 87 (December 2005): 254–264.

9. Munavvar, *Ocean* States, 27.

10. Ibid., 29.

11. Ibid., 28.

12. Jean Lacouture, "The First Conference of the Third World," *Le Monde Diplomatique* (May 2005), http://mondediplo.com/2005/05/.

13. Ibid.

14. Walter Mignolo, *Local Histories/Global Designs: Coloniality, Subaltern Knowledges and Border Thinking* (Princeton, N.J.: Princeton University Press, 2000), ix.

15. Wright, *Color Curtain*, 13.

16. Ibid., 13, 141.

17. Ibid., 140 [italics in original].

18. Richard Wright, "Introduction," in George Lamming, *In the Castle of My Skin* (New York: McGraw-Hill Book, 1953), vi. As Wright states: "Notwithstanding the fact that Lamming's story, as such, is his own, it is, at the same time, a symbolic repetition of the story of millions of simple folk who, sprawled over half of the world's surface and involving more than half of the human race, are today being catapulted out of their peaceful, indigenous earthy lives and into the turbulence and anxiety of the twentieth century."

19. Wright, *Color Curtain*, 13–14.

20. Vijay Prashad, *The Darker Nations: A People's History of the Third World* (New York: New Press People's History, 2008), 33.

21. A discussion of the Caribbean as a biodiversity hotspot, with a range of accompanying maps, can be found at http://www.cepf.net/where_we_work/regions/CaribbeanIslands/Pages/default.aspx. A discussion of the Caribbean islands as an area of forestation can be found at http://www.fao.org/docrep/004/Y1997E/y1997e28.jpg. What is of interest here is the use of a regional boundary line to mark off the archipelagic area under consideration, much as the maritime baselines of the ocean states sought to represent archipelagic nations as one terraqueous unit.

22. As Munavvar describes further in *Ocean States*: "The naval powers feel that a sovereign archipelagic regime, with straits threatening as choke points, could represent a death blow to mobility," that is, their free passage through archipelagic waters (42).

23. Ibid., 185.

24. This exilic consciousness can be seen as another aspect of the forms of postcolonial melancholia Paul Gilroy describes as afflicting the colonizer in the metropole in *Postcolonial Melancholia* (New York: Columbia University Press, 2006).

25. Richard Wright, *The Outsider* (New York: HarperCollins, 1953); James Baldwin, *Giovanni's Room* (New York: Dial Press, 1956); George Lamming, *The Emigrants* (London: McGraw-Hill, 1954); Samuel Selvon, *The Lonely Londoners* (London: Allan Wingate, 1956).

26. Harold Barratt, "An Island Is Not a World: A Reading of Sam Selvon's 'An Island Is a World,'" *ARIEL: A Review of International English Literature* 27, no. 2 (April 1996): 25–34, 26.

27. James Baldwin, "Princes and Powers," in *Nobody Knows My Name: More Notes of a Native Son* (New York: Dial Press, 1961), reprinted in *James Baldwin: Collected Essays* (New York: Literary Classics of the United States, 1998), 143–169.

28. Ibid., 160–161.

29. See bell hooks, "Feminism as a Persistent Critique of History: What's Love Got to Do with It?" in *The Fact of Blackness: Frantz Fanon and Visual Representation*, ed. Alan Read (Seattle: Bay Press, 1996), 76–85, for more on the ways this Manichaean struggle shapes a black, diasporic, postcolonial, male sensibility.

30. C. L. R. James, *Mariners, Renegades and Castaways: The Story of Herman Melville and the World We Live In* (Lebanon, N.H.: Dartmouth University Press, 2001).

31. Paul Gilroy, *The Black Atlantic: Modernity and Double Consciousness* (Cambridge, Mass.: Harvard University Press, 1993), 17.

32. James, *Mariners, Renegades and Castaways*, 18.

33. Ibid.

34. Ibid.

35. Ibid.

36. Ibid., 13.

37. C. L. R. James, *Modern Politics* (Detroit: Bewick/Ed., 1973), 70.

38. Anna Grimshaw, ed., *The C. L. R. James Reader* (Cambridge, Mass.: Blackwell, 1992), 308.

39. C. L. R. James, *At the Rendezvous of Victory: Selected Writings* (London: Allison and Busby, 1984), 91–92.

40. James, *Modern Politics*, 84.

41. James, *At the Rendezvous of Victory*, 95.

42. Stuart Hall, "The Formation of a Diasporic Intellectual: An Interview with Stuart Hall by Kuan-Hsing Chen," in *Stuart Hall: Critical Dialogues in Cultural Studies*, ed. David Morley and Kuan-Hsing Chen (New York: Routledge, 1996), 492–502.

43. George Lamming, *The Pleasures of Exile* (1960; repr., Ann Arbor: University of Michigan Press, 1992), 155.

Epilogue: Coming of Age in the Fifties

EDWARD BAUGH

I entered the University College of the West Indies (UCWI) at Mona, Jamaica, in October 1954 to read for a degree in English, with Latin as subsidiary subject. This development helped to foster in me an interest in what was to become known as West Indian literature, which was just then coming into full bloom. However, my contact with West Indian writing owed nothing to my formal studies at university. There was, in those early days, no suggestion of it on the syllabus, which was that of the University of London, to which the UCWI was affiliated. The syllabus that I followed covered the history of the literature of England, from *Beowulf* to the work of Joseph Conrad and T. S. Eliot, two honorary English writers, so to speak.

I came into stimulating contact with West Indian writing through extra-curricular factors: the discovery of the literary magazine *Bim* and the BBC's *Caribbean Voices* program; getting to know Cedric Lindo (then the college's public relations officer); the activities of the student Literary Society and Scribblers Group; and the proximity of Derek Walcott, who had left Mona the term before I entered, but who was still around, teaching in high school and writing on books and theater for the weekly *Public Opinion*, and visiting the campus. I had read, in March 1954, a few months before I was to enter university, a review in the *Daily Gleaner* of a play, *Henri Christophe*, staged by the Dramatic Society at Mona and written and directed by a student, one Derek Walcott. My eager anticipation of becoming a part of such a milieu was heightened. There were also, of course, the seminal, ground-breaking novels that were appearing during the Fifties, novels by George Lamming, Sam Selvon, John Hearne, Roger Mais, Edgar Mittelholzer, most of which I read.

At school, I had come to know and like one or two Jamaican poems, such as J. E. Clare McFarlane's "On National Vanity," Claude McKay's "Flame Heart," and Roger Mais's "All Men Come to the Hills." The Mais I had had to recite as a member of a verse-speaking group at a school function, and I seem to remember reciting the McFarlane in an elocution competition in a parish festival of music and speech. There was also Louise Bennett, on popular lips, special, but not received then as "literature."

It may also have been while I was at school, in the Sixth Form, that I discovered *Caribbean Voices*. One of my channels of contact then with the international world, and one of my special sources of pleasure, was the table-model short-wave radio that my father had bought secondhand during "the war years" in order to listen to news of the war on the BBC and to hear Winston Churchill. A special delight for me was the half-hour *Caribbean Voices* program on a Sunday evening, at 6:15 if I remember correctly. It was like a secret pleasure. I had discovered it through my own "surfing," and no one else in the family would have been interested in it. No particular short story or poem stuck in my mind from then, only the general excitement, a solitary excitement, of hearing them, and hearing West Indian voices reading them.

That experience was a major factor in my entry into West Indianness, all the more significant because I had been brought up in an insular environment, in which people from the other West Indian islands were dismissed as "small island people," never mind the great success at that time of the West Indies cricket team. My initial contact with West Indianness was widened and deepened, exhilaratingly, by my contact with the variety of West Indians from other territories who were among my fellow students at the UCWI. What is more, the idea of a West Indian Federation, which was to become a reality, though short-lived, in 1958, found heady expression among the student body during the mid-to-late Fifties. This mood contributed to the sense of the emergence of West Indian literature. As for cricket, the historic West Indian victory in the 1950 test match at Lords cricket ground in London was like a herald to the development of the West Indian idea in the Fifties. It is no mere coincidence that an impressive body of West Indian creative writing about cricket has evolved since then, with C. L. R. James as its godfather, so to speak.

My going to Mona extended my contact with *Caribbean Voices*. I was able to listen to the program only when I went home for the vacations, because I did not have a radio. However, my interest in it deepened as a result of my getting to know and chat with Cedric Lindo, who, I discovered, was the local agent for the program. His wife, Gladys, was for a time the official contact, but he was the person who chiefly made the decisions and also solicited material. All material being submitted from within the region had to go through the Lindos. They selected what they thought fit to send on to Henry Swanzy, the program's editor, in London.

Eventually, before the end of my four-year stay at Mona, and through Cedric Lindo's encouragement, I was to enjoy the excitement of having a poem and a short story read on *Caribbean Voices*. The pleasure was heightened by the fact that I was paid for them, one guinea per minute of reading time. The poem, an uncollected apprentice piece, was very much the sort of thing one might expect from would-be poets at that stage of life: about the *angst* of growing up, losing one's sense of innocent fantasy and wonder to the harsh light of the real world and the demons of introspection. With regard to the story, more on that below.

I cannot claim to have had any feeling of mission to be a West Indian writer, or any clearly thought-out idea of what that would entail. It was, rather, that my love of literature, whether as reader or potential writer—a love nurtured by English literature—seemed to take on new meaning in a milieu in which I could feel that I naturally belonged, and out of which it would be natural and allowable to write.

I can't remember how I first got to know about *Bim*, but here again Cedric Lindo may have played a crucial role, because he was in postal contact with Frank Collymore, and there was appreciable traffic of material between *Caribbean Voices* and *Bim*. (I knew hardly anything about *Kyk-over-al* at that time.) What I remember vividly though is reading *Bim* on many an afternoon in the periodicals stacks of the Mona library. Arts students did not have classes in the afternoons, and my afternoons were pleasurable. Lunch was followed by a siesta. I then had a shower and went for tea (or, preferably, "postcolonial" lemonade); then I would browse in the library before returning to my room to dress for dinner. One of the most pleasurable and eye-opening objects of that browsing was *Bim*, and the sense it gave me of a literature emerging, a literature to which I could feel a kind of familial affinity.

I don't remember many specific pieces from that time, but I do carry a few names and titles that marked my sense of discovery. It meant something to be reading the short stories of the few who had already become celebrated as a result of having had novels published in London that would endure: Lamming, Mittelholzer, and Selvon. Then there was Walcott, who, although he had not yet had a book published internationally (and wouldn't until 1962), was causing a stir in the still small West Indian literary circles because of his exceptionally promising talent, in poetry and in drama. My most vivid memory from my encounter with *Bim* at that time came at the end of the period. There in the stacks, one afternoon in 1958, turning the pages of No. 26 (January–June 1958), I came upon Walcott's "Tales of the Islands" and saw new vistas suddenly open before me.

This variation on the traditional sonnet sequence—and I had been absorbing appreciatively, in my formal studies, the sonnets of Shakespeare, the Elizabethans, and Milton—carried a contemporary and West Indian quality in respect of content, form, and style, even as it exploited conventional strengths of the sonnet and of English. In pursuing his stated aim of bringing back to poetry something of what prose fiction had taken from it, Walcott made his quasi-sonnets into succinct short stories, giving poetic life to West Indian characters and definitive sociocultural issues. As for language, there was the dramatic exploitation of West Indian, in this case Trinidadian, vernacular, in a verse form traditionally associated with "proper" English, as in the unforgettably startling opening "Poopa, da' was a fête!" I felt impelled to share my excitement in a review of that issue of *Bim* for the student newspaper, the *Pelican*. The review dealt almost entirely with "Tales."

There were others in the *Bim* of my Mona years (Nos. 20–26, 1954–1958) whose talent and promise were striking, but who would have to wait a good little while, or interminably long, to get wide or even modest acclaim. Kamau (then "L.E.") Brathwaite was a regular contributor throughout the Fifties, of notable craft, although one might not have foreseen then the revolutionary breakthrough in subject matter and form that was to be marked by the publication of *Rights of Passage* in 1967. Still, there were signals: "The Spade," *Bim*, No. 25 (July–December 1954) and "South," *Bim*, No. 28 (January–June 1959), which were both to take their justifiable places in *Rights*.

I also remember being elated by the new sound and subject matter, the particular West Indianness of Ian McDonald's "Jaffo the Calypsonian" (No. 22, June 1955) and "The Stick Fighters" (No. 24, January–June 1957), his first two contributions to the magazine. Here again it was a matter of bringing into "serious" poetry the West Indian folk, this time folk heroes, and in a natural-voiced, long-lined, post-Whitman, post-Lawrence free verse. Earl Lovelace, in his novels, was subsequently to give major space to the calypsonian and the stick-fighter as folk hero. Other writers, notably Selvon, also featured the calypso and calypsonians. McDonald continued to be engagingly productive over the years, gaining reasonably wide recognition.

Then there was the consistent authority of E. M. Roach, his "passionate intensity," metaphorical inventiveness, and eloquent riding of the iambic wave. In addition to his *Bim* contributions and poems read on *Caribbean Voices* between 1950 and 1955, Roach had only one very limited, local collection published in his lifetime, the chapbook *A Collection of Poems by a Poet of Tobago* (Scarborough, Tobago [1967]). Consequently, he missed out on being recognized as one of the major West Indian poets. That deficiency was somewhat corrected, long after his death, with the publication in 1992 of *The Flowering Rock: Collected Poems 1938–1974*, followed by Laurence A. Breiner's close and insightful critical study, *Black Yeats: Eric Roach and the Politics of Caribbean Poetry* (2008). But Roach is still to enjoy his true status in the ranks of Caribbean poets.

There was also John Figueroa, a regular, long-standing contributor, who had had a collection of prose and poetry, *Blue Mountain Peak*, published as early as 1944. Such attention as he commanded was enhanced with the subsequent publication of two collections of poetry: *Love Leaps Here* (1962) and *Ignoring Hurts* (1974). My sense of the possibility of literature as being alive in my immediate surroundings was augmented by Figueroa's imposing presence on campus as professor of education. At Mona too I became aware (as who in the extracurricular literary circle didn't?), though not through *Bim* but through "the grapevine," of Martin Carter's historic 1953 *Poems of Resistance*, which established the validity of urgent West Indian political concerns as accessible to first-rate artistic expression.

With regard to the short story, there was John Wickham, a meticulous craftsman of lucid, unhurried prose, who, thanks to three collections—*Casuarina Row* (1974), *World Without End: Memoirs of a Time* (1982), and *Discoveries: Short Stories* (1993)—did establish a fair reputation in his lifetime. Interestingly, one of his pieces in *Bim* was an extract from an unpublished novel, "The Living Image" (No. 24, January–June 1957). The novel was never published. No doubt if it had been it would have added to his reputation.

To look back now, and more closely, at the *Bim* issues of my four Mona years, is to confirm in hindsight that there were some writers who fell through the cracks of opportunity, but who would or might otherwise have taken their place in the canon. I think of Owen Campbell, poet, and especially of Karl Sealy, short story writer. Campbell's work was somewhat in the mode of Roach's, but not so taut or authoritative. He continued to contribute, sporadically, up to 1967, but then disappeared from the West Indian literary scene.

The no doubt understandable relative neglect of Sealy is the most regrettable case of all. He is one of the finest, most compelling West Indian writers of prose fiction. The twenty short stories of his that appeared in *Bim* between 1945 and 1965 (nineteen of them by 1958) would have made (could still make) an impressive collection. "The Sun Was a Slaver" (in the same issue as Walcott's "Tales of the Islands") is a masterpiece, but so are others of his stories. His name is hardly known now, except to the few who read literary histories and those who have looked into or have had to engage with one or other of a few anthologies.

Although the first number (undated) of *Bim: Arts for the 21st Century*, the successor to *Bim*, was devoted to a selection of "*Bim* Classics," there was no Sealy story among them. However, the next number, "Special Edition" (November 2007), carried "The Bargain" (from No. 6). "The Sun Was a Slaver" appeared in *From the Green Antilles*, edited by Barbara Howes (1971). "My Fathers Before Me" was reprinted in *Caribbean Stories*, edited by Michael Marland (1978), while "The Pieces of Silver" appeared in *Insights: An Anthology of Short Stories*, edited by Roy Narinesingh and Clifford Narinesingh (1980); in *Global Tales:*

Stories from Many Cultures, edited by Beverley Naidoo, Chris Donovan, Alan Hicks, and Michael Marland (1997); and again in *Response: A Course in Narrative and Comprehension and Composition for Caribbean Secondary Schools*, edited by Cecil Gray (2000), which also carried "The Fields Are High" (No. 9). Most readers of these will have become acquainted with just one Sealy story, without being aware of the body of achievement around it. Gray was himself one of *Bim*'s early contributors of short stories, in due course turning to poetry, in which he has become prolific in his late years. He would have been familiar with Sealy's work, and no doubt thought highly of it.

Amusingly, by virtue of "The Pieces of Silver," Sealy has, however innocently and unknowingly, scored a sort of poetic justice against neglect, as an agent of what Louise Bennett mischievously called "Colonization in Reverse." Wonderful to relate, "The Pieces of Silver" has long been on the English literature syllabus of England's General Certificate of Secondary Education, perhaps as a result of being available in one of the anthologies just mentioned. It has consequently enjoyed some small fame.

Mention of anthologies prompts reflection on possible reasons for the fact that the less-than-major writers of the Fifties (and later periods) have been rather too neglected. One possible reason has to do with anthologies, their availability and use. Some West Indians know poems and short stories by these otherwise neglected writers because the pieces have been taught in schools largely from readers for which the material is chosen primarily with regard to subject matter, rather than in terms of whether the authors are classics. Still, the major authors are usually well represented. However, at university level in the West Indies the situation has been otherwise, syllabuses being drawn up in terms of major authors, sometimes exclusively so, unlike what has traditionally prevailed in the North American system, where there is great reliance on anthologies, such as, notably, the Norton anthology.

In my Mona years, there were other incidental events that encouraged, however half-knowingly, my sense of being in personal touch with the coming-of-age of West Indian literature. I heard talks by Lamming and Walcott to the student Literary Society, of which I was an active member. One Sunday morning, Walcott turned up at a meeting of the Scribblers Group, of which he had been an active member. He read for us e. e. cummings's humorous, witty, idiosyncratic "I Sing of Olaf," which opened my ears to kinds of modern poetry that departed radically from the sort of traditional English poetry on which I had been nurtured, and encouraged my openness to the world of poetry, to the idea that finding oneself as a West Indian poet did not mean cutting oneself off from that wider world. I made a note of the book from which Walcott had read, Oscar Williams's *Little Treasury of Modern Poetry*.

I subsequently acquired a copy, which I still have, and from which I derived much knowledge and pleasure over the years. By a happy turn of events, I was to teach from it during my year (1959–1960) as instructor in English at Victoria College (now Victoria University) on Vancouver Island.

Then there was my contact with Garth St. Omer, a now regrettably neglected novelist. Happily, that neglect is being corrected. Three of his novels have recently been republished by Peepal Tree Press. It was mainly through Cedric Lindo that I first heard of St. Omer and of the buzz of excitement about his talent. Of particular mention was St. Omer's novella *Syrop*, which was doing the little round of insiders, but which was not to see publication until 1964, in Faber's *Introduction 2: Stories by New Writers*. St. Omer had five pieces of prose fiction published in *Bim* between 1951 and 1957. Two of these, "La Revendeuse" and "The Departure," as well as two or three others, were also read on *Caribbean Voices*. Then, in 1956, at the beginning of my third year on campus, St. Omer entered the College to read for a degree in modern languages (French and Spanish). Cedric Lindo was influential in getting him to apply for the scholarship that took him to Mona. As chance would have it, he was assigned a room next to mine in hall. We became good friends. My trying my hand at the short story at that time must have had something to do with his example. I remember him offering constructive comment on my story, which was later read on *Caribbean Voices*.

That story, a vignette really, was based on the experience of seeing a Poco-mania preacher and one of his church sisters, clad in appropriate costumes, meet at the bus stop at Papine near the Mona campus, and take the bus, presumably to go to "keep a meeting" in some other part of the city. Interestingly, as it strikes me now, the next piece of writing I was fortunate to have published was in the same thematic area. It was a short poem, "The Daughters of Music," about the street-side, drum-and-tambourine revivalist services that I used to pass as I walked home from Sunday evening service at the Methodist church in Port Antonio. It appeared in *The Independence Anthology of Jamaican Literature* (1962), edited by A. L. Hendriks and Cedric Lindo. If I remember correctly, the poem had been written before the end of the Fifties. It gave me an additional fillip to have my poem included in this historic anthology, one that was another illustration of the synergy between the blossoming West Indian literature and the watershed national-political developments of the time.

Another campus friendship also contributed, in a more peripheral way, to my sense of having some contact with "the action." In my very first week on campus, I made two close friendships, one of which turned out to be with Michael Sloly, a nephew of Roger Mais, whose *The Hills Were Joyful Together* had appeared in 1953, while his other two novels, *Brother Man* and *Black Lightning*, were to appear in 1954 and 1955, respectively. It was from Michael that I learned that Mais had returned to Jamaica in 1954, and was in the university hospital dying of cancer. Michael would walk over from Taylor Hall to the hospital to visit Uncle Roger, and he told me how irascible Roger sometimes was with the nurses. It was also through my friendship with Michael that I met, at his family's house, John Hearne, a close friend of Mais, who was also his mentor. Hearne had himself recently returned from England. His first novel, *Voices under the Window*, was published in 1955, to be followed by four others in the Fifties.

My sense of being close to significant new developments in literature also owed something to the proximity of fellow undergraduates, in addition to St. Omer, whose literary talents showed great promise. I think particularly of Mervyn Morris, Slade (later Abdul-Rahman Slade) Hopkinson, Cliff Lashley, Aston Mullings, and Jean D'Costa (then Creary). Lashley published only a sprinkling of poems, but there is reason to believe that at his death he left behind a fair-sized collection. D'Costa, who at that time signaled her gift for poetry, was later to earn a reputation as a writer of novels for children.

Hopkinson's first slim volume of poetry, *The Four and Other Poems*, privately published and not widely circulated, appeared in 1954, in his first undergraduate year. It was not until the 1960s that a good few of his pieces appeared in *Bim*, and not until 1976 that two other small collections, *The Madwoman of Papine* and *The Friend*, were published in his native Guyana. It was only in 1992, the year of his death, that *Snowscape with Signature*, a substantial collection, appeared, published by Peepal Tree Press and boosting recognition of him.

It was fitting that the introduction to *Snowscape with Signature* was written by Mervyn Morris, Hopkinson's fellow hall-resident. In their time on campus, Morris was known mainly as a promising short story writer. By the time of the publication of *Snowscape*, he had had four collections of poetry published in London, and had established himself as a major West Indian poet with a distinctive voice. Like Hopkinson, it was in the Sixties that he first began to appear in *Bim*. He became one of the magazine's most substantial contributors.

Aston Mullings, my senior by one year in the English Honours program, was perhaps the one most productive during the Fifties, but the one who was to remain least known. Fastidious of taste, rigorous of intellect and style, he absorbed well the influences from the European poetry he studied at school and university, noticeably that of the Elizabethan and seventeenth-century periods, with a fondness for the sonnet. He never appeared in *Bim*, but had nearly twenty poems broadcast on *Caribbean Voices*, all between 1953 and 1958. One of these was a translation of Apollinaire's "Le Pont Mirabeau." He left Jamaica not long after graduating, and has not been heard of since.

I spent the last year-and-a-bit of the Fifties in Canada, and that period fortuitously provides a fitting rounding-out to my story of coming of age in the Fifties, for myself, for West Indian literature, and for the relationship between us. In the academic year 1958–1959, when I was a graduate student at Queen's University, Ontario, I read a Selvon novel/story (I think it was Selvon) in which a Trinidadian returns home with a white English wife. Here again I was engaged in extracurricular reading; there was no thought then of Commonwealth or least of all West Indian literature on the Queen's University curriculum. In the story that I read there was a brilliantly funny scene that had to do with local reaction to the man's bringing home an English wife. The effect of the scene depended partly on Selvon's path-finding use of Trinidadian speech. (I hope I am not making all this up, but if I am, then I am illustrating the truth of fiction.) One of the students in my class was a Trinidadian, my friend, who had done his first degree at another Canadian university. Thinking that a "Trini" would respond even more knowledgeably and animatedly than I to the scene, I showed it to him. I watched him read it without animation. His only response was, "But will Canadians understand it?" My heart sank. I felt that my eyes were being opened to something of what West Indian literature was up against. I rationalized (to myself) the difference in the reactions of my friend and myself in terms of the fact that *I* had spent my coming-of-age years in the West Indies and had done my first degree at the University College of the West Indies.

Then, just three or four months before I left Canada to return home, Canada's prestigious *Tamarack Review* published an issue (No. 14, Winter 1960) devoted to "the West Indies." It was an impressive selection of work by writers who were already on their way to becoming the "classics": Martin Carter, John Hearne, George Lamming, Victor Reid, Samuel Selvon, and Derek Walcott. An essay by Reid, "The West Indies: A New Nation," provided the historical background to the literature, while Frank Collymore gave an overview of the literature in his essay, "Writing in the West Indies." Also there, holding their own, were poems by Cecil Herbert, Eric Roach, and Philip Sherlock. I still have my copy of the *Review*. It represented the first substantial recognition of West Indian literature in a big, First World country other than Great Britain. This recognition was curiously deepened by the fact that, as I was surprised to discover at the time, Canada was itself in a self-interrogating mode as to the viability of the idea of a Canadian literature identifiably distinct from English or American literature. The *Tamarack* special issue confirmed my sense of self and identity there in a foreign country. It nicely rounded out my own coming of age in relation to West Indian literature, just as it seemed to underscore the coming of age of the literature.

Contributors

Edward Baugh is emeritus professor of English at the University of the West Indies, Mona, Jamaica. An internationally acclaimed critic and poet for over four decades, his works include *West Indian Poetry 1900–1970: A Study in Cultural Decolonisation* (1971), *Critics on Caribbean Literature* (1978), *Derek Walcott* (2006), and *Black Sand: New and Selected Poems* (2013).

J. Dillon Brown is an associate professor of English and African and African American studies at Washington University in St. Louis. His book *Migrant Modernism: Postwar London and the West Indian Novel* (2013) examines the interrelations between Windrush novelists and British modernism.

Michael A. Bucknor is a senior lecturer in literatures in English at the University of the West Indies, Mona, Jamaica. He has published extensively on Caribbean Canadian literature and Caribbean masculinity. He is an editor of the *Journal of West Indian Literature*, coeditor of *The Routledge Companion to Anglophone Caribbean Literature* (2011), and the immediate past chair of the Association for Commonwealth Literature and Language studies (ACLALS).

Raphael Dalleo is an associate professor of English at Florida Atlantic University. He is the coauthor of *The Latino/a Canon and the Emergence of Post-Sixties Literature* (2007) and the author of *Caribbean Literature and the Public Sphere: From the Plantation to the Postcolonial* (2011).

Alison Donnell is professor of Modern Literatures in English at Reading University (United Kingdom). She is the author of *Twentieth Century Caribbean Literature: Critical Moments in Anglophone Literary and Critical History* (2006) and the coeditor of *The Routledge Reader in Caribbean Literature* (1996) as well as of *The Routledge Companion to Anglophone Caribbean Literature* (2011).

Nadia Ellis is an assistant professor of English at the University of California, Berkeley. Her book *Territories of the Soul: Modes of Belonging in the Black*

Diaspora (forthcoming) reexamines central authors of the Windrush era such as George Lamming and Andrew Salkey.

Donette Francis is currently an associate professor in the Department of English and director of the American studies program at the University of Miami. Her research and teaching interests include Caribbean literary and cultural studies, African Diaspora literary studies, globalization and transnational feminist studies, and theories of sexuality and citizenship. *Fictions of Feminine Citizenship: Sexuality and the Nation in Contemporary Caribbean Literature* (2010) is her first monograph. She is currently at work on her second book, *The Novel 1960s: Form and Sensibilities in Caribbean Literary Culture.*

Glyne A. Griffith is an associate professor of English and of Latin American, Caribbean, and US Latino studies at SUNY Albany. He is the author of *Deconstruction, Imperialism and the West Indian Novel* (1996), the editor of *Caribbean Cultural Identities* (2001), and the coeditor, with Linden Lewis, of *Color, Hair and Bone: Race in the Twenty-First Century* (2008).

Kate Houlden is a lecturer in English literature and cultural history at Liverpool John Moores University, following an AHRC-funded Ph.D. at Queen Mary, University of London. Her research is focused on questions of gender and sexuality in postwar Caribbean fiction, and her monograph *Sexuality, Gender and Nationalism in Caribbean Literature* will be published in 2015. She has also published essays in journals such as *English Studies in Africa, Interventions, Journal of West Indian Literature,* and *Memory Studies.*

Evelyn O'Callaghan is a professor of West Indian literature in the Department of Language, Linguistics, and Literature at the University of the West Indies, Barbados. She is the author of *Woman Version: Theoretical Approaches to West Indian Fiction by Women* (1993) and *Women Writing the West Indies 1804–1939: A Hot Place, Belonging to Us* (2003). She serves as an editor for the *Journal of West Indian Literature.*

Lisa Outar, who formerly taught postcolonial literature at St. John's University and is now an independent scholar, researches Anglophone and Francophone Caribbean literature. She specializes in writings by and about Indo-Caribbeans. Her work has appeared in the *South Asian Review, Caribbean Journal of Education, South Asian History and Culture, Caribbean Review of Gender Studies, Stabroek News,* and *South Asian Diaspora,* and in the edited collection *South Asian Transnationalisms.* She is working on an edited book collection with Gabrielle Hosein called *Beyond Gender Negotiations: Indo-Caribbean Feminist Thought* and is also completing a manuscript about the production of the category of Indianness in the Caribbean within discourses of nationalism, creolization, and diasporic identity.

Atreyee Phukan is an associate professor of English at the University of San Diego. Her dissertation, "East Indianness in the West Indies: Representations of Post-Indentureship in Indo-Trinidadian Literature" (2006), and her current book project examine Indo-Caribbean identity and literature in the context of theories of hybridity and creolization. She is coeditor of *Reading the Exotic: South Asia and Its Others* (2009).

Kim Robinson-Walcott is the editor of *Caribbean Quarterly*, University of the West Indies, and *Jamaica Journal*, Institute of Jamaica. Her publications include *Out of Order! Anthony Winkler and White West Indian Writing* (2006); *Jamaican Art* (1989, 2011), which she coauthored; and the children's book *Dale's Mango Tree* (1992), which she also illustrated. Her scholarly articles, short stories, and poems have been published in a number of journals and anthologies.

Leah Reade Rosenberg is an associate professor of English at the University of Florida and the author of *Nationalism and the Formation of Caribbean Literature* (2007).

Faith Smith is an associate professor of African and Afro-American studies and of English at Brandeis University. She is the author of *Creole Recitations: John Jacob Thomas and Colonial Formation in the Late 19th-Century Caribbean* (2002) and the editor of *Sex and the Citizen: Interrogating the Caribbean* (2011).

Michelle A. Stephens is an associate professor of English and Latino and Hispanic Caribbean studies at Rutgers University. She is the author of *Black Empire: The Masculine Global Imaginary of Caribbean Intellectuals in the United States, 1914 to 1962* (2005) and *Skin Acts: Race, Psychoanalysis and the Black Male Performer* (2014).

Index